D0350211

TWO NATIONS

TWO NATIONS

BLACK AND WHITE, SEPARATE, HOSTILE, UNEQUAL

ANDREW HACKER

CHARLES SCRIBNER'S SONS
New York
MAXWELL MACMILLAN CANADA
Toronto
MAXWELL MACMILLAN INTERNATIONAL
New York Oxford Singapore Sydney

Charles Scribner's Sons
Macmillan Publishing Company
866 Third Avenue, New York, NY 10022

Maxwell Macmillan Canada, Inc.
1200 Eglinton Avenue East, Suite 200
Don Mills, Ontario M3C 3N1

Library of Congress Cataloging-in-Publication Data
Hacker, Andrew.
Two Nations: black and white, separate, hostile, unequal / Andrew Hacker.
p. cm.
Includes index.
ISBN 0-684-19148-2
1. United States—Race relations. 2. Racism—United States.
3. Afro-Americans—Social conditions—1975– I. Title.
E185.615.H23 1992
305.8'00973—dc20 91–34003 CIP

Macmillan books are available at special discounts for bulk purchases for sales promotions, premiums, fund-raising, or educational use. For details, contact:

Special Sales Director
Macmillan Publishing Company
866 Third Avenue
New York, NY 10022

10 9 8 7 6

Designed by M 'N O Production Services, Inc.

Printed in the United States of America

For My Students and Colleagues,
Cornell University and Queens College

CONTENTS

PREFACE

Every one of us could write a book about race. The text is already imprinted in our minds and evokes our moral character. Dividing people into races started as convenient categories. However, those divisions have taken on lives of their own, dominating our culture and consciousness, coloring passions and opinions, contorting facts and fantasies.

So race is more than simply a subject to be studied or an issue for debate. Given these conditions, objectivity is hardly possible. Which brings us back to the book that each of us might write. The volume in your hand offers one author's understanding of the role and meaning of race in the contemporary United States. Its title borrows from Benjamin Disraeli's remarks on the rich and poor of his Victorian England, and applies them to the two major races in America today: "Two nations, between whom there is no intercourse and no sympathy; who are as ignorant of each other's habits, thought, and feelings, as if they were dwellers in different zones, or inhabitants of different planets."

The subtitle, "Separate, Hostile, Unequal," has several sources. First, there has been the continuing debate in our courts and conversations over whether racially separated facilities can ever be equivalent in status and social worth. Another reflects the conclusion presented by the National Advisory Commission on Civil Disorders in 1968: "Our nation is moving toward two societies, one black, one white, separate and unequal." Yet these two nations, these two separate societies, have existed from the start. And, to be utterly frank, their relations have never been amiable. Alexis de Tocqueville noted this hostility a century and a half ago. "The most formidable of all the ills that threaten the future of the Union arises from the presence of a black population upon its territory," he observed during his visit to the United States. If he wrote these words during the days of slavery, they describe our racial reality today. Indeed, he could have been in our midst when he saw how "the danger of a conflict between the white and the black inhabitants perpetually haunts the imagination of the Americans, like a painful dream." We can benefit by returning to Tocqueville's analysis in the concluding chapter.

My early training was in philosophy, where I soon discovered that we should not expect a consensus on social and moral issues. Not the least reason is that we frequently differ on what we feel are the facts. While research can be useful, past a certain point, we must bring intuition and imagination to bear. On this premise, the first part of this book will expand on some personal impressions concerning race in our time. These chapters will include observations on how we define and divide people into races; on what it is like to be black in the United States; and why white Americans react as they do to people of African ancestry. So the reader should be forewarned: this section will rely on subjective interpretations, since statements about how we behave in the realm of race are seldom amenable to evidence, let alone conclusive proof.

At the same time, in treating these and other topics, I have tried to provide enough plausibility to keep the conversation going. While the reader will not be asked to agree at every stage, it may be hoped that he or she may say, "you could have a point, I'm still willing to listen." Some of what will be said may seem overstated or unwilling to acknowledge exceptions. Here, too, indulgence is asked. Race is a tense terrain, where we often try to hide crucial truths from ourselves. One way to bring these premises to the surface is by making them as vivid as possible.

Part II of *Two Nations* will focus more precisely on the role race plays in such spheres as education and family life, as well as the economy, politics, and crime. This section, too, reflects the author's outlook and interests. Much of my career has been spent as a social scientist, which carries a commitment to revealing how the world really works. One way to array information is in statistical form. While numbers in and of themselves cannot pronounce final truths, they can offer insights and illumination if they are collated with care.

It is revealing that so much information about ourselves is classified according to race. We publish separate black and white breakdowns on whether mothers breast-feed their babies, and for persons who have been arrested for embezzlement. The census even has separate racial columns for people who bicycle to work. But it would be a mistake to view such tabulations as depersonalized data. On the contrary, they can tell a very human story. And, as will be seen, statistics often surprise us with unexpected findings.

Nor will Part II rely entirely on tables. It will also offer a broader analysis of conditions impinging upon race. Thus the rise in fatherless households may emerge not as just one race's problem, but as having larger social causes. In the same way, what we call crime can be explained in terms of class as well as race. Or, by exploring forces that run deeper, we may come closer to realizing why so many men commit the crime of rape. Also, any discussion of unequal education should be conjoined with at least a few comments on what we want our offspring to learn, and why we place so much emphasis on multiple-choice tests. These chapters will also seek to explain why some conditions related to race have changed over time, while others manage to persist, and still others have become more painful and pronounced. Given the breadth of these issues, the reader should not be surprised if more than a few impressions find their way into these analytical chapters.

One or two more remarks should suffice. No one could possible tally all the books and articles that have been written about race in America. A host of scholars, journalists, and commentators have produced an impressive literature. Prominent among these are authors who have actually lived on the nation's racial frontiers. J. Anthony Lukas's *Common Ground* about Boston; Elijah Anderson's *Streetwise* on Philadelphia; as well as Chicago as depicted in Nicholas Lemann's *The Promised Land* and Alex Kotlowitz's *There Are No Children Here* have all added dimensions to our understanding that statistics can never satisfy. For this reason, each book on race should be seen as part of a collective enterprise. If each of us focuses on certain aspects and issues, and explains them in our own way, we are all dependent on what others have discovered and said.

So separate mention should be made of America's most notable book on race. Fifty years ago, Gunnar Myrdal was completing his classic study *An American Dilemma: The Negro Problem and Modern Democracy*, which ultimately appeared in 1944. By every measure, it was a masterful enterprise and one that can never be rivaled. If few people read him today, many of Myrdal's insights remain relevant and applicable. For example, he stressed the idea that race in America is essentially a caste condition, so that for all basic purposes, black people never escape their birth. And as his title made clear, Myrdal's central theme was that the United States was and is beset by an apparent paradox: the nation's commitments to universal justice and equality are contradicted by the way it treats its principal minority race. Myrdal, an eminent Swedish scholar, took seriously Americans' declarations about justice and equality. Perhaps, as a good guest, he did not want to accuse his hosts of hypocrisy.

As it happens, the pages that follow will contain relatively few citations or references. This should not be taken as suggesting that what others have written lacks significance. Rather, it is that too many allusions to fellow authors can end up as a book devoted to other books. Real issues like employment and welfare can become deflected into a debate over Charles Murray's formulations versus those of William Julius Wilson. Or questions of education and culture may become a battle of competing quotations from Diane Ravitch and Molefi Kete Asante. While this can often be a fruitful approach, especially for academic audiences, it has not been the one chosen here. References, listing source materials, have been gathered in a separate section.

The book's title might seem to intimate that a full portrait of America can be rendered in black and white. Obviously this is not the case. While persons we classify as black or white still comprise America's major races, they currently account for a smaller share of the population than at any time in our history. Since we want a full perspective, Asians and Hispanics and other ethnic groups will obviously appear on these pages. Still, *Two Nations* will adhere to its title by giving central attention to black and white Americans, and the reasons for this emphasis will be made evident. In many respects, other groups find themselves sitting as spectators, while the two prominent players try to work out how or whether they can coexist with one another.

Two Nations will also seek to explain why so much behavior regarding race remains so obdurate and ingrained. Not the least of its conclusions will be that racial tensions serve too many important purposes to be easily ameliorated, let alone eliminated or replaced. The reader should be advised not to expect this book to end on an optimistic note. Nor should he or she look for a closing chapter with proposals for reducing discrimination and ending prejudice. *Two Nations* is not that kind of book. I leave it to others to mention measures they feel can break down racial barriers, and bring more amity and equity to the racial sphere.

Of course, there are things that should be done, and some may be within the realm of possibility. At the same time, there is scant evidence that the majority of white Americans are ready to invest in redistributive programs, let alone give of themselves in more exacting ways. As will be shown, not only is the taxpaying electorate overwhelmingly white, but it is also middle class, middle-aged, and—increasingly—ensconced in insulated suburbs. In short, our time is not one receptive to racial remedies. One aim of this book will be to show why this is the case.

—Andrew Hacker

PART ONE

CHAPTER ONE

DIVIDING AMERICAN SOCIETY

RACE HAS BEEN an American obsession since the first Europeans sighted "savages" on these shores. In time, those original inhabitants would be subdued or slaughtered, and finally sequestered out of view. But race in America took on a deeper and more disturbing meaning with the importation of Africans as slaves. Bondage would later be condemned as an awful injustice and the nation's shame, even as we have come to acknowledge the stamina and skill it took to survive in a system where humans could be bought and sold and punished like animals. Nor are these antecedents buried away in the past. That Americans of African origin once wore the chains of chattels remains alive in the memory of both races and continues to separate them.

Black Americans are Americans, yet they still subsist as aliens in the only land they know. Other groups may remain outside the mainstream—some religious sects, for example—but they do so voluntarily. In contrast, blacks must endure a segregation that is far from freely chosen. So America may be seen as two separate nations. Of course, there are places where the races mingle. Yet in most significant respects, the separation is pervasive and penetrating. As a social and human division, it surpasses all others—even gender—in intensity and subordination.

If white Americans regard the United States as their nation, they also see it beset with racial problems they feel are not of their making. Some contrast current conditions with earlier times, when blacks appeared more willing to accept a subordinate status. Most whites will protest that they bear neither responsibility nor blame for the conditions blacks face. Neither they nor their forebears ever owned slaves, nor can they see themselves as having held anyone back or down. Most white Americans believe that for at least the last generation blacks have been given more than a fair chance and at least equal opportunity, if not outright advantages. Moreover, few white Americans feel obliged to ponder how membership in the major race gives them powers and privileges.

America is inherently a "white" country: in character, in structure, in culture. Needless to say, black Americans create lives of their own. Yet, as a people, they face boundaries and constrictions set by the white majority. America's version of *apartheid*, while lacking overt legal sanction, comes closest to the system even now being reformed in the land of its invention.

That racial tensions cast a pall upon this country can hardly be denied. People now vent feelings of hostility and anger that in the past they repressed. Race has become a national staple for private conversation and public controversy. So it becomes necessary to ask what in recent decades has brought the issue and reality of race to the center of the stage.

The idea of race is primeval. Humans have given names to their varied strains since physical differences first began to appear. Nor are there signs that racial lines have grown dimmer in modern times. On the contrary, race continues to preoccupy the public mind, a reminder of a past that cannot be willed away.

Since race is part of common parlance, people have used the term in many ways. Little will be gained by asking for clear-cut definitions; or, for that matter, trying to decide exactly how many different races occupy this planet. Anthropologists have their lists, but even they disagree on criteria and classifications. Still, some major groupings recur: Negroid, Mongoloid, Australoid, Caucasoid, and Indic, with American Indians and Pacific Islanders added as two encompassing categories. But there are also finer racial divisions, such as Aryans and Semites and Dravidians. Tribes like the Watusi and Navahos have also been given racial designations. Indeed, since there is no consensus when it comes to defining "race," the term has been applied to a diversity of groups. The Irish have been called a race in their own right, as have Jews and Hindus. Many find these ambiguities unsettling, but then so is much of life. In the United States, what people mean by "race" is usually straightforward and clear, given the principal division into black and white. Yet, as it happens, not all Americans fit into "racial" designations.

In theory, Native Americans taken together belong to what most anthropologists would call a basic race. Yet on the whole, they tend to be a loose residue of tribes, rather than a racial entity. A single primal consciousness cannot be said to bind the aspirations and interests of Chippewas and Seminoles and Aleuts. As it happens, the Native American population has undergone an unusual increase. Between 1970 and 1990, the number of persons claiming tribal antecedents rose from 827,268 to 1,516,540, which works out to more than three times the growth rate for the nation as a whole. The chief reason is that a lot of people who had concealed their native origins are now reclaiming them as their primary identity. As it happens, another group can claim an even firmer racial cohesion. It consists of descendants of Hawaii's original inhabitants, most of whom have Polynesian origins. Their growth has mirrored the Native American model, doubling from 100,179 in 1970 to 210,907 in 1990.

Until just a decade or so ago, Americans spoke of "Orientals," and the individuals so described are certainly members of what the anthropologists call the "Mongoloid" race. However, these terms—along with "yellow"—are now hardly ever heard. For one thing, many of those subsumed under the "Oriental" rubric never liked that designation. After all, it was invented and imposed by Europeans, who saw their own continent as the center of civilization, and relegated the "Orient" to Europe's eastern horizon.

Today, we have the generic term "Asian," which includes not only Japanese and Chinese and Koreans, but also Indonesians and Indians, along with Burmese and Thais, plus Filipinos and Pakistanis. Geographically speaking, Asia extends from the Kurile Islands to Istanbul and Israel. In fact, "Asian Americans" did not chose this title for themselves. Rather, the larger society has found it convenient to collect them into a single category that mingles racial and national origins. For this reason, obviously, "Asian" itself cannot be a race, since it embraces not only persons once described as "Mongoloid," but also Indics and Dravidians and Caucasians. Even the Koreans and Chinese and Japanese, who belong to the common "Mongoloid" race, seldom mix with one another and have few activities or interests in common. Rather than racial, their images of their identities are almost wholly national. So while in textbook terms, most Americans of Asian origin have specific racial origins, in social and political terms those identities have only a residual significance. In 1970, the census counted 1,438,544 people in what is now the Asian category. By 1990, due mainly to immigration, that group had grown fivefold to 7,273,662. (See the table on page 15.)

Nor can it be contended that Americans of Hispanic—or Chicano or Latino—heritage comprise a race. On the contrary, among their numbers can be found persons of almost pure European ancestry, as well as some of partial but visible African origins, along with individuals of unblemished Indian descent. But far outnumbering them are people of such varied parentages as to render any talk of race impossible. Since 1970, the Hispanic group has increased from 9,072,602 to 22,354,059, almost three times the rate for the population as a whole.

In fact, the "nonracial" character of Hispanics has been reflected in recent census reports, where individuals are allowed to describe themselves as they choose. Accordingly, in one census question, individuals may indicate that they are Latin or Hispanic. In another place, they may also fill in a race. Thus in 1990, the census located 7,687,938 residents of California who selected the Latin or Hispanic designation. Within this group, just under half—49.5 percent—chose to say that they also had a race: black or white, or, in a few cases, Asians or Native Americans. However, the other 50.5 percent told the census that in their own view, they had no "race" at all. For them, to be Hispanic was a sole and sufficient identity. (The same eschewal of "race" may be observed among Islamic immigrants from the Middle East.)

So it would seem that the country's fastest-growing groups prefer to emphasize their cultural and national identities rather than traits associated with race. However, the same cannot be said for the rest of the nation, which remains either black or white.

To give the names "black" and "white" to races might seem, on its face, quite ludicrous. Clearly, no human beings have skins of either color. Indeed, very few come even close to those tones. But then "white" and "black" stand for much more than the shades of epidermal coverings. To start, they refer to the "Caucasian" and "Negroid" races, whose facial appearances differ as prominently as their colors.

But more is involved than color or facial features or skeletal structure. The terms also carry cultural connotations. In its basic meaning, "white" denotes European antecedents, while "black" stands for Africa. Since the human species began in Africa, we can say that black people are those whose ancestors remained on that continent, while whites descend from those who embarked on migrations to cooler climates. This has led some to the presumption that the races are at different levels of evolutionary development. For at least half a dozen centuries, and possibly longer, "white" has implied a higher civilization based on a superior inheritance.

Europeans who colonized the western hemisphere sought to recreate it in their image, and to transform North and South America into "white" continents. With conquest comes the power to impose your ways on territories you have subdued. The treatment of the Native Americans simply ratified that view. (In some places, the native populations remained large enough to exert a reciprocal influence, as in India and most of Africa. This was not to be the case in the United States.) Still, something can be learned by looking at how "white" was originally conceived, and the changes it has undergone.

From the colonial period through the Jacksonian era, most white Americans were of English ancestry. Alexis de Tocqueville, during his visit in the 1830s, found he could characterize the country and its people as "Anglo-Americans."

Given the expansion of the population, this epithet could not last. Even so, the Anglo-American model has remained remarkably durable, with most subsequent immigrants adapting to its canons. They not only learned English, the single national language, but also adjusted their lives to the economy and technology associated with that prototype. This does not mean that the majority of white Americans regard themselves as "English" in a literal sense. They can and do identify with other origins. Even so, it could be argued that most contemporary citizens associate themselves to a greater degree with Anglo-American culture than with their actual country of origin.

To say this would seem to resurrect the conception of the melting pot, which argued that immigrants would shed their older identities and assimilate to the new culture they encountered. That view has been challenged in many quarters. Rather than as a cauldron, many commentators today prefer to see America as a mosaic or even a lumpy stew. At best, the pot still contains plenty of unmelted pieces. Hence the renewed emphasis on "ethnicity," with its focus on the country's racial and national and religious diversity.

Even so, assimilation has taken place and it continues apace. One of the earliest examples came with Germans, who in terms of sheer numbers made up the nation's largest immigrant group. Yet for at least a generation, it has been hard to find many people who qualify as "German-Americans" in any serious sense. Soon after their arrival, which gathered momentum following 1848, Germans quickly learned English and studied the customs of their new land. Many were merchants or farmers, familiar with the rules of a market economy. In addition, it became evident that they were not particularly committed to the country they had left behind. (In fact, there was no unified Germany at that time.) Each generation saw more intermarriage, accompanied by moves to mixed neighborhoods. Service in the Union Army during the Civil War speeded the assimilation process, which was effectively completed during the First World War. With the suburbanization of Milwaukee, only Cincinnati retains the vestiges of a German flavor.

What also eased acceptance of German immigrants was the realization by Americans of English origin that they needed an ally. For one thing, their own stock was not being renewed by immigration. And, as often happens with groups that arrive early, the offspring they produce begin to feel they should no longer have to do society's less pleasant chores. German-Americans could see why they were being co-opted, and they welcomed the chance to show their ambitions and skills. The English had a further motive: encouraging the Germans, who were mainly Protestant, helped to hold the Catholic Irish at bay.

It took the Irish longer to shed an alien identity. Although they arrived already knowing English, rural folkways slowed their adjustment to an urban world. Furthermore, at the time of their arrival, Catholics were not regarded as altogether "white." (Thomas Nast's political cartoons gave Irish immigrants subhuman features.) Italians may have been less fervidly Catholic than the Irish, but their acceptance was hampered by peasant habits. Many chose to return to Italy after brief sojourns here; and some of those who chose to stay took their time learning the new language.

Jews, who arrived in large numbers at the turn of the century, were at first kept at the margin of "white" America simply because they were not Christians. Still, by a generation after their arrival, they had set themselves to mastering the tests for college admission, civil service posts, and many professions. World War II speeded the process of assimilation. At its end, people from every corner of Europe were considered fully "white." By 1990, two Americans of Irish extraction had been elected President, and being a Catholic was seldom a bar to promotion or preferment. The Chrysler Corporation has had a Lee (from Lido) Iacocca for its chairman, while an Irving Shapiro headed DuPont, and several Ivy League universities have had Jewish presidents.

By this time, it should be clear that the question is not "Who *is* white?" It might be more appropriate to ask "Who *may* be considered white?" since this suggests that something akin to permission is needed. In a sense, those who have already received the "white" designation can be seen as belonging to a club, from whose sanctum they ponder whether they want or need new members, as well as the proper pace of new admissions.

Recent immigration from Asia and Latin America complicates any discussion of race. To start, we might ask if persons arriving from countries like Korea or Pakistan might somehow "become white." (Nor is this to say that they might desire the designation.) As was noted earlier, Koreans and others who were once portrayed as belonging to the "yellow" race now reject that description. Their membership in the "Asian" category conjoins them with people as far west as Istanbul. Armenians are now considered "white," as are most Lebanese and Iranians. While in theory, some Asian Indians might be thought too dark to be "white," the appellation has shown itself to possess remarkable elasticity.

In many respects, therefore, color is becoming less important. Most Asian immigrants arrive in this country ready to compete for middle-class careers. Many come with a level of educational preparation at least as good as our own. Schools in Seoul and Bombay now offer coursework as sophisticated as any in Seattle or Baltimore. As hardly needs repeating, Asia has been catapulting itself into the modern world; so if most Asians are not literally "white," they have the technical and organizational skills expected by any "Western" or European-based culture.

How Asians are currently being viewed has much in common with the ways earlier generations co-opted new talents and energies as their own were winding down. To cite a single example, which will be amplified in a later chapter, studies show that white students today spend less time on homework than their Asian classmates. At college, white undergraduates tend to select easier majors, and are opting for comfortable careers in the more sociable professions. Right now, it is in science and technology where Asian talents are being co-opted. But a glance at the list of editors of the *Harvard Law Review* suggests that they are destined for broader representation in the professions and management.

As Asians find places in the economy, they are allowed to move upward on social and occupational ladders. Middle-class whites do not object if Asian children attend their local schools or populate their neighborhoods. Even now, we are beginning to see an increasing incidence of intermarriage, although with the caveat that the first pairings will most usually involve an Asian woman and a white man. The grandchildren will undoubtedly be regarded as a new variant of white.*

Much the same process can be observed among Hispanics. Of course, large numbers are already quite "white." This is clearly the case with Cubans, a prominent example being Roberto Goizueta, the Yale-educated chairman of the Coca-Cola Corporation. Most Central and South Americans can claim a strong European heritage, which eases their absorption into the "white" middle class. While skin color and features still figure in social grading, they are less obstacles to mobility than was once the case. More at issue is the divide between unskilled laborers, who will continue pouring across the border for the foreseeable future, and others with the skills and schooling that allow them to enter legally.

With the absorption of increasing numbers of Hispanics and Asians, along with Middle Eastern immigrants, being "white" will cease to carry many of the connotations it did in the past. The future

* Nor should all Asians be categorized as immigrants. Americans of Chinese and Japanese ancestry have been in this country for many generations, particularly in California and Hawaii. Indeed, in Hawaii, these citizens hold many of its prominent positions.

population will reflect a more varied array of national origins rather than races, since—as has been stressed—the new groups cannot be easily assigned to racial classifications.

Nor should we be too quick in proclaiming that America will become "multicultural" as well. True, one can point to exotic neighborhoods, with their parades and festivals, to foreign-language newspapers and television channels, along with calls for new kinds of courses in colleges and schools. It would be more accurate to say that the United States will continue to have a single dominant culture. It doesn't really matter whether it is called "white" or "Western" or European or Anglo-American or by another title. It would be better simply to describe it as a structure of opportunities and institutions that has been willing to use the energies and talents of people from various origins. The reception given to recent immigrants is essentially similar to that accorded to successive waves of Europeans. In neither case have the newcomers been given a very cordial welcome. Indeed, they have often met with mistrust, not to mention violence and hostility. Despite the felicitous words on the Statue of Liberty, immigrants are allowed entry on the condition that they serve as cheap labor and live unobtrusively. Many will tell you that now, as in the past, they find their religions scorned, their customs ridiculed, and their features caricatured.

Throughout this nation's history, the expectation has been that newcomers will adapt to the models they encounter on their arrival. If that means relinquishing old-country customs, there are signs that many are prepared to do just that, or at least watch as their children assimilate. Perhaps the first instance of the expanded purview of "white" was when the English founders sought the services of two talented Scots—James Madison and Alexander Hamilton—to help found this nation. The process is still going on.

As with "white," being "black" is less one's particular shade of color than physical features and continent of ancestry. Of course, very few Americans are entirely African in origin. As is well known, slave owners and other whites felt free to force themselves on black women. Still, no matter how light their skin tones, if they retained any vestige of African features, they and their descendants continue to be delineated as "black."

The United States, unlike other countries and cultures, no longer uses terms specifying finer gradations. Hence "mestizo" and "mulatto" have disappeared from our parlance, as have "creole" and "quadroon." Nor has this country retained the generic term "colored" for people whose ancestries are obviously mixed. (The last use of an intermediate term was in the 1910 census, in which interviewers identified about 20 percent of the "Negro" group as "Mulattoes.") It has been far from accidental that this country has chosen to reject the idea of a graduated spectrum, and has instead fashioned a rigid bifurcation.

For all practical purposes, "whites" of all classes and ethnicities now prefer to present a common front. Unlike in the past, there are no pronounced distinctions of "purer" versus "lesser" whites, or of those with older claims as against newer arrivals. While immigrants from Colombia and Cyprus may have to work their way up the social ladder, they are still allowed as valid a claim to being "white" as persons of Puritan or Pilgrim stock.

Americans of African ancestry were never given that indulgence. The reason is not that their coloration was too "dark" to allow for absorption into the "white" classification. After all, the swarthiness of some Europeans did not become a barrier to their admission. Had white America really believed in its egalitarian declarations, it would have welcomed former slaves into its midst at the close of the Civil War. Indeed, had that happened, America would not be two racial nations today. This is not to suggest how far blacks themselves would have assimilated, since a lot depends on how far members of a group want to preserve their special heritage. The point is that white America has always had the power to expand its domain. However, in the past and even now, it has shown a particular reluctance to absorb people of African descent.

How do blacks feel about this bifurcation? Today, most express pride in their African origins, especially those who make a point of calling themselves African-Americans. While, like it or not, a lighter color remains an advantage for women, social advantage is no longer gained by alluding to white elements in one's ancestry. Black Americans are aware that much in the "black" designation represents how whites have defined the term. Still, despite attempts by whites to describe and define them, black Americans have always sought to create their own lives and sustain their sentiments and interests. It started when the first slaves created a culture of their own. Similarly, the drive to replace "colored" with "negro," followed by the move to

"Negro," and then on to "black" and "African-American," have all reflected a desire to maintain an autonomous identity.

For most black Americans to be an African-American means literally that in that continent lies the primal origin of your people. The experiences of capture and transportation, of slavery and segregation, never diminished or erased the basic culture and character of tribal ancestries. Yet it is also instructive that blacks from the West Indies and other islands of the Caribbean seek to retain an independent history. Their forebears also originated in Africa and served as slaves, but blacks born in Barbados and Jamaica, or Haiti and Martinique, make clear the British or French connections that distinguish them from others of their race. This emphasis is not intended to render Haitians or Jamaicans "less black" in terms of color. Rather, they wish it known that their antecedents are not exclusively African, but also bear a European imprint.

Black Americans came from the least-known continent, the most exotic, the one remotest from American experience. Among the burdens blacks bear is the stigma of "the savage," the proximity to lesser primates. Hence the question in many minds: Can citizens of African origin find acceptance in a society that is dominantly white, Western, and European?

Even at a time when Americans of European backgrounds are giving less emphasis to their ancestries, it is not as easy for black men and women to assimilate into the American mainstream. Even those who aspire to careers in white institutions, and emulate white demeanor and diction, find that white America lets them only partly past the door.

Arguably, this is because the "Africa" in African-American contrasts with much of the European structure of technology and science, of administrative systems based on linear modes of reasoning. Today, Africa is the least developed and most sorrow-ridden of continents. It has more than its share of malnutrition and debilitating diseases, and at least its share of tribal rancor and bloodshed. It seems always to be petitioning the rest of the world for aid. Since the close of the colonial era, over a generation ago, there have not been many African success stories.

Yet the actual Africa of today is not really the model black Americans have in mind. Of much greater significance is how the continent is construed as a symbol: what it says about the human spirit, what it connotes as a way of life. It is more the Africa of history, before the imperial powers arrived. It is also an Africa of the imagination, of music and dance and stories. This Africa speaks for an ancestral humanity, for an awareness of the self, the bonds of tribe and family and community. If the European heritage imposes the regimens of standardized tests, the African dream inspires discursive storytelling celebrating the soul and the spirit.

But as much as anything, being "black" in America bears the mark of slavery. Even after emancipation, citizens who had been slaves still found themselves consigned to a subordinate status. Put most simply, the ideology that had provided the rationale for slavery by no means disappeared. Blacks continued to be seen as an inferior species, not only unsuited for equality but not even meriting a chance to show their worth. Immigrants only hours off the boat, while subjected to scorn, were allowed to assert their superiority to black Americans.

And in our own time, must it be admitted at the close of the twentieth century, that residues of slavery continue to exist? The answer is obviously yes. The fact that blacks are separated more severely than any other group certainly conveys that message. Indeed, the fear persists that if allowed to come closer they will somehow contaminate the rest of society.

What other Americans know and remember is that blacks alone were brought as chattels to be bought and sold like livestock. As has been noted, textbooks now point out that surviving slavery took a skill and stamina that no other race has been called upon to sustain. Yet this is not what others choose to recall. Rather, there remains an unarticulated suspicion: might there be something about the black race that suited them for slavery? This is not to say anyone argues that human bondage was justified. Still, the facts that slavery existed for so long and was so taken for granted cannot be erased from American minds. This is not the least reason why other Americans—again, without openly saying so—find it not improper that blacks still serve as maids and janitors, occupations seen as involving physical skills rather than mental aptitudes.

The recollections of the past that remain in people's minds continue to shape ideas about the character and capacities of black citizens. Is it possible to erase the stigmas associated with slavery? After all, a very considerable number of black Americans have achieved impressive careers, winning many of the rewards bestowed by white America. Still, there is no way that even the most talented of these men and women will be considered eligible for the honorific of "white." They are, and will remain, accomplished blacks, regarded as role models for their race. But white Americans, who both grant and impose racial memberships, show little inclination toward giving full nationality to the descendants of African slaves.

The subject of this book is race: in particular, America's two principal races who, in Alexis de Tocqueville's words, "are fastened to each other without intermingling." As it happens, taken together, black and white Americans now comprise a dwindling share of the nation's population. Census counts over the last two centuries illuminate some of the changes.

At the time of the first census in 1790, blacks were at their highest point as a proportion of the population. In each succeeding decade through 1940, their share grew smaller, due to growing waves of white immigration. Since 1940, the black quotient has been rising by about half a percentage point each decade, due to the fact that black Americans have a higher birthrate. (Although, as will be seen in a later chapter, the black rate is always a constant multiple of the white rate.) Still, as the following table shows, each decade finds the two races accounting for declining proportions of the national population:

	1970	1980	1990*	1990**
Whites	83.3%	79.6%	75.3%	74.2%
Blacks	10.9%	11.5%	11.9%	12.5%
Hispanics	4.5%	6.4%	9.0%	9.5%
Asians / Others	1.3%	2.5%	3.8%	3.8%
	100.0%	100.0%	100.0%	100.0%

*Official count **Using adjustments for undercount.

As has been noted, Hispanics, Asians, Native Americans, and Hawaiians are now the nation's fastest growing groups. By 1990, they together outnumbered black Americans, and were also helping to erode white predominance. For this reason, it might seem that a book that focuses on only two races will be woefully incomplete. Why not simply describe America's two nations as composed of whites and people of color? There is much to be said for such an argument. Certainly, all persons deemed to be other than white can detail how they have suffered discrimination at the hands of white America. Any allusions to racist attitudes and actions will find Cherokees and Chinese and Cubans agreeing with great vigor.

Yet, as has already been suggested in this chapter, members of all these "intermediate" groups have been allowed to put a visible distance between themselves and black Americans. Put most simply, none of the presumptions of inferiority associated with Africa and slavery are imposed on these other ethnicities. Moreover, as has also been noted, second and subsequent generations of Hispanics and Asians are merging into the "white" category, partly through intermarriage and also by personal achievement and adaptation. Indeed, the very fact that this is happening sheds light on the tensions and disparities separating the two major races.

CHAPTER TWO

RACE AND RACISM

INFERIORITY VS. EQUALITY

THROUGHOUT THIS NATION'S HISTORY, race has always had a central role. Until recently, however, most notions concerning the races and relations between them either went unquestioned or remained relatively muted. As recently as a generation ago, white Americans in both the South and the North would say that so far as they could see their region had no overpowering racial problems. Most of them really wanted to believe that blacks and whites coexisted quite amiably; separately, to be sure, but that was a matter of mutual choice.

For almost a century after the abolition of slavery, America's black population subsisted under a system of controls. In the South, physical force was blatant and unabashed. The whims of a sheriff, an employer, even the driver of a bus, could hold black lives in thrall. In the North, intimidation and oppression were less explicit but nonetheless real. Fear of the police obviously helped to maintain this submission, for in those days precinct houses were less attentive to legal processes than they seem to be today. An equally effective control lay in the understanding that members of subordinate races did not touch or threaten their betters. This is not to suggest that black Americans were happy with their condition. Many were resentful, if not totally enraged. But given the panoply of power they faced, the most common posture was one of resignation: a minority with barely an avenue of appeal.

Little attention was paid to the conditions under which black Americans lived. It was assumed, for example, that a docile pool would always be available for the arduous labors required by white society. No one thought to ask what domestic servants did after their working hours. Black Americans remained unobtrusive, and apparently uncomplaining, for all intents invisible to white eyes.

These were placid years for white Americans. No serious movements or organized protests arose to upset white sensibilities. No talk of black power was in the air, and only the barest whispers of egalitarian aspirations could be heard. Black Americans knew they were regarded as marginal members of the nation, and realized that white America saw them as an alien appendage.

The real change began during the Second World War, when for the first time black Americans were courted by white society. A shortage of civilian labor forced employers to offer jobs to workers who previously had been excluded. More than a million black women left domestic service never to return. At the outset of the war, blacks were drafted into the armed forces to serve in labor battalions. By its end, they were given the right to fight and die, as many did. Once a society has told men and women that it cannot function without their talents, they will not willingly revert to a subordinate status. Notions of civil rights and racial integrations, of social equality and economic progress, received their impetus in those wartime years. During the decades that followed, they took coherent shape.

In particular, college students in the South decided it was time to end the ignominies inflicted on educated men and women, who could not even order a sandwich at a local lunch counter. Shortly thereafter, ordinary citizens began to demand that most elemental of rights which was still denied to most members of their race: to be allowed to vote for the officials who legislate and tax and exercise power over you.

Most white Americans saw these and related activities as dignified and responsible, and embodying legitimate aims. That black groups eschewed violence also set white minds at ease. Certainly, they felt safe with Martin Luther King, Jr., the most prominent leader in the civil rights movement. Not only was he a minister born into a patrician family, but he had studied and received a doctoral degree at a Northern university. Moreover, he welcomed whites to join in marches and demonstrations, making it a biracial cause.

So until the middle 1960s, there was little talk of a racial crisis or tensions that had grown out of control. Then came the so-called riots in cities like Los Angeles and Newark and Detroit, marked by looting and burning within black neighborhoods. In fact, these were not "race riots," if by that is meant actual confrontations of black and white citizens. The violence never reached downtown business districts or areas where whites lived. However, race became the central issue. The chief response, including gunfire in which many blacks lost their lives, came from white police and national guardsmen. To more than a few observers, the conduct of the police was much more callous and indiscriminate than that of the civilians they had been ordered to control.

After those disturbances, race relations never returned to their former plane. Whites ceased to identify black protests with a civil rights movement led by students and ministers. Rather, they saw a resentful and rebellious multitude, intent on imposing its presence on the rest of the society. Blacks were seen as trying to force themselves into places and positions where they were not wanted or for which they lacked the competence. As the 1970s started, so came a rise in crimes, all too many of them with black perpetrators. By that point, many white Americans felt they had been misused or betrayed. Worsening relations between the races were seen as largely due to the behavior of blacks, who had abused the invitations to equal citizenship white America had been tendering. It is this setting that creates the context of racism.

Something called racism obviously exists. As a complex of ideas and attitudes, which translate into action, it has taken a tragic toll on the lives of all Americans. Unfortunately, the term has been so used and overused that it loses serious meaning. It has served as a rallying cry, a bludgeon, and as a diversion from other issues. But racism is real, an incubus that has haunted this country since Europeans first set foot on the continent. It goes beyond prejudice and discrimination,

and even transcends bigotry, largely because it arises from outlooks and assumptions of which we are largely unaware.

Racism expresses itself in three distinct but related ways. Of course, this or any trifurcation may seem oversimple, and undoubtedly is. Still, a graphic presentation can expand our understanding of an elusive reality.

Taxicab drivers who refuse to stop for black riders base that decision on the only information they have: the race of the person raising his or her hand. Even if the driver has had some bad experiences, he understands that most black men are law-abiding citizens. At the same time, he knows that some have been known to pull a gun on taxicab drivers. And that "some" is enough to make him wary about every black man. When he drives by a middle-aged black woman without stopping, it is because he thinks she may ask to be taken to a part of the city he would rather not enter. Of course, he has no way of knowing her destination, but he does not want to take the risk. In these and similar cases, his decision not to stop is patently racist, especially since he then proceeds to pick up the first white passenger he sees further down the block.

Racism has much in common with other "isms." We already have the term "sexism." Other generalizations may apply to height or weight, or age or physical handicaps. "Homophobia" is also an "ism," although it carries connotations of hatred as well. Whether a taxi driver dislikes black people is not really the issue. He may actually feel sorry for the person he left standing in the rain.

In some cases, expressions of racism admit of no exceptions. This was the case with the Nazi ideology, which said that *all* human beings of Jewish origin carried the seeds of depravity. The fact that infants were included in the Holocaust made this conviction clear. (This is not to say that Jews are a race. Still, that Nazis chose to see them that way is itself a fact.)

Racism need not be so rigid or absolute. In fact, few whites insist that the traits they dislike in some black people are to be found in every member of the race. Most are pleased to point to black men and women who are not like "the rest." They may watch black performers regularly on film or television, cheer them at athletic events, and even claim some black people as their friends.

Making—and acting upon—limited impressions is a part of ordinary life. Each day, like the taxicab driver, we base decisions on the one or two facts we gather about people, which may simply be their outward appearance, or their addresses on an application, or how they sound over the telephone. Such presumptions are obviously unfair to the individuals involved. Constraints of time do not always allow us to obtain the fuller information we would like or need.

Racism, we are sometimes told, rests largely on ignorance. If we get to know people better, we will discover that they are quite different from what we have been led to think they are. That is surely so. For example, very few white Americans have ever set foot inside a black family's home. They might be surprised to discover that simply in terms of furniture, appliances, meals, and television-watching, blacks live very much like whites of their own class. While some differences in style can be identified, members of the two races share many common characteristics. Quite obviously, the United States would be a much more harmonious nation if there were fewer racial barriers. Yet even blacks who attain economic and educational parity find that social obstacles remain. How often does one see a party of two couples, one black and one white, on an outing together?

Still, racism is not always based on ignorance. There can be cases where stereotyped judgments contain some elements of truth. While we can agree that taxicab drivers often make decisions on a racist basis, we might grant that in doing so they show a modicum of rationality. Some black men—a higher proportion than among whites—do have intentions that are in fact dangerous. It is one thing for a passenger to refuse to pay a taxi fare; it is another if he holds a loaded gun to the driver's head. And the latter has been a frequent enough occurrence to give many drivers pause. Sad to say, actions that are often unfair can also be reasonable, at least insofar as they are based on sufficient experience to give them a degree of validity.

To reply that taxicab drivers draw on rational odds hardly comforts those subjected to such calculations. Tendencies attributed to common felons get shunted onto surgeons and scholars. Nor does it help to point out that this kind of unfairness is inevitable in a world where we can never come to know each individual in an intimate way. Judgments based on race cut more deeply and cause more harm than other presumptions Americans may make about one another. What every black American knows, and whites should try to imagine, is how it feels to have an unfavorable—and unfair—identity imposed on you every waking day.

* * *

In addition to the outlooks and actions of individuals like taxicab drivers, there is also a condition called "institutional racism." The institutions can be colleges and churches, or business firms or governmental bureaus. The Federal Bureau of Investigation and the Los Angeles Police Department, for example, have long had reputations for antipathy toward blacks and other minorities. But not all organizations are so blatant in their biases. Most develop more subtle cultures of their own, which their members usually internalize, often without pause or reflection. Of course, organizational cultures take many forms. But in the United States, an overarching feature is that they tend to be inherently "white."

This is not to say that churches and colleges and corporations actually proclaim a racial preference. All will assert that they welcome parishioners and students and employees of every color, and they hope to increase that diversity. Executives at firms like General Motors and General Electric would be shocked if told that they headed racist firms, as would administrators at Cornell or Columbia. Indeed, the issue barely arises in the minds of their members. So if someone files a lawsuit, the complaint generally comes as a surprise. The organizations reply that they do not discriminate; more than that, most who speak this way truly believe what they say.

Simply stated, most white people prefer not to perceive their nation and its major institutions as "white," and consequently racist. They will say that the United States is a multiracial society, and becomes more so every day. The same strictures, they will add, hold for its major organizations and associations. To claim that the white race holds so preponderant a sway is both untrue and gratuitous.

Black Americans seldom see the reality this way. Black students at Yale University, black members of the Omaha police force, even black passengers on an airline flight, never cease being aware of their white surroundings. When black Americans go to movies, turn on television, or simply scan the comic strips, it seems as if their nation hardly knows or cares that they exist. (They are quite aware of well-known black figures, ranging from Oprah Winfrey to Colin Powell. Still, institutional images are overwhelmingly white.)

American institutions begin with an initial bias against black applicants, since the presumption is that most blacks cannot or will not meet the standards the organization has set. Historically, virtually all of the people associated with Yale University, United Airlines, and the

Omaha police force have been white, which has in turn created both the image of these institutions and the way they operate. In this sense, they are "white" organizations, from which it follows that their members are expected to think and act in white ways. This is not as difficult for white people, although some have to make an extra effort if they wish to master class-based aspects of the manner and style. However, for blacks the situation is qualitatively different, since they see themselves as being judged by more coercive criteria, which call on them to deny large parts of themselves.

Black Americans spend much of their lives at a distance from white Americans, in part because they feel more comfortable that way, and partly because their separation has been imposed by white America. As will be seen later, this helps to explain why even better-off blacks tend to do less well than whites on tests used by schools and employers. Since blacks of all classes are more likely to be raised in segregated surroundings, they grow up with less exposure to the kinds of reasoning that standardized examinations expect.

From slavery through the present, the nation has never opened its doors sufficiently to give black Americans a chance to become full citizens. White Americans often respond that it rests with blacks to put aside enough of their own culture so they can be absorbed into the dominant stream. Blacks can only shake their heads and reply that they have been doing just that for several centuries, with very little to show for it.

Many black men and women are concluding that they can best be described as African-Americans, considering how much their character and culture owe to their continent of origin. A pride in this heritage and history has helped them survive slavery and subsequent discrimination. Indeed, the nation as a whole has benefited from black Americans who bring to life the rhetoric and rhythms of their ancestral origins.

However, most white Americans interpret the African emphasis in another way. For them, it frequently leads to a more insidious application of racism. As has been reiterated, there persists the belief that members of the black race represent an inferior strain of the human species. In this view, Africans—and Americans who trace their origins to that continent—are seen as languishing at a lower evolutionary level than members of other races.

Of course, this belief is seldom voiced in public. Still, the unhappy fact remains that most white people believe that, compared with other races, persons with African ancestries are more likely to carry primitive traits in their genes. Given this premise—and prejudice—the presumption follows that most individuals of African heritage will lack the intellectual and organizational capacities the modern world requires.

Most whites who call themselves conservatives hold this view, and proclaim it when they are sure of their company. Most liberals and those further to the left deny that present racial disparities are based on genetic inheritance. If they harbor doubts, they keep them to themselves. Their intellectual forebears were not so constrained. Thomas Jefferson offers a case in point.

As the principal author of the Declaration of Independence, he enunciated the new nation's commitment to human equality. Most Americans can recite his phrases from memory:

> We hold these truths to be self-evident: that all men are created equal; that they are endowed by their creator with certain unalienable rights; that among these are life, liberty, and the pursuit of happiness.

To refer to some truths as self-evident means that all reasonable people should be able to agree on their veracity, without need for further proof or evidence. They are empirical first principles and moral starting points. It is noteworthy that Jefferson set down as the first of these verities the premise "all men are created equal."

There have been endless discussions over what "created equal" could have meant to Jefferson and what it might connote for us today. One thing can be said at the outset: it must refer to more than the possession of equal rights, since those entitlements are listed later and separately in the passage just quoted. Moreover, those who take the egalitarian position are well aware of human differences. No one will deny that some people are taller or gain weight more readily, or can run faster, or have perfect pitch.

However, our current concern is not whether all human beings everywhere are "created equal" in terms of personal potential, but whether this tenet applies to the groups of individuals we have come to call races. Here the terms of the argument can allow for ranges of possible talents *within* racial groups. So what racial equality *does* posit is that within each race there will be a similar distribution of talents, if all members of all races are given a chance to discover and develop those traits. Ideally, then, white Americans and black Americans could be brought to a point where both racial groups would have a virtually identical range of IQ scores. Or, even more ideally, on tests we might devise to gauge more important human qualities.

What is revealing is that while Thomas Jefferson was prepared to affirm an equality among the people to whom the Declaration of Independence applied, he was not so sure about that principle where the slaves of his day were involved. In a letter written fifteen years later, he said:

> Nobody wishes more then I do to see proofs that nature has given to our black brethren talents equal to those of the other colors of men, and that the appearance of a lack of them is owing merely to the degraded condition of their existence in Africa and America.

Can this be the same Jefferson who had earlier affirmed it was "self-evident" that all human beings everywhere are conceived with equal potential to pursue the fullest life? What, we may wonder, led him to make blacks a special case, and now to plead for "proofs" that they had faculties equal to those of other races? We may also speculate about what manner of evidence would have been sufficiently persuasive to Jefferson to undo doubts that have proved so durable. One might think that even in his day at least some blacks had shown sufficient accomplishments to quell his misgivings. As has been noted, racial equality only asks us to assume a comparable range of potentialities within every racial group.

Jeffersonian doubts remain relevant for another reason. Note how much he *wanted* to believe that persons of African origin had capacities equal to those of other races. Why, then, could not Jefferson simply pronounce the inherent equality of blacks also to be a "self-evident" truth? Any deficiencies he might find could be attributed to the oppressive environment of segregation and slavery. That has always been the egalitarian answer. Sadly, even for those who allude to blacks as their "brethren," a desire to believe does not always bring that result. Warring within the minds of Jeffersonians, both in his time and ours, is the hope that blacks are equal—accompanied by the suspicion that they are not.

* * *

Not all expressions of racism have been as beset by misgivings as Jefferson's. Since Europeans first embarked on explorations, they have been bemused by the "savages" they encountered in new lands. In almost all cases, these "primitive" peoples were seen as inferior to those who "discovered" them. While they were often described as peaceful and pastoral, as innocent and caring, those were viewed as attributes of children, not fully-formed adults. On the whole, the presumption was that these natives could never attain to a stage where they might emulate European achievements.

Many people still hold views similar to these. Indeed, terms even cruder than "savages" can be heard in private interchanges. But in public discourse, ours is much more a scientific age. So those who believe in the inherent inferiority of certain races feel obliged to allude to research based on experimentation, evidence, and an objective point of view.

One of the most prominent has been William Shockley, a winner of the Nobel Prize, who argued that evidence showed people of African origin to be lower on an evolutionary scale. Another well-known name is Arthur Jensen, a professor of psychology at the University of California. His stated position has been that because black children are genetically inferior, even compensatory programs like Head Start will fail because the native talents are not there.

In the past, this quest was called "eugenics," and it had practical as well as scholarly aims. For it hoped to warn people of supposedly superior strains that they should not mate with their genetic inferiors. The fear was of "mongrelization," a phrase then commonly used, wherein the best human breeds would marry down and produce lesser heirs. Today, such sentiments are seldom stated in so direct a way. Rather than counseling against intermarriage, it will be hinted that even social racial mixing can have deleterious effects. Hence we hear it argued that allowing too many blacks into elite colleges will not only lower intellectual standards, but will undo what those august institutions have sought to achieve.

In rational terms, there is an easy rebuttal to research and reasoning based on racist suppositions. In simplest terms, it is the environmental answer. To begin, while we know that heredity has a role in shaping human beings, this is best considered on an individual level. Within races, through parents or other forebears certain attributes are passed on to successive offspring, although it is not always possible to trace who got what from whom. After all, many permutations and combinations are involved.

Of course, races differ in some outward respects. Each race, taken as a group, carries a pool of genes that gives its members their identifiable color and anatomical structure. But even here there are shades and variations, since very few Americans belong to a "pure" race. (This is particularly true of the growing group of Hispanics.) However, despite more than a century of searching, we have no evidence that any one of those pools of race-based genes has a larger quotient of what we choose to call intelligence or organizational ability or creative capacities.

If more members of some races end up doing better in some spheres, it is because more of them grew up in environments that prepared them for those endeavors. If members of other races had similar rearings, they would display a similar distribution of success. So in terms of potential capacities, our best knowledge is that all races have a comparable range of geniuses and morons and people of average ability. We can test people as much as we please. But there is no way to factor out whether any part of the results reflect "racial" elements in some genetic sense, since we would have to adjust for every specific environmental influence as it has affected each individual. (Indeed, even when a white family adopts a black infant, the child knows that she is "black" and that image of herself will affect how she adapts to a "white" environment.)

Of course, remarks such as these will not deflect individuals like Arthur Jensen and William Shockley from sifting through research reports for evidence of racial superiority. Other citizens who are not scientists will settle for deductions of their own or cite accounts that seem to back their suppositions. Indeed, there is reason to believe that most white Americans still share Thomas Jefferson's belief that in terms of evolution and genetics theirs is the most developed race.

At a certain point, the suspicion arises that we are less in the realm of science than of ideology. Scientists, no less than lay people, have political dispositions. And, like the rest of us, the sentiments they hold give shape to what they see. More than that, even Nobel Prize winners can end up seeing not what is actually there, but what they want to see. We are not talking about dishonesty or hypocrisy, but the way human minds—indeed brilliant minds—tend to work.

So it should not be surprising that scientists who stress the role of heredity tend to be politically conservative, while those who emphasize environment veer toward the liberal side of the spectrum. By the same token, lay people select scientific views that support their ideological positions. Even individuals who have never taken a science course feel free to cite some studies as authoritative, if they agree with their findings. Thus racism has always been able to come up with a scientific veneer. This is certainly true today of those who wish to claim that one race or another is by nature inferior. They are fully persuaded that they are citing biology, not displaying bigotry.

Thus the racism blacks face runs deeper than judgments about culture. From the premise of genetic inferiority, there follows the corollary that members of a lesser race should be content to perform tasks unsuited to other strains. This was the rationale for slavery, and it has by no means disappeared. (There are even hints of this in the plea to create more blue-collar jobs for black men.) Nor is the racism applied to blacks found only among persons of European ancestry. Today, inhabitants of every other continent like to think that they have evolved further than those who trace their origins to the region south of the Sahara.

Certainly, compared with other continents, Africa remains most like its primeval self. Even today, white Americans as individuals, and white America's institutions, are unwilling to absorb the people and patrimony of humanity's first continent. This expression of racism goes well beyond personal prejudice and discriminatory institutions. It rests on judgments about culture and civilization, and who dictates the meaning of science and history.

All the observations offered thus far have focused on beliefs and behavior of white Americans. Quite obviously, racism arises in other places and guises. Most Japanese, for example, feel that they represent the highest evolution of humanity, and have cited Chinese, Koreans, and Americans as their genetic inferiors.

And what about blacks in America; cannot they harbor racist sentiments as well? Some certainly talk that way. One well-known black scholar has designated whites as "ice people," labeling them materialistic, greedy, and inherently driven to domination. By way of contrast, he calls blacks "sun people," whose chief traits are kindness and caring and communal responsibility. More than that, this scholar has argued, the melanin that makes for darker pigmentation imparts a mental and moral superiority to persons who trace their ancestries to Africa. So blacks can also employ stereotypes that impute inferiority to human beings of another race. Some whites worry about these views, seeing them as mirror images of white displays of racism, supremacy, and bigotry.

Some blacks reject that symmetry. Thus Coleman Young, the mayor of Detroit, a predominantly black city, has argued that blacks within the United States cannot be called racists, for the simple reason that they are an oppressed people. Racism, he has said, should be attributed only to those who have the power to cause suffering. What he is suggesting is it is insufficient to define racism as a set of ideas that some people may hold. Racism takes its full form only when it has an impact on the real world. While most white people may dispute the mayor's reasoning, he raises an important point. If we care about racism, it is because it scars people's lives. Individuals who do not have power may hold racist views, but they seldom cause much harm. (No one cares if homeless people believe the earth is flat.) The significance of racism lies in the way it consigns certain human beings to the margins of society, if not painful lives and early deaths. In the United States, racism takes its highest toll on blacks. No white person can claim to have suffered in such ways because of ideas that may be held about them by some black citizens.

Ideas about equality and inferiority and superiority are not simply figments in people's minds. Such sentiments have an impact on how institutions operate, and opinions tend to be self-fulfilling. If members of a minority race are believed to be deficient in character or capacities, the larger society will consign them to subordinate positions.

America has always been the most competitive of societies. It poises its citizens against one another, with the warning that they must make it on their own. Hence the stress on moving past others, driven by a fear of falling behind. No other nation so rates its residents as winners or losers.

If white America orchestrates this arena, it cannot guarantee full security to every member of its own race. Still, while some of its members may fail, there is a limit to how far they can fall. For white America has agreed to provide a consolation prize: no matter to what depths one descends, no white person can ever become black. As James Baldwin has pointed out, white people need the presence of black people as a reminder of what providence has spared them from becoming.

If white people are compelled to compete against one another, they are also urged to believe that any advances blacks may make will be at their expense. Here government and politics reflect a harsh economy. Indeed, this country is less a society, certainly less a community, than any of the countries with which it compares itself. A reason commonly given is that the United States is a large and diverse country. What is less commonly acknowledged is that its culture makes a point of exaggerating differences and exacerbating frictions. This appears most vividly in the stress placed on race.

Competition and whites' fears of failure help to explain the resistance to ensuring opportunities for black Americans, let alone more equitable outcomes. Even allowing for interludes like the New Deal and the Great Society, government is expected to take on obligations only as a late and last resort. Hence the presence in the United States of more violent crime, more of its people in prison, more homeless families and individuals, more children created virtually by accident, more fatal addiction and disease, more dirt and disorder—why prolong the list?—than any other nation deemed industrially advanced and socially civilized.

A society that places so great a premium on "getting ahead" cannot afford to spare much compassion for those who fall behind. If the contest were racially fair, it would at least be true to its own principle of assessing all individuals solely on talent and effort. But keeping black Americans so far behind the starting line means most of the outcomes will be racially foreordained.

CHAPTER THREE

BEING BLACK IN AMERICA

MOST WHITE AMERICANS will say that, all things considered, things aren't so bad for black people in the United States. Of course, they will grant that many problems remain. Still, whites feel there has been steady improvement, bringing blacks closer to parity, especially when compared with conditions in the past. Some have even been heard to muse that it's better to be black, since affirmative action policies make it a disadvantage to be white.

What white people seldom stop to ask is how they may benefit from belonging to their race. Nor is this surprising. People who can see do not regard their vision as a gift for which they should offer thanks. It may also be replied that having a white skin does not immunize a person from misfortune or failure. Yet even for those who fall to the bottom, being white has a worth. What could that value be?

Let us try to find out by means of a parable: suspend disbelief for a moment, and assume that what follows might actually happen:

THE VISIT

You will be visited tonight by an official you have never met. He begins by telling you that he is extremely embarrassed. The organization he represents has made a mistake, something that hardly ever happens.

According to their records, he goes on, you were to have been born black: to another set of parents, far from where you were raised.

However, the rules being what they are, this error must be rectified, and as soon as possible. So at midnight tonight, you will become black. And this will mean not simply a darker skin, but the bodily and facial features associated with African ancestry. However, inside you will be the person you always were. Your knowledge and ideas will remain intact. But outwardly you will not be recognizable to anyone you now know.

Your visitor emphasizes that being born to the wrong parents was in no way your fault. Consequently, his organization is prepared to offer you some reasonable recompense. Would you, he asks, care to name a sum of money you might consider appropriate? He adds that his group is by no means poor. It can be quite generous when the circumstances warrant, as they seem to in your case. He finishes by saying that their records show you are scheduled to live another fifty years—as a black man or woman in America.

How much financial recompense would you request?

When this parable has been put to white students, most seemed to feel that it would not be out of place to ask for $50 million, or $1 million for each coming black year. And this calculation conveys, as well as anything, the value that white people place on their own skins. Indeed, to be white is to possess a gift whose value can be appreciated only after it has been taken away. And why ask so large a sum? Surely this needs no detailing. The money would be used, as best it could, to buy protections from the discriminations and dangers white people know they would face once they were perceived to be black.

Of course, no one who is white can understand what it is like to be black in America. Still, were they to spend time in a black body, here are some of the things they would learn.

In the eyes of white Americans, being black encapsulates your identity. No other racial or national origin is seen as having so pervasive a personality or character. Even if you write a book on Euclidean algorithms or Renaissance sculpture, you will still be described as a "black author." Although you are a native American, with a longer lineage than most, you will never be accorded full membership in the nation or society. More than that, you early learn that this nation feels no need or desire for your physical presence. (Indeed, your people are no longer in demand as cheap labor.) You sense that most white citizens would heave a sigh of relief were you simply to disappear. While few openly propose that you return to Africa, they would be greatly pleased were you to make that decision for yourself.

Your people originated in Africa, and you want to feel pride in your homeland. After all, it was where humanity began. Hence your desire to know more of its peoples and their history, their culture and achievements, and how they endure within yourself. W. E. B. Du Bois said it best: "two thoughts, two unrecognizable stirrings, two warring ideals in one black body."

Yet there is also your awareness that not only America, but also much of the rest of the world, regards Africa as the primal continent: the most backward, the least developed, by almost every modern measure. Equally unsettling, Africa is regarded as barely worth the world's attention, a region no longer expected to improve in condition or status. During its periodic misfortunes—usually famine or slaughter—Africa may evoke compassion and pity. Yet the message persists that it must receive outside help, since there is little likelihood that it will set things right by itself.

Then there are the personal choices you must make about your identity. Unless you want to stress a Caribbean connection, you are an American and it is the only citizenship you have. At the same time, you realize that this is a white country, which expects its inhabitants to think and act in white ways. How far do you wish to adapt, adjust, assimilate, to a civilization so at variance with your people's past? For example, there is the not-so-simple matter of deciding on your diction. You know how white people talk and what they like to hear. Should you conform to those expectations, even if it demands denying or concealing much of your self? After all, white America gives out most of the rewards and prizes associated with success. Your decisions are rendered all the more painful by the hypocrisy of it all, since you are aware that even if you make every effort to conform, whites will still not accept you as one of their own.

So to a far greater degree than for immigrants from other lands, it rests on you to create your own identity. But it is still not easy to follow the counsel of Zora Neale Hurston: "Be as black as you want to be." For one thing, that choice is not always left to you. By citizenship and birth, you may count as an American, yet you find yourself agreeing with August Wilson when he says "We're a different people." Why else can you refer to your people as "folks" and "family," to one another as "sisters" and "brothers," in ways whites never can?

There are moments when you understand Toni Morrison's riposte, "At no moment in my life have I ever felt as though I were an American." This in turn gives rise to feelings of sympathy with figures like Cassius Clay, H. Rap Brown, Lew Alcindor, and Stokely Carmichael, who decided to repatriate themselves as Muhammad Ali, Jamil Abdullah al-Amin, Kareem Abdul-Jabbar, and Kwame Touré.

Those choices are not just for yourself. There will be the perplexing—and equally painful—task of having to explain to your children why they will not be treated as other Americans: that they will never be altogether accepted, that they will always be regarded warily, if not with suspicion or hostility. When they ask whether this happens because of anything they have done, you must find ways of conveying that, no, it is not because of any fault of their own. Further, for reasons you can barely explain yourself, you must tell them that much of the world has decided that you are not and cannot be their equals; that this world wishes to keep you apart, a caste it will neither absorb nor assimilate.

You will tell your children this world is wrong. But, because that world is there, they will have to struggle to survive, with scales weighted against them. They will have to work harder and do better, yet the result may be less recognition and reward. We all know life can be unfair. For black people, this knowledge is not an academic theory but a fact of daily life.

You find yourself granting that there are more black faces in places where they were never seen before. Within living memory, your people were barred from major league teams; now they command the highest salaries in most professional sports. In the movies, your people had to settle for roles as servants or buffoons. Now at least some of them are cast as physicians, business executives, and police officials. But are things truly different? When everything is added up, white America still prefers its black people to be performers who divert them as athletes and musicians and comedians.

Yet where you yourself are concerned, you sense that in mainstream occupations, your prospects are quite limited. In most areas of employment, even after playing by the rules, you find yourself hitting a not-so-invisible ceiling. You wonder if you are simply corporate wallpaper, a protective coloration they find it prudent to display. You begin to suspect that a "qualification" you will always lack is white pigmentation.

In theory, all Americans with financial means and a respectable demeanor can choose where they want to live. For over a generation, courts across the country have decreed that a person's race cannot be a reason for refusing to rent or sell a residence. However, the law seems to have had little impact on practice, since almost all residential areas are entirely black or white. Most whites prefer it that way. Some will say they would like a black family nearby, if only to be able to report that their area is integrated. But not many do. Most white Americans do not move in circles where racial integration wins social or moral credit.

This does not mean it is absolutely impossible for a black family to find a home in a white area. Some have, and others undoubtedly will. Even so, black Americans have no illusions about the hurdles they will face. If you look outside your designated areas, you can expect chilly receptions, evasive responses, and outright lies: a humiliating experience, rendered all the more enraging because it is so repeated and prolonged. After a while, it becomes too draining to continue the search. Still, if you have the income, you will find an area to your liking; but it will probably be all black. In various suburbs and at the outer edges of cities, one can see well-kept homes, outwardly like other such settings. But a closer view shows all the householders to be black.

This is the place to consider residential apartheid—and that is what it is—in its full perspective. Black segregation differs markedly from that imposed on any other group. Even newly arrived immigrants are more readily accepted in white neighborhoods.

Nor should it be assumed that most black householders prefer the racial ratios in areas where they currently reside. Successive surveys have shown that, on average, only about one in eight say they prefer a neighborhood that is all or mostly black, which is the condition most presently confront. The vast majority—some 85 percent—state they would like an equal mixture of black and white neighbors. Unfortunately, this degree of racial balance has virtually no chance of being realized. The reason, very simply, is that hardly any whites will live in a neighborhood or community where half the residents are black. So directly or indirectly, white Americans have the power to decide the racial composition of communities and neighborhoods. Most egregious have been instances where acts of arson or vandalism force black families to leave. But such methods are exceptional. There are other, less blatant, ways to prevent residential integration from passing a certain "tipping" point.

Here we have no shortage of studies. By and large, this research agrees that white residents will stay—and some new ones may move in—if black arrivals do not exceed 8 percent. But once the black proportion passes that point, whites begin to leave the neighborhood and no new ones will move in. The vacated houses or apartments will be bought or rented by blacks, and the area will be on its way to becoming all black.

What makes integration difficult if not impossible is that so few whites will accept even a racial composition reflecting the overall national proportion of 12 or 13 percent. In this regard, one or two attempts have been made to impose ceilings on the number of black residents in housing projects and developments, so as not to frighten away whites. Starrett City in New York has used this strategy, as has Atrium Village in Chicago. According to some legal readings these procedures are unconstitutional, since they treat racial groups differently. Those administering such "benign quotas" have found they must maintain two sets of waiting lists. This has been necessary to ensure that the next families chosen for vacant apartments will preserve the prevailing racial ratio. Given the preference of most blacks for integrated housing, quite a few tend to apply, and they invariably outnumber the whites on the list. The result is that black applicants have to wait longer, and are less likely to get their first choice of accommodation.

Whites and blacks who want to achieve and maintain interracial housing—itself a rarity—find they are forced to defend "benign quotas" that are biased against some blacks, since there are fewer "black" places. Racial quotas also tend to put blacks on the spot. On the one hand, few are willing to publicly support a ceiling for people of their race. Even so, most of the black householders already in residence would prefer that the racial ratio remain stabilized. After all, they themselves underwent a wait because they wanted to live in a racially integrated setting. Yet preserving the equation pits them against other blacks impatient to get in.

If many whites say they support racial integration in principle, even if this only means a token black neighbor, at least as many do not want any blacks living near them at all. One question, certainly, is how far this resistance is based solely on race, or whether the reasons have more to do with culture or class. White people themselves vary in income and other signals of status, and every section of the nation has hierarchies among white neighborhoods. Even in an area where everyone earns essentially the same income, many residents would not want a homosexual couple on their block, or a neighbor who parked a business van ("PARAGON PEST CONTROL") in his driveway every night. Simply being a fellow white is not enough to make a person a desired neighbor.

This granted, we can try to isolate the element of race by positing some "ideal" black neighbors: persons with professional credentials or those who hold administrative positions in respected organizations. Give them sophisticated tastes; make them congenial in demeanor; and have them willing to care about their property and the area as a whole. And allow, further, that a fair number of whites might not object to having one or two such households nearby. Why, then, would such open-minded neighbors start worrying if the number of black families—granting that all of them are impeccably middle class—seems to be approaching a racial "tipping" point?

The first reason is that there is no assurance that the black proportion will stay below the "tipping" figure. Word gets around among black families when a "white" neighborhood appears willing to accept a measure of integration. Rental and real estate agents are also quick to note this fact and begin recommending the area to black customers. As a result, whenever homes and apartments become vacant, a visible number of those coming to look at them appear to be black. Nor should this be surprising. Some black Americans want more interracial exposure for themselves and their children. Others may not share this wish, but they know that better schools and safer streets are more apt to be where whites are.

Longitudinal studies, based on tracing census tracts, show that whites begin to move out once the black proportion reaches somewhere between 10 and 20 percent. Moreover, this happens even when the blacks who move in have the same economic and social standing as the white residents. What is it, then, that makes white Americans unwilling to risk having black neighbors? Some of the reasons are familiar and openly stated. Others involve fears less easily articulated or admitted.

To the minds of most Americans, the mere presence of black people is associated with a high incidence of crime, residential deterioration, and lower educational attainment. Of course, most whites are willing to acknowledge that these strictures do not apply to all blacks. At the same time, they do not want to have to worry about trying to distinguish blacks who would make good neighbors from those who would not. To which is added the suspicion that if more black families arrive, it would take only one or two undesirables to undermine any interracial amity.

Even if all one's black neighbors were vouchsafed to be middle class or better, there may still be misgivings about their teenaged children. To start, there is the well-known wariness of white parents that their children—especially their daughters—could begin to make black friends. Plus the fear that even less intimate contacts will influence the vocabulary and diction, even the academic commitments, of their own offspring. And if white parents are already uneasy over the kinds of music their children enjoy, imagine their anxieties at hearing an even greater black resonance. Along with the worry that some of the black youths on the block might display a hostile demeanor, clouding the congenial ambience most Americans seek.

Americans have extraordinarily sensitive antennae for the colorations of neighborhoods. In virtually every metropolitan area, white householders can rank each enclave by the racial makeup of the residents. Given this knowledge, where a family lives becomes an index of its social standing. While this is largely an economic matter, proximity to blacks compounds this assessment. For a white family to be seen as living in a mixed—or changing—neighborhood can be construed as a symptom of surrender, indeed as evidence that they are on a downward spiral.

If you are black, these white reactions brand you as a carrier of contaminations. No matter what your talents or attainments, you are seen as infecting a neighborhood simply because of your race. This is the ultimate insult of segregation. It opens wounds that never really heal and leaves scars to remind you how far you stand from full citizenship.

* * *

Except when you are in your own neighborhood, you feel always on display. On many occasions, you find you are the only person of your race present. You may be the only black student in a college classroom, the only black on a jury, the sole black at a corporate meeting, the only one at a social gathering. With luck, there may be one or two others. You feel every eye is on you, and you are not clear what posture to present. You realize that your presence makes whites uncomfortable; most of them probably wish you were not there at all. But since you are, they want to see you smile, so they can believe that you are being treated well. Not only is an upbeat air expected, but you must never show exasperation or anger, let alone anything that could look like a chip on your shoulder. Not everyone can keep such tight control. You don't find it surprising that so many black athletes and entertainers seek relief from those tensions.

Even when not in white company, you know that you are forever in their conversations. Ralph Ellison once said that to whites, you are an "invisible man." You know what he meant. Yet for all that, you and your people have been studied and scrutinized and dissected, caricatured, and pitied or deplored, as no other group ever has. You see yourself reduced to data in research, statistics in reports. Each year, the nation asks how many of your teenagers have become pregnant, how many of your young men are in prison. Not only are you continually on view; you are always on trial.

What we have come to call the media looms large in the lives of almost all Americans. Television and films, newspapers and magazines, books and advertising, all serve as windows on a wider world, providing real and fantasized images of the human experience. The media also help us to fill out our own identities, telling us about ourselves, or the selves we might like to be.

If you are black, most of what is available for you to read and watch and hear depicts the activities of white people, with only rare and incidental allusions to persons like yourself. Black topics and authors and performers appear even less than your share of the population, not least because the rest of America doesn't care to know about you. Whites will be quick to point out that there have been successful "black" programs on radio and television, as well as popular black entertainers and best-selling authors. Yet in these and other instances, it is whites who decide which people and productions will be underwritten, which almost always usually means that "black" projects will have to appeal to whites as well. You sometimes sense that much that is "black" is missing in artists like Jessye Norman and Toni Morrison, Paul Robeson, and Bill Cosby, who you sense must tailor their talents to white audiences. You often find yourself wishing they could just be themselves, among their own people.

At the same time, you feel frustration and disgust when white America appropriates your music, your styles, indeed your speech and sexuality. At times, white audiences will laud the originality of black artists and performers and athletes. But in the end, they feel more comfortable when white musicians and designers and writers—and athletic coaches—adapt black talents to white sensibilities.

Add to this your bemusement when movies and television series cast more blacks as physicians and attorneys and executives than one will ever find in actual hospitals or law firms or corporations. True, these depictions can serve as role models for your children, encouraging their aspirations. At the same time, you do not want white audiences to conclude that since so many of your people seem to be doing well, little more needs to be done.

Then there are those advertisements showing groups of people. Yes, one of them may be black, although not too black, and always looking happy to be in white company. Still, these blacks are seldom in the front row, or close to the center. Even worse, you think you have detected a recent trend: in advertisements that include a person of color, you see Asians being used instead of blacks.

To be sure, textbooks and lesson plans now include allusions to "contributions" made by Americans of many ancestries. Children are taught how the Chinese built the railroads, and that Hispanics have a vibrant and varied culture. Even acknowledging these nods, the curriculums of the nation's schools and colleges focus mainly on the achievements of white people. The emphasis is on English origins, and that those settlers brought their institutions and ideas from the British Isles. Most Americans with European ancestors can identify with this "Anglo-Saxon" past. Descendants of slaves do not find it as easy. Whether black children are alienated by the content of the curriculum is a matter of controversy, which will be considered later on. At this point, it can be said that few teachers attempt to explain how the human beings consigned to slavery shaped the structure and sensibilities of the new nation. Apart from brief allusions to a Sojourner Truth or a Benjamin Banneker, your people appear as passive victims and faceless individuals.

In much the same vein, white children can be led to see how the travails of Shakespeare's heroes shed light on the human condition. Or that Jane Austen's heroines have messages for Americans of today. Nor is this impossible for black Americans. Ralph Ellison, raised in rural Alabama, recalled that reading Ezra Pound and Sigmund Freud give him a broader sense of life. Jamaica Kincaid has cited Charlotte Brontë as her first literary influence. Yet no matter how diligently you think about these authors and their ideas, you find that much of your life is not reflected in European learning. You often feel that there is a part of yourself, your soul, that Europe cannot reach. As in Countée Cullen's lines:

> What is Africa to me:
> Copper sun or scarlet sea,
> Jungle star or jungle track,
> Strong bronzed men, or regal black,
> Women from whose loins I sprang
> When the birds of Eden sang?

Whether you would like to know more white people is not an easy question to answer. So many of the contacts you have with them are stiff and uneasy, hardly worth the effort. If you are a woman, you may have developed some cordial acquaintances among white women at your place of work, since women tend to be more relaxed when among themselves. Still, very few black men and women can say that they have white "friends," if by that is meant people they confide in or entertain in their homes.

Of course, friendships often grow out of shared experiences. People with similar backgrounds can take certain things for granted when with one another. In this respect, you and white people may not have very much in common. At the same time, by no means all your outlooks and interests relate to your race. There probably are at least a few white people you would like to know better. It just might be that some of them would like to know you. But as matters now stand, the chances that these barriers will be broken do not appear to be very great.

Societies create vocabularies, devising new terms when they are needed, and retaining old ones when they serve a purpose. Dictionaries list words as obsolete or archaic, denoting that they are no longer used or heard. But one epithet survives, because people want it to. Your vulnerability to humiliation can be summed up in a single word. That word, of course, is "nigger."

When a white person voices it, it becomes a knife with a whetted edge. No black person can hear it with equanimity or ignore it as "simply a word." This word has the force to pierce, to wound, to penetrate, as no other has. There have, of course, been terms like "kike" and "spic" and "chink." But these are less frequently heard today, and they lack the same emotional impact. Some nonethnic terms come closer, such as "slut" and "fag" and "cripple." Yet, "nigger" stands alone with its power to tear at one's insides. It is revealing that whites have never created so wrenching an epithet for even the most benighted members of their own race.

Black people may use "nigger" among themselves, but with a tone and intention that is known and understood. Even so, if you are black, you know white society devised this word and keeps it available for use. (Not officially, of course, or even in print; but you know it continues to be uttered behind closed doors.) Its persistence reminds you that you are still perceived as a degraded species of humanity, a level to which whites can never descend.

You and your people have problems, far more than your share. And it is not as if you are ignorant of them, or wish to sweep them under a rug. But how to frame your opinions is not an easy matter. For example, what should you say about black crime or addiction or out-of-wedlock pregnancies? Of course, you have much to say on these and other topics, and you certainly express your ideas when you are among your own people. And you can be critical—very critical—of a lot of behavior you agree has become common among blacks.

However, the white world also asks that black people conduct these discussions in public. In particular, they want to hear you condemn black figures they regard as outrageous or irresponsible. This cannot help but annoy you. For one thing, you have never asked for white advice. Yet whites seem to feel that you stand in need of their tutelage, as if you lack the insight to understand your own interests. Moreover, it makes sense for members of a minority to stand together, especially since so many whites delight in magnifying differences among blacks. Your people have had a long history of being divided and conquered. At the same time, you have no desire to be held responsible for what every person of your color thinks or does. You cannot count how many times you have been asked to atone for some utterances of Louis Farrakhan, or simply to assert that he does not speak for you. You want to retort that you will choose your own causes and laments. Like other Americans, you have no obligation to follow agendas set by others.

As it happens, black Americans can and do disagree on racial matters, not to mention a host of other issues. Thus a survey conducted in 1990 found that 78 percent of those polled said they preferred to think of themselves as "black," and another 20 percent chose "African-American," while the remaining 2 percent stayed with "Negro." Another study by a team of black social scientists found that less than a quarter of the blacks they polled felt that black parents should give their children African names. Indeed, on a wide range of matters, there is no fixed, let alone official, black position. Yet it is amazing how often white people ask you to tell them how "black people" think about some individual or issue.

Then there are the accusations of inconsistency. As when you seem to favor taking race into consideration in some areas, but not in others. Or that you support a double standard, which allows separate criteria to be used for blacks in employment or education. Well, as it happens, you do believe:

- That discrimination against blacks remains real and calls for radical remedies; yet you cannot take seriously the argument that these compensatory actions will cause whites to suffer from "reverse" discrimination.
- That blacks have every right to attend dominantly white schools; yet once they are there, they should not be taken to task for spending much of their time with classmates of their own race.
- That it is important to preserve historically black colleges; yet you would feel entitled to object if some other schools were to designate themselves as "historically white."
- That racism is often the key reason why white voters rally behind

white candidates; yet when blacks support a candidate of their own race, you do not see this as expressing racism.

- That while you reject censorship, you would prefer that a book like *Huckleberry Finn* not be assigned in high school classes, since its ubiquitous use of "nigger" sustains a view of blacks that can only hurt your people. Nor are you persuaded that the typical teacher can make clear Mark Twain's intentions, or put them in perspective, for white teenagers.

It will often seem to you as if black people's opinions are constantly under scrutiny by the white world. Every time you express an opinion, whites seem to slap it on their dissecting table, showing that blacks want the best of both ways. In fact, you have answers on these issues, but whites take so much delight in citing alleged "inconsistencies" that they hardly hear what you have to say.

You may, by a combination of brains and luck and perseverance, make it into the middle class. And like all middle-class Americans, you will want to enjoy the comforts and pleasures that come with that status. One downside is that you will find many white people asking why you aren't doing more to help members of your race whom you have supposedly left behind. There is even the suggestion that, by moving to a safer or more spacious area, you have callously deserted your own people.

Yet hardly ever do middle-class whites reflect on the fact that they, too, have moved to better neighborhoods, usually far from poorer and less equable persons of their own race or ethnic origins. There is little evidence that middle-class whites are prepared to give much of themselves in aid of fellow whites who have fallen on misfortune. Indeed, the majority of white Americans have chosen to live in sequestered suburbs, where they are insulated from the nation's losers and failures.

Compounding these expectations, you find yourself continually subjected to comparisons with other minorities or even members of your own race. For example, you are informed that blacks who have emigrated from the Caribbean earn higher incomes than those born in the United States. Here the message seems to be that color by itself is not an insurmountable barrier. Most stinging of all are contrasts with recent immigrants. You hear people just off the boat (or, nowadays, a plane) extolled for building businesses and becoming productive citizens. Which is another way of asking why you haven't matched their achievements, considering how long your people have been here.

Moreover, immigrants are praised for being willing to start at the bottom. The fact that so many of them manage to find jobs is taken as evidence that the economy still has ample opportunities for employment. You want to reply that you are not an immigrant, but as much a citizen as any white person born here. Perhaps you can't match the mathematical skills of a teenager from Korea, but then neither can most white kids at suburban high schools. You feel much like a child being chided because she has not done as well as a precocious sister. However, you are an adult, and do not find such scolding helpful or welcome.

No law of humanity or nature posits a precise format for the family. Throughout history and even in our day, households have had many shapes and structures. The same strictures apply to marriage and parental relationships. All this requires some emphasis, given concerns expressed about "the black family" and its presumed disintegration. In fact, the last several decades have seen a weakening of domestic ties in all classes and races.

Black Americans are fully aware of what is happening in this sphere. They know that most black children are being born out of wedlock and that these youngsters will spend most of their growing years with a single parent. They understand that a majority of their marriages will dissolve in separation or divorce, and that many black men and women will never marry at all. Black Americans also realize that tensions between men and women sometimes bear a violence and bitterness that can take an awful toll.

If you are black, you soon learn it is safest to make peace with reality: to acknowledge that the conditions of your time can undercut dreams of enduring romance and "happily ever after." This is especially true if you are a black woman, since you may find yourself spending many of your years without a man in your life. Of course, you will survive and adapt, as your people always have. Central in this effort will be joining and sustaining a community of women—another form of a family—on whom you can rely for love and strength and support.

If you are a black woman, you can expect to live five fewer years than your white counterpart. Among men, the gap is seven years. Indeed, a man living in New York's Harlem is less likely to reach sixty-five than is a resident of Bangladesh. Black men have a three times greater chance of dying of AIDS, and outnumber whites as murder victims by a factor of seven. According to studies, you get less sleep, are more likely to be overweight, and to develop hypertension. This is not simply due to poverty. Your shorter and more painful life results, in considerable measure, from the anxieties that come with being black in America.

If you are a black young man, life can be an interlude with an early demise. Black youths do what they must to survive in a hostile world, with the prospect of violence and death on its battlefields. Attitudes can turn fatalistic, even suicidal: gladiators without even the cheers of an audience.

When white people hear the cry, "the police are coming!" for them it almost always means, "help is on the way." Black citizens cannot make the same assumption. If you have been the victim of a crime, you cannot presume that the police will actually show up; or, if they do, that they will take much note of your losses or suffering. You sense police officials feel that blacks should accept being robbed or raped as one of life's everyday risks. It seems to you obvious that more detectives are assigned to a case when a white person is murdered.

If you are black and young and a man, the arrival of the police does not usually signify help, but something very different. If you are a teenager simply socializing with some friends, the police may order you to disperse and get off the streets. They may turn on a searchlight, order you against a wall. Then comes the command to spread your legs and empty out your pockets, and stand splayed there while they call in your identity over their radio. You may be a college student and sing in a church choir, but that will not overcome the police presumption that you have probably done something they can arrest you for.

If you find yourself caught up in the system, it will seem like alien terrain. Usually your judge and prosecutor will be white, as will most members of the jury, as well as your attorney. In short, your fate will be decided by a white world.

This may help to explain why you have so many harsh words for the police, even though you want and need their protection more than white people do. After all, there tends to be more crime in areas where you live, not to mention drug dealing and all that comes in its wake. Black citizens are at least twice as likely as whites to become victims of violent crimes. Moreover, in almost all of these cases, the person who attacks you will be black. Since this is so, whites want to know, why don't black people speak out against the members of their race who are causing so much grief? The reason is partly that you do not want to attack other blacks while whites are listening. At least equally important is that while you obviously have no taste for violence, you are also wary of measures that might come with a campaign to stamp out "black crime." These reasons will receive fuller consideration in a later chapter. At this point you might simply say that you are not sure you want a more vigorous police presence, if those enforcers are unable to distinguish between law-abiding citizens and local predators. Of course, you want to be protected. But not if it means that you and your friends and relatives end up included among those the police harass or arrest.

The national anthem sings of America as "the land of the free." The Pledge of Allegiance promises "liberty and justice for all." The Declaration of Independence proclaims that all human creatures are "created equal."

If you are black, you cannot easily join in the anthem's refrain, reciting the pledge, or affirming that your country is committed to equality. While you grant that the United States is "your" country, you may define your citizenship as partial and qualified. It is not that you are "disloyal," if that means having your first allegiance elsewhere. Rather, you feel no compelling commitment to a republic that has always rebuffed you and your people.

We know from surveys that during the Cold War era, black Americans felt less antipathy toward nations then designated as our enemies, since they saw themselves less threatened by the Soviet Union or Cuba or China than did most white Americans. Nor were they so sure why they or their children were asked to risk their lives fighting people of color in places like Vietnam and Panama and the Middle East. And if the United States finds itself increasingly at odds with Islamic countries or other movements in the Third World, even more black Americans may find themselves wondering where their own allegiances lie.

As you look back on the way this nation has treated your people, you wonder how so many have managed to persevere amid so much adversity. About slavery, of course, too much cannot be said. Yet even within living memory, there were beaches and parks—in the North as well as in the South—where black Americans simply could not set foot. Segregation meant separation without even a pretense of equal facilities. In Southern communities that had only a single public library or swimming pool, black residents and taxpayers could never borrow a book or go for a swim. Indeed, black youths were even forbidden to stroll past the pool, lest they catch a glimpse of white girls in their bathing costumes.

How did they endure the endless insults and humiliations? Grown people being called by their first names, having to avert their eyes when addressed by white people, even being expected to step off a sidewalk when whites walked by. Overarching it all was the terror, with white police and prosecutors and judges possessing all but total power over black lives. Not to mention the lynchings by white mobs, with victims even chosen at random, to remind all blacks of what could happen to them if they did not remain compliant and submissive.

You wonder how much that has changed. Suppose, for example, you find yourself having to drive across the country, stopping at gasoline stations and restaurants and motels. As you travel across the heart of white America, you can never be sure of how you will be received. While the odds are that you will reach your destination alive, you cannot be so sure that you will not be stopped by the police or spend a night in a cell. So you would be well advised to keep to the speed limit, and not exceed it by a single mile. Of course, white people are pulled over by state troopers; but how often are their cars searched? Or if a motel clerk cannot "find" your reservation, is it because she has now seen you in person? And are all the toilet facilities at this service station really out of order?

The day-to-day aggravations and humiliations add up bit by bitter bit. To take a depressingly familiar example, you stroll into a shop to look at the merchandise, and it soon becomes clear that the clerks are keeping a watchful eye on you. Too quickly, one of them comes over to inquire what it is you might want, and then remains conspicuously close as you continue your search. It also seems that they take an unusually long time verifying your credit card. And then you and a black friend enter a restaurant, and find yourselves greeted warily, with what is obviously a more anxious reception than that given to white guests. Yes, you will be served, and your table will not necessarily be next to the kitchen. Still, you sense that they would rather you had chosen some other eating place. Or has this sort of thing happened so often that you are growing paranoid?

So there is the sheer strain of living in a white world, the rage that you must suppress almost every day. No wonder black Americans, especially black men, suffer so much from hypertension. (If ever an illness had social causes, this is certainly one.) To be black in America means reining in your opinions and emotions as no whites ever have to do. Not to mention the forced and false smiles you are expected to contrive, to assure white Americans that you harbor no grievances against them.

Along with the tension and the strain and the rage, there come those moments of despair. At times, the conclusion seems all but self-evident that white America has no desire for your presence or any need for your people. Can this nation have an unstated strategy for annihilating your people? How else, you ask yourself, can one explain the incidence of death and debilitation from drugs and disease; the incarceration of a whole generation of your men; the consignment of millions of women and children to half-lives of poverty and dependency?* Each of these debilities has its causes; indeed, analyzing them has become a minor industry. Yet with so much about these conditions that is so closely related to race, they say something about the larger society that has allowed them to happen.

This is not to say that white officials sit in secret rooms, plotting the genocide of black America. You understand as well as anyone that politics and history seldom operate that way. Nor do you think of yourself as unduly suspicious. Still, you cannot rid yourself of some lingering mistrust. Just as your people were once made to serve silently as slaves, could it be that if white America begins to conclude that you are becoming too much trouble, it will find itself contemplating more lasting solutions?

*In 1990, when a sample of black Americans were asked if they thought that the government was deliberately encouraging drug use among black people, 64 percent felt that this might be true. When asked if they suspected that AIDS had been purposely created by scientists to infect black people, 32 percent believed there might be some truth in this view.

CHAPTER FOUR

WHITE RESPONSES

RIGHT AND LEFT, GUILT AND SEX

LEFT AND RIGHT, we often hear, have lost their relevance in a complex and changing age. That view has validity for many issues, especially as fewer people screen the world through an ideological lens. Yet race remains an area where it still makes sense to locate the attitudes of white Americans along a liberal-conservative continuum.

As used here, the term "liberal" will range from a moderate posture to the radical left. While liberalism is not a detailed doctrine with positions on every issue, it has a quite coherent outlook concerning what white America owes to its black citizens.

Conservatives also range across a spectrum; but, as with liberals, some generalizations can be ventured. Conservatives will be considered first, because their views are more straightforwardly stated, and have a less ambiguous basis.

Most conservative Americans tend to disclaim responsibility for issues and tensions associated with race. They reject the suggestion that they bear any personal guilt. In their view, black Americans are the ones who should change their attitudes and conduct. Conservatives believe that for at least a generation, black people have been given plenty of opportunities, so they have no one but themselves to blame for whatever difficulties they face. Also, when among themselves, conservatives may be heard to wonder whether many blacks truly want to make an effort to adapt to the demands of this nation. Nor are they persuaded that many have the talents needed for positions of authority. For this and related reasons, in political contests involving a choice between candidates of different races, they usually end up voting for whomever happens to be the white candidate.

For their own part, conservatives prefer to believe that whatever success they have achieved has been due to their own efforts; and they feel this standard should apply to everyone. They may add that special assistance erodes the character of those so benefitted, by allowing them to get by too easily. In objecting to calls for preferential treatment, they cite other ethnic groups that started at or near the bottom and have, by their own efforts, pulled ahead of black Americans. Conservatives tend not to be moved by arguments that immigrants face fewer obstacles than the descendants of slaves.

One of the more interesting hallmarks of white conservatives is the amount of energy they expend attacking policies intended to aid blacks. Among their targets are affirmative action in employment and education, along with contracts earmarked for minority businesses. At first glance, the sheer volume of these broadsides—books and articles and speeches, backed by lawsuits and administrative challenges—might seem a case of overkill given the impact of these programs. As will be noted in later chapters, the number of whites who have suffered due to affirmative action has been relatively small. Still, preferred treatment for blacks hits a conservative nerve. It is not simply that they want everyone to play by the same rules. In other areas, conservatives defend inherited privileges and advantages. With affirmative action, there is something about the race of the recipients that bothers conservatives in ways they cannot always articulate in a coherent manner.

On the whole, conservatives don't really care whether black Americans are happy or unhappy. At the same time, they remain vigilant for signs of discontent, especially if stirrings have ominous overtones. Hence their support for close police control of the black population. So when crime rates rise, conservatives do not call for confronting basic causes—unemployment, for example, or inferior education—but rather invoke a firmer use of force. Since they see themselves as bearing no onus for whatever problems blacks face, they do not really care if blacks feel aggrieved or unfairly treated. To support their position, they cite black conservatives—Thomas Sowell, Clarence Thomas, Shelby Steele—who assure them that blacks have played the victim too long and must be judged by the same standards as other Americans.

For the past several decades, a majority of white Americans have said that they support racial integration, equality of opportunity, and a better life for their black fellow citizens. Are these statements more than cosmetic?

What has changed in recent years is the way people speak in public. Indeed, even in private conversations, the coarser kinds of descriptions are less often heard. Hence recourse to roundabout phrases, like "underclass" and "inner city." There are several reasons for this shift. At the center has been the extension of schooling. To what extent, if at all, lessons taught in a classroom can make people more tolerant is not easy to ascertain. Obviously, some teachers have influenced the way their pupils perceive the world, as students will attest. But young minds are shaped by many forces, and what happens in classrooms may play only a marginal role. What we can say with certainty is that the choice to go on with formal learning usually reflects a wish to raise one's self socially and professionally, which in turn calls for more caution in speech and demeanor.

Given these new sensitivities, it is not surprising that surveys find majorities of white Americans avowing that they would not object to having some black families on their block. Nor, they say, would they mind were their children's schools to have a greater mixture of races. Nor should such responses be dismissed as dishonest or hypocritical, at least not at a conscious level. For a further effect of education is to encourage people to think of themselves as tolerant and open-minded.

The term "liberal" tends to be associated with men and women who are at least minimally middle class. (In contrast, conservative beliefs can be found on every rung of the social ladder.) What often distinguishes liberals from others at the same economic level is their greater willingness to pay for programs aimed at resolving social and racial ills. To that extent, then, they seem ready to share some of what they have with others less fortunate than themselves. In this respect, liberals like to feel they are altruistic, and justified in criticizing conservatives for being tightfisted, if not downright selfish.

At the same time, the new taxes liberals tend to propose are unlikely to be so severe as to reduce their own living standard in a serious way. If a few choose to live in multiracial neighborhoods and send their children to racially balanced schools, at least as many find reasons to settle in outlying towns or more insulated suburbs. They may try to make up for this by expressing a willingness to pay taxes for social programs, as well as writing checks for progressive causes and organizations.

As was seen in the preceding chapter, Thomas Jefferson used the phrase "our black brethren" to refer to fellow beings consigned to slavery, including those he owned himself. Liberals continue to profess this fellowship, affirming that in character and potential, blacks and whites are full and complete equals. Hence the inclination to empathize; to murmur, when seeing what so many blacks endure, that there but for an accident of birth, go I.

Moreover, liberals are also prone to accept personal responsibility for racial conditions that prevail in this country. Even if their forebears never owned slaves, they nevertheless believe that their own privileged status has contributed to keeping blacks in a degraded state. For example, liberals are ready to acknowledge how they have benefited from the availability of cheap black labor, whether as domestic servants or the people who pick the fruit and vegetables they buy. As an earnest of atonement, they give larger tips to blacks who serve or wait on them.

Liberals also express more ambiguities than conservatives about the attainments of the white and Western world. They are more likely to focus on colonial conquests and exploitation, on technologies that destroy nature and corrupt the human spirit. Alongside the grandeur of Mozart and Michelangelo have been the horrors of Auschwitz and Hiroshima and chattel slavery. Thus on campuses, liberals urge a more multicultural content for the curriculum, which can mean compressing courses on Shakespeare to make room for offerings with less traditional origins.

Liberals also hold a theory about the sweep and tenor of human history. While seldom stated as a coherent philosophy, its premises occasionally become explicit. One such tenet is that the era of white dominance is coming to an end. If nothing else, birthrates dictate that the approaching century will belong to people of color, just as immigration is changing the texture of the United States. True, the Western world still has military might; but it lacks social goals and moral purpose. Hence the desire of liberals to find a place for themselves in the new era: so the future will note that they were among the few white persons who foresaw what was coming and were prepared to accept their diminished status.

How far we hold adults responsible for their acts hinges largely on moral judgments we make about social and psychological conditions. Children may be deemed insufficiently mature to realize the implications of their actions; similar exemptions are often granted to people diagnosed as mentally ill. However, liberals seldom stop there. They frequently use psychology and the social sciences to excuse certain black behavior, on the ground that it is an understandable response to the way their race has been treated by an oppressive society.

This raises key questions about the meaning of crime and the rationale for punishment, which will be considered in a later chapter. What can be said here is that liberals are more apt to express compassion for the large numbers of black men and women currently languishing in prisons. They want to learn more about the conditions that may have turned these blacks to crime, especially circumstances that might exonerate them from guilt. Seen in this way, individuals who have been condemned as culpable may be recast as victims, since they were driven to destructive conduct by forces beyond their control.

Liberals can thus conclude that the real guilt rests with white society, which forces blacks into demeaning segregation, consigns them to low-paid employment, and gives so many so little hope. That some black Americans may react in ways seen as antisocial should not be surprising, considering the constrictions on their lives. Of course, this raises the issue of how far individuals who have been treated unjustly should be held responsible for their acts. Conservatives have no problem with their answer. They believe that to exonerate irresponsible conduct is not only condescending, but that it does little to improve the character of the culprits. Liberals tend to reply that the issue is not so simple. At the least, we ought to give more thought to the conditions that cause so many people who are black to end up being judged and condemned and punished by public opinion and official institutions.

Liberals account for most of the white faces in the audiences for serious African and African-American music, art, and theater. A similar interest holds for books by black authors. Of course, white people of all ages and political persuasions are drawn to black entertainers, whether on television and movie screens or in athletic arenas. However, for those on the left, the attraction runs deeper than art and entertainment. For them, Africa—and much of black America—remains symbolic of a mode of life that the white and Western world has effaced or destroyed.

As has been intimated, white liberals want to be liked by black people, as if having their goodwill is a seal of approval. Hence the frequency with which they allude to black friends, black workmates, and—when possible—black neighbors. (Having only a single black family in an apartment complex allows all the others to announce that they live in an "integrated" area.) Hence also the mentions of black schoolmates their children may bring home, affirming their choice of integrated classes, even if in private schools. On the other side are the feelings of dismay when one receives rebuffs from blacks, or simply the anonymous but scornful stares often encountered in public places. Liberals hope blacks will acknowledge that some whites—themselves, as it happens—are not The Enemy, but rather can be counted as friends and allies. For blacks to grant this, if only by bestowing a smile, serves to certify one's moral stature.

This search for approval also occurs in associational settings. Here we can observe an experience common among professional groups of professors, social workers, and librarians, which have large liberal memberships. These organizations usually elect their officers by ballots distributed through the mail. On an accompanying sheet, the candidates summarize their activities and affiliations, since in many cases they are not personally known to everyone taking part in the voting. If one of the persons running for office signals his or her race, perhaps by mentioning a position once held in an African-American group, the odds are all but certain that he or she will end up among those elected. The individual's credentials may be excellent; however, that was not why that person got so many votes. Simply filling in the box by one or more "black" names allows a lot of white members to feel better about themselves.

Hence, too, the tendency to applaud longer and more strenuously following the remarks by a black participant in a panel discussion. In many instances, of course, such praise is deserved: the panelist may have offered original and important observations. But it is also possible that the comments made by the black member are no more profound than those by the others at the table. If that was the case, then the prolonged applause is not so much to acclaim the presentation as to make someone who is black feel he is in the company of friendly whites. This will, they hope, serve as some recompense for the wrongs their race has done to his.

Often, in conversations where members of the two races are present, one or another of the white persons will say something that prompts a heated reply from a black member of the group. When it happens that the offending statement was made by someone who prides himself on being liberal, his reaction is usually to stammer plaintively, either retracting what he said or protesting that he had been misunderstood. Here, as elsewhere, liberals stand in dread of black disfavor, which must be mollified by admitting to oversight or error. This is especially evident when blacks charge whites with racism. Rather than deny the indictment, the liberal tendency is to admit to such bias, and pledge renewed vigilance against future errors.

Upon hearing a report of a violent crime, many liberals find themselves half-consciously hoping that the perpetrator will turn out to be white. If that proves to be the case, their response will often be a sigh of relief. Given that liberals—much like everyone else—deplore violence of any kind, why should they have a preference about the race of the perpetrators?

The answer relates to the general tendency among Americans to associate blacks with crimes that threaten or inflict physical injury. As it happens, this belief has some basis in fact, since blacks do account for a disproportionate number of crimes like murder, rape, and robbery. An unfortunate consequence of this association is that law-abiding blacks find themselves perceived as possible criminals.

So, as liberals see it, any increase in the number of whites arrested for violent crimes would help to redress racial images in the public mind, which would in turn relieve blacks from the burden they bear due to current stereotypes about race and crime.

* * *

Since the opening years of this century, America's variant of liberalism has maintained that governmental action can ameliorate serious social problems. Although less confident now than in the past, most liberals still put their faith in public policies. Hence the view that a variety of programs, many of them quite expensive, will be needed if black Americans are to be brought to parity with whites. By this time, the agenda is fairly familiar. Much more will have to be spent in areas such as education, health services, housing, and job training. Other programs would include better foster care for children, birth control education, and aid to men and women coming out of prison, along with drug treatment and counseling. The list could be easily extended, in light of the disabilities besetting so much of the black population.

Liberals continue to have confidence in the competence of government to achieve social change. They do not view the "Great Society" of the 1960s as a failure. On the contrary, it had some signal successes. Head Start classes, for example, have enabled children to carry on through high school and beyond. Food stamps, really a kind of currency, have improved nutritional levels among millions of the poor. In both cases, black Americans were major beneficiaries. The sad part, liberals would add, is that funding for such programs was reduced or rescinded just when results were beginning to show.

Therefore, governmental intervention is not just "throwing money" at social—and racial—problems. Liberals believe that both social science research and practical experience have amassed useful funds of knowledge. Thus, they would claim, we know how to make racial integration work, and how to motivate youngsters to apply themselves in school. These aims have been attained in varied settings, and their lessons can be applied elsewhere. Faith in government rests on more than urging funding and authority for public agencies. It also arises from a belief in our ability to expand knowledge and understanding; a faith in the capacity of reason to triumph over prejudice and superstition; and the application of research and rationality to the betterment of society. So government should not be defined simply as coercive force. It should also be seen as an instrument of service, and a vehicle for organized action. Despite the presence of political pressures and parochial interests, we can still cite many cases where governmental agencies have pursued the public good and registered impressive successes.

As these arguments would suggest, liberals often rely on the presumed knowledge and objectivity of public service professionals. Whether the area is child abuse, contraceptive counseling, or managing low-income housing, liberals have sought a central role for experts with academic training. This has, however, stirred charges of "elitism," often with racial overtones, since the major decisions in health, education, and similar services tend to be made by white men and women with civil service tenure and graduate degrees. While these individuals have respectable credentials, questions have been raised concerning how much they truly know about the lives and aspirations of the people they are supposed to be assisting.

One consequence has been demands for "community control" of schools and other social programs, as a democratic counterweight to professional power. One proposal calls for giving committees of parents the authority to choose and supervise the principals of their youngsters' schools. At the time this is written, Chicago has adopted this plan, replacing a centralized system that had had little success in educating the city's children, especially in schools with enrollments that were largely or entirely black. Not surprisingly, most principals and many teachers have misgivings about giving over power to people they regard as amateurs.

There is a real issue here, and it beleaguers contemporary liberals. Some have joined in the calls for community control, arguing that familiarity with local conditions should have higher priority than formal credentials and degrees. Others have resisted, saying that professional competence cannot be compromised. One resolution has been to co-opt more blacks as administrators, and then use them as spokesmen for official positions.

All of these approaches are susceptible to perversion or corruption. Despite progressive intentions, social research can turn into arid methodologies of interest only to academics. Professionalism can become a wall of degrees and diplomas having little relation to the jobs that need to be done. Community control may end up with local groups diverting the resources of social agencies for purposes of their own.

If these and similar divisions sometimes daunt the liberal spirit, its faith in amelioration usually arises again. Despite the caricatures drawn by critics, few liberals go so far as to assert that the human condition is perfectible. But they do tend to affirm that progress is possible; that we can learn from experience; and that with good will and ingenuity, human beings can evolve new solutions that need not repeat the errors of the past.

Professions of sympathy and support have yet another source. Here the springs are more subtle, going beyond the way people want to be seen by the outside world. Rather, they reflect an unease within individuals stirred by distress over what this country has made of race.

Guilt is a tangled maze of emotions and reactions. Nor is there much consensus among psychologists about how it should be analyzed or explained. It is not a sentiment one can uncover by social surveys or opinion polls, since short answers to set questions seldom probe beneath the surface. Moreover, guilt can be rational or irrational. When it is rational, human beings admit that they have behaved badly, and they are right to blame themselves for such conduct. But guilt can also be irrational, in that people can flagellate themselves for conditions in which they did not participate. (Unless, of course, one believes that the mere fact of being white is enough to vest one with some responsibility for the plights of black Americans.) Some people enjoy feeling guilty, indeed savor the sensation. It can also express a desire for punishment: a conscience-stricken oppressor asks to be told how he has erred, so that he may mend his ways. We have seen how this operates with white people who seek the approval of blacks, which is taken as absolving them of racism.

Just what makes some people feel guilty, while others do not, cannot be answered in any conclusive way. We see that guilt is more apparent among academics and social service professionals than, say, corporation executives and self-made businessmen. It appears to run deeper among Jews and Congregationalists than, say, Baptists or Mormons. But it is not enough to say that people have learned in their schools or from their families to judge themselves in certain ways. Imagine two sisters, raised in the same home during their formative years. Now, visiting them as adults, we find one sister plagued by racial guilt, while her sibling denies having any such feelings. Doubtless, close analysis of the two women could produce "explanations." We have no shortage of analysts willing to try their hand at psychobiography. In fact, though, we have little reliable knowledge about what may have moved one person in one direction and the other in another.

* * *

We now come to a more perplexing aspect of this subject of guilt: what to say about individuals who assert that they feel no guilt at all, who insist they have nothing to feel guilty about, and disclaim any responsibility for creating or maintaining the misfortunes of others. Are we to accept their own analysis, and simply end the discussion? For better or for worse, in our educated age, this is no longer possible. We all experience situations when we feel we can see through a person's protestations. It is clear to us that they feel guilty about something, but have set up barriers to avoid facing an unpleasant sensation. At one time or another, all of us have refused to admit certain truths about ourselves. By engaging in what Psychology 101 calls "denial," we seek to convince others—and ourselves—of our innocence of blame.

This said, it will be proposed here that all white Americans, regardless of their political persuasions, are well aware of how black people have suffered due to inequities imposed upon them by white America. As has been emphasized, whites differ in how they handle that knowledge. Yet white people who disavow responsibility deny an everyday reality: that to be black is to be consigned to the margins of American life. It is because of this that no white American, including those who insist that opportunities exist for persons of every race, would change places with even the most successful black American. All white Americans realize that their skin comprises an inestimable asset. It opens doors and facilitates freedom of movement. It serves as a shield from insult and harassment. Indeed, having been born white can be taken as a sign: your preferment is both ordained and deserved. Its value persists not because a white appearance automatically brings success and status, since there are no such guarantees. What it does ensure is that you will not be regarded as *black,* a security which is worth so much that no one who has it has ever given it away.

This helps to explain why white conservatives so vehemently oppose programs like affirmative action. They simply do not want to admit to themselves that the value imputed to being white has injured people who are black. Nor is this reaction surprising. Most people do not like feeling guilty. It can be an unpleasant, even painful, sensation. Hence the tendency to turn, often angrily, on those who stir us in this way. Rather than do something substantial to help people who have been treated unfairly, we find ourselves saying that they brought their afflictions on themselves. By this device, guilt can be made to disappear, or at least seem less burdensome. As we were taught in Psychology 101, we erase our self-blame by projecting—or simply dumping—it onto someone else.

Guilt is often associated with fear. In particular, fear of those aspects of ourselves we would prefer not to confront. This is why white people devised the word "nigger" and gave it so charged a meaning. As was indicated earlier, it implies a creature so debased and degraded, that such a person must represent a lower level of humanity. There was a need for such a term to justify slavery. And its current use rationalizes much of segregation and subordination today. James Baldwin, in *The Fire Next Time,* saw that the word served a further purpose. White people "need the nigger," he wrote, because it is "the nigger" within themselves that they cannot tolerate.

Construed in this way, "nigger" represents components of the human condition that may be found in all peoples and races. Whatever it is that whites feel that "nigger" signifies about blacks—lust and laziness, stupidity or squalor—in fact exists within themselves. Baldwin's message is that any person of any race can be a "nigger." The capacity is there, waiting to be released.

Needless to say, white people—paragons of civilization—cannot allow that "niggerness" is part of their being. Were that admitted, they would have to grant that they could plunge to a degradation from which their white skin cannot shield them. So, Baldwin concluded, white people "need the nigger." By creating such a creature, whites are able to say that because only members of the black race can carry that taint, it follows that none of its attributes will be found in white people. This also explains why many whites react as they do to interracial marriage and mating, and to rapes involving a black man and a white woman. There is the fear that the offspring of such couplings could dilute a superior strain with degraded traits.

A half-century ago, Gunnar Myrdal observed that "sex and race fears are the main defense for segregation and, in fact, the whole caste order." In his *An American Dilemma,* he cited the insistence of white men that they had to protect their women from advances of black men. Hence periodic lynchings, often preceded by castrations, to warn all black men that they would do well to avert their eyes when white women were in view. While lynchings are no longer used as means of control, anxieties over interracial sex have far from abated.

Myrdal was too polite a guest to draw out the full implications of the sexual emphasis he proposed. So he forbore from suggesting that white Americans also envy "the nigger" in ways they but dimly realize and are loathe to acknowledge. Here we enter that very murky realm of sexual potency and performance, of sexual conquest and competition. Certainly, among the capacities that make for manhood, sexual potency continues to rank high even in our modern times. Compounding the ordinary insecurities most men have in this sphere, white men face the mythic fear that black men may outrival them in virility and competence. At issue, of course, is not whether this is actually true, but the fact that the stereotype persists. Aggravating this unease is a further foreboding: that white women may wonder whether black men could provide greater sexual satisfaction than they now get from their white mates. Notice, also, how white men glance a second time when they see a racially mixed couple: what, they seem to ask, does *she* see in—or do with—him? In a similar vein, white women may wonder if they can offer the sexual abandon that their men may desire. What, they may ask themselves, draws so many white men to black prostitutes?

To be white is to be "civilized," which brings acceptance and imposition of sexual constraints. True, the freedoms that arose with the sexual revolution permit more experimentation than in the past. Still, fantasies persist that black men and women are less burdened by inhibitions, and can delight in primal pleasures beyond the capacities of whites. (The erotic abandon displayed in black dancing has no white counterpart.) Nor is it surprising that much of the commentary concerning women on welfare adds the charge that they share their beds with successions of men. Underwriting indolence is bad enough. That taxes also subsidize sexual excess stirs anger and, just possibly, envy. (Not the least reason for demanding that women on welfare be made to work is that they will have less time for recreational sex.)

There are signs that race now has a more problematical place on the liberal agenda. White support for racial justice reached its high point in the 1960s, when dogs and cattle prods were used on blacks engaging in peaceful protests. The viciousness and violence so common in the South shocked even white conservatives. When blacks organized for voter registration—the most elemental of rights—scores of their churches were burned to the ground. Local leaders such as Medgar Evers were openly gunned down, while civil rights workers were murdered with the connivance of public officials. Perhaps the most shocking act of all came in 1963, with the dynamiting of a black church in Birmingham, taking the lives of four little girls attending a Sunday school class. Yet throughout these travesties, there was something stoic, even saintly, about the demeanor of Southern blacks. Equally important for sustaining white opinion, blacks remained respectful and deferential toward their liberal well-wishers.

If one person embodied these tendencies, it was Martin Luther King, Jr. He was—and remains—the leader that whites would have chosen for black Americans if they had that power to choose. To white eyes, King was safe and respectable. It is hardly accidental that they invariably referred to him as "Dr. King," as if to draw assurance from the credentials he had earned in the white world. King stood for civil rights and peaceful change, as opposed to the fists of black power. (Shortly before his death, he was coming to conclude that sustained solutions would require a huge economic cost.) He also represented a mainstream religion, Baptist, which gave his movement moral impetus as well as political stature. Colleges and universities literally lined up to give him honorary degrees.

Of course, King was a genuine leader with an unequaled following. Still, his adoption by whites gave him an ambiguous status. One reason why many white Americans worked to have his birthday made a holiday was to ensure that this honor would go to someone with whom they could feel comfortable. Blacks could not object, nor was that their wish. At the same time, they sensed that he was essentially a white choice. This feeling surfaced in New York at the time when the city council changed Harlem's 125th Street to Martin Luther King, Jr., Boulevard. Soon afterward, local residents aired their own sentiments by renaming Lenox Avenue after Malcolm X.

White attitudes began to shift when black activism started to show a more assertive posture. First came the urban disorders of the mid-1960s, where disaffection expressed itself in looting and burning. There soon followed the message that white advice and assistance were no longer wanted nor needed. The deference blacks had shown earlier had come to an end; they now sought to define their own goals and pursue them on their own terms. This in turn led many whites to dissociate themselves from demands that moved beyond the basic entitlements covered by the rubric of civil rights. Affirmative action, autonomous control, and separate development made up a new agenda, in which whites were not asked to participate.

Most liberals who have reached middle age like to recall the fellowship they felt in civil rights marches and integrated meetings. As liberals see it, the erosion of the interracial alliance did not come from a decline in white commitment. Rather, blacks turned from building bridges to shriller forms of politics that seem to indict all whites.

Racial relations have also been affected by the high incidence of crime, the fraying of family ties, and other behavior whites find frightening. Liberals can claim they worked for open housing, better schools, and vocational training. So some feel they have been let down, if not actually betrayed. In their eyes, rather than making the most of opportunities opened by progressive programs, all too many blacks appear to have embarked on self-destructive spirals downward, dooming themselves and taking a toll on the rest of society. Perhaps the most vivid evidence of altered attitudes comes from soundings by Democratic candidates and officeholders, who sense dwindling interest for wars on poverty and racial redress.

Recent decades have seen new issues command the concern and attention once given to race. One of the most prominent has been the environment. Here objects of compassion include dolphins and whales, fur-bearing animals and those used in laboratories, along with rain forests and the ozone layer. While these are clearly worthy causes, working on behalf of flora and fauna brings an additional satisfaction. These beneficiaries never grumble, or turn resentful or ungrateful. Nor is it likely that dolphins will present themselves one day and proclaim that they henceforward wish to assume control of their own struggle.

PART TWO

CHAPTER FIVE

PARENTS AND CHILDREN

DO THE RACES REALLY DIFFER?

AT FIRST SIGHT, even the statistics are dismaying. Nearly two thirds of black babies are now born outside of wedlock, and over half of black families are headed by women. The majority of black youngsters live only with their mother; and in over half of these households, she has never been married. At last count, over half of all single black women have already had children, and among women in their mid- to late-thirties, less than half have intact marriages. These figures are from three to five times greater than for white households, and markedly higher than those recorded for black Americans a generation ago.

How people reside and reproduce can be sensitive subjects, so it would be well to guard against generalizations that oversimplify the facts. There is no generic "black family," any more than white families come in a single form. Black Americans account for more than 10 million households, ranging from young adults in condominiums to suburban couples with two children and a swimming pool. So nothing in this chapter should be construed as claiming that specific domestic arrangements are "typical" for one race or the other. At the same time, it is possible to point to trends and tendencies, so long as it is understood that they refer to developments within a varied reality.

Similar cautions apply to interracial comparisons. Much of our knowledge of household life comes from government reports, which tally the races in separate tables. But even those figures must be placed in a larger context. Too great an emphasis on race can divert attention from forces that have been reshaping the entire society.

This becomes apparent from the figures in the table below, which trace rates and ratios for families headed by women over the last four decades. As can be seen, the proportion of black families headed by women has always been higher than among white households, and remains so today. But those numbers, by themselves, convey only part of the picture. An equally pervasive pattern becomes apparent when the black percentages are transformed into multiples of the white figures. Once this is done, it turns out that the biracial ratio has remained remarkably stable throughout the forty-year period. This raises the possibility that what we have been seeing are not so much racial differences as concurrent adaptations to common cultural trends.

During the past generation, single-parent households—which in most cases means homes headed by the mother—have become increasingly common in America and the rest of the world. That this arrangement now accounts for over half of black families has aroused

HOUSEHOLDS HEADED BY WOMEN: 1950–1990

Year	Black	White	Multiple
1950	17.2%	5.3%	3.2
1960	24.4%	7.3%	3.3
1970	34.5%	9.6%	3.6
1980	45.9%	13.2%	3.5
1990	56.2%	17.3%	3.2

Figures focus on families that have no husband present and with children under 18. Hispanic families are omitted after 1960.

great concern. For one thing, the loss of male breadwinners has done much to perpetuate poverty. More homes now lack a man's earnings, which means more are falling below the level of subsistence. In addition, some observers perceive an erosion of potential controls—especially over teenagers—which were once maintained by fathers in the home.

On the whole, these changes are relatively recent. In 1950, only 17 percent of black households were headed by women, equal to today's white rate. So within living memory, homes with two parents present were very much the black norm. This makes it difficult to describe the matrifocal families that preponderate today as being a "legacy" of slavery. Since legal servitude ended well over a century ago, the claim that it continues to exert a force should be made with some care. We know that in the slave system, adult pairings were denied legal standing, since owners did not want their chattels committed to lifetime covenants. Slaves were always subject to sale, which meant wives and husbands, parents and children, could be wrenched apart. Also, women had to endure assaults by white men, including bearing their offspring. Such circumstances might not seem a forerunner for enduring marriages.

Yet it is now apparent that arrangements imposed by the owners were never accepted by the slaves themselves. Once freed, blacks sought the durable unions they had been denied. For almost a century following the Civil War, black families remained remarkably stable. Despite low incomes and uncertain employment, most black households had two parents in residence, even if bound by common-law marriages. Then as now, however, their rates for female-headed households always exceeded those of other races. But figures for even as recently as the 1950s show that such families were exceptions and not the rule. So it seems clear that more recent increases in homes headed by single parents cannot be attributed to a plantation past. Not only have other developments been at work, but they cut across racial lines. While many factors are at work, for present purposes two may be emphasized here.

One such force has been aptly described as "men's liberation." More married men than ever in the past apparently feel free to leave their wives and children, often to start again with a younger companion. Nowadays, they can do this with comparatively little social censure, and often at small economic cost. Government studies show that most departing fathers either end up paying no child support at all or remit less than the agreed-upon amounts. Moreover, even the full payments seldom cover all the children's costs, leaving mothers to struggle with the bills. Ex-husbands are also more likely to remarry, in many cases starting a second round of children.

In the past, community opinion, religious canons, and an inner sense of duty kept most marriages intact. Legal divorces were much harder to obtain. If passion and romance were less apt to be expected or experienced, spouses grew accustomed to one another and built settled routines. As has been seen, these conventions encompassed both races; black couples as well as whites spent their entire married lives together. A correlative duty was for young men to "do the right thing" when informed that a baby was on the way. Shotguns were seldom needed, since social pressure combined with conscience to achieve the desired result.

A second development may be called "the right to reproduce." In theory, women have always been free to bear a child. (Despite much murmuring on the subject, forced sterilization has never been widely practiced.) In the past, girls who became pregnant usually got married before the baby came. When this did not happen, social censure set in. In some states, birth certificates were stamped "ILLEGITIMATE" in capital letters. Unwed women were often deemed unfit for parenthood. Prior to World War II, institutions assisting unmarried mothers made it clear that the women would not be allowed to keep their babies. (This is one reason why so many infants were available for adoption.)

Today, the decision of a woman to produce a child, under any conditions she chooses, is viewed as a personal right. Stated another way, no one can forbid her from following through with her decision: she cannot be ordered to have an abortion; nor can she be made to give up her baby for adoption. Of course, many people will not applaud her decision. However, the critics tend to be far removed from the settings where youthful parenthood occurs, so the censure is seldom heard. The mother may be fifteen years old. She may drink excessively or take drugs throughout the pregnancy. Indeed, she can insist on giving birth even if early tests show she has transmitted AIDS to the child she carries. In short, the right of any woman—and fifteen-year-olds now receive this designation—to use her reproductive powers cannot be vetoed or overruled. Proponents of freedom of choice join with right-to-life activists in supporting the right of any teenager to use her body to make a baby.

Under the imprint of this freedom, more single women than ever before are deciding they want to be mothers. In the great majority of cases—now well over 90 percent of the time—those who decide to carry the pregnancy to completion also opt to take the infant home and raise it themselves. So if the liberation of men has helped to increase the number of households headed by women, the choice of single women to reproduce and start families of their own has pushed the figure even higher.

Perhaps the clearest racial parallel can be found in the basic natal measure: fertility rates, which represent the number of annual births per 1,000 women from fifteen to forty-four, the most common child-bearing years. Black women have always tended to have more children, due to a desire for larger families, coupled with less sustained use of birth control. Once again, though, racial differences can conceal common causes. The table below shows that for the past half-century, fertility indexes for white and black women have moved up and down with remarkable consistency. For example, both races were swept up by the baby boom of the 1950s and 1960s. More than that, the figures show that, when they wish, black women can and do have fewer children. Their fertility rate in 1940 was actually lower than the one recorded for white women twenty years later. Moreover, black women have joined white women in reducing childbearing in recent years.

The facts and figures considered here suggest that much of the

FERTILITY RATES: 1940–1988

	White Women	Black Women	Multiple
1940	77.1	102.4	1.33
1950	102.3	137.3	1.34
1960	113.2	153.5	1.36
1970	84.1	115.4	1.37
1980	64.7	88.1	1.36
1988	63.0	86.6	1.38

sexual behavior of black Americans may be defined as less "racial" than within the national mainstream. In fact, it would have been rather surprising had black men and women remained unaffected by such forceful currents. Given the ubiquity of these trends, little will be gained by lecturing only one race on its domestic duties. To ask black Americans to show greater discipline carries the implication that only they have deviated from national norms. In fact, if any strictures are in order, they apply equally to white Americans.

Even given their tie to national trends, households headed by women and births outside of wedlock have become basic facts of life within much of black America. Most matrifocal families still adhere to the "nuclear" model of a mother on her own raising one or more children. Among black households, however, other configurations have begun to emerge. The fastest-growing group consists of three generations residing in a single household. One common arrangement consists of a mother, one or more of whose adolescent daughters has come home from the hospital with her own child. Thus the original family headed by the mother, who has become a grandmother, now includes a "subfamily" headed by the daughter.

Since 1970, black multigenerational households have increased threefold. Three quarters of the child-mothers have never been married, and many have dropped out of school to bear and care for their babies. While more white daughters than ever before are living with their parents, they tend to be older and have been married, and are now separated or divorced. Their sojourn home is more apt to be a relatively shorter stay, during which they prepare for becoming self-supporting.

Another growing group of black households are those where aunts and grandparents or other relatives are bringing up the children. According to the most recent census survey, upward of 20 percent of black adults are taking care of some youngsters other than their own. Sometimes, the mother may have died or is being treated for an illness or drug dependency, or simply lacks the resorces to act as a parent. In other cases, she may be serving a prison term, or has an occupation where she cannot stay with her children. Not infrequently, she lives in a Northern state, and has sent them to grandparents in the South.

This is not the place to debate whether optimal family life requires the full-time presence of two parents bound by a legal marriage. What can and should be stressed is that millions of American children have grown up in homes with a single parent, almost always their mother. Andrew Cherlin, a sociologist at the Johns Hopkins University who is an authority on marriage and divorce, notes it has yet to be shown that "absence of a father was directly responsible for any of the supposed deficiencies of broken homes." Still, single parents are more likely to experience emotional and physical exhaustion than couples, who can share parental responsibilities.

However, there is a social dimension as well. In depressed black neighborhoods, hardly any of the households has a male parent in residence. As a functional alternative, boys spend much of their time with groups of youths of their own age, where they devise their own definitions of masculinity. In many cases, their mothers all but cease having any influence over them. Indeed, even if more fathers were present, they would have their work cut out for them. Given the temptations of guns and drugs, as well as disdain for formal schooling, the most dedicated fathers might find it hard to impose a countervailing discipline.

The real issue, Professor Cherlin points out, "is not the lack of a male presence but the lack of a male income." If all too many families must live in dangerous terrain, it is because they cannot afford to move out. Many of those headed by single mothers get by at close to a subsistence level. In 1990, the most recent year for figures, half such households had incomes of less than $14,000. Here is where the "feminization of poverty" takes its greatest toll. Some 38 percent of white single mothers and 56 percent of their black counterparts are trying to clothe and feed their children on incomes below the poverty threshold, which in 1990 stood at $10,530 for a family of three. Many single mothers work hard at underpaid jobs and support their children in a creditable way. Yet only one in four manages to earn over $25,000 a year. White women are more apt to be in this group, since they tend to have more education and to be older when they find they must manage on their own. At the same time, it should be noted that approximately half of all black single mothers are fully self-supporting; and many on welfare do off-the-books work to supplement their stipends. Given the levels of public assistance, some outside income must be found to provide their kids with shoes and school supplies.

* * *

As the table below shows, more than half of black mothers have never been married, which works out to three times the white rate and five times what it was for their own race a generation ago. In the past, the chief reason black women ended up as heads of households was that their original marriages were dissolved by death or separation or divorce. Today, most such families come into being because an unmarried woman decides to become a mother. Nor does this always result from unfamiliarity with birth control or lack of access to abortion facilities. Often her pregnancy was intended from the start, all but assured by a conscious refusal to use contraception.

Single status may be found not only on the welfare rolls, but is becoming common for middle-class professionals as well. Among black women aged thirty-five to fifty-five, who have had four or more years of college, only about half are currently married, compared with 72 percent of white women of similar age and education. One cause of the imbalance is that women tend to want a partner at their own educational level. Unfortunately, for every 100 black women currently being awarded bachelor's degrees, only 67 black men are also receiving diplomas.

The pool of "marriageable" black men gets smaller every year. A traditional requisite for marriage has been having a steady job or the prospect of one, a status not readily achieved given current unemployment rates, which will be detailed in the next chapter. At the time of this writing, over half a million black men are in jails or prisons, and as many more could be sent or returned there if they violate their parole or probation. And perhaps as many as a million more have records as felons, not the best credential for employment. Another large group is debilitated by drugs or alcohol or mental

HOUSEHOLDS HEADED BY UNMARRIED WOMEN

Marital Status of Head of Household	Black 1990	White 1990	Black 1960
Divorced or Separated	39.9%	73.8%	64.5%
Widowed	5.0%	8.1%	24.0%
Never Been Married	55.1%	18.1%	11.5%

illness. In addition, the death rates for younger men have reached terrifying levels. In the fifteen to twenty-five age group, the mortality rate for black men is now 3.25 times that for black women, with the principal cause being gunned down by a member of their own race. The fact that in some areas as many as 20 percent of the men are missed by the census would point up their lack of even a settled address. And of those who were contacted by the census, fewer than half held full-time employment during the previous year.

When middle-class marriages break up, as millions do every year, economic reasons are seldom cited. This ought to remind us that low-income households can also fall prey to emotional tensions. (It is patronizing—and inaccurate—to presume that poorer people lack sensitivities found in the well-to-do.) For this reason, if no other, we should think twice before presuming that giving husbands steady jobs will keep poor families from falling apart.

What we do know is that some racial factors seem to have an influence of their own. For example, special studies conducted by the census allow us to look at the marital experience of black and white men of comparable ages and education. Among those aged thirty-five to fifty-four, who have had five or more years of college, it turns out that black men are twice as likely to be separated or divorced. This need not mean that black men take wedding vows less seriously. Rather, it suggests that the strains that come with being black put extra burdens on a marriage. There is reason to believe that most black Americans, like Americans of every race, would like to settle in with someone they love for a sustained period of years. However, this eventuality is less and less likely, due to the factors and forces thwarting the aspirations of black Americans.

The increase in out-of-wedlock births is often taken as evidence that black Americans are evolving a separate sexual culture. Here, too, race-based explanations must be handled with care. As has been noted, many white women are making essentially the same decisions and usually for quite similar reasons. We know of women with professional careers who decide to conceive a child without asking more from the father than an anonymous donation. Still, there are racial differences. In far fewer white neighborhoods are out-of-wedlock pregnancies and motherhood seen as customary and ordinary. The next table makes clear that black teenagers are much more likely to start sexual activity earlier. Moreover, we know that blacks are less

TEENAGED PREGNANCIES, ABORTIONS, AND BIRTHS	Black	White
Girls who have had sexual intercourse by age 15	68.6%	25.6%
Girls who have become pregnant by age 18	40.7%	20.5%
Pregnancies among 15–19-year olds that eventuate in births	51.2%	46.4%
Pregnancies among 15–19-year-olds terminated by abortions	35.0%	40.3%
Unmarried mothers aged 15–19 who keep and raise their babies	99.3%	92.6%
Total births per 1,000 women who have never married (all ages)	1,020	127

apt to use contraception, which accounts for their higher pregnancy rates. And black girls are more apt than white girls to carry their pregnancies to completion. Moreover, it would be well to remind ourselves that the four basic steps—sex, pregnancy, birth, and keeping the baby—do not always follow from one another. That is, not all sexual activity ends up in pregnancies; not all pregnancies eventuate in births; and not all babies are kept by the mother.

Teenagers the world over are pubescent earlier and increasingly independent; they are also exposed to similar erotic influences. In many other countries, young people are just as sexually active as they are in the United States; but youths elsewhere take more care with contraception, which means that many fewer of them become pregnant. And if they do, they are more likely to arrange for abortions.

The next page gives figures for several countries, showing how many of their teenagers become pregnant during a given year. The United States now leads other Western nations in out-of-wedlock births. In part, this is because other nations' schools and governments generally do more to encourage the use of birth control and make abortions available. But the chief difference is cultural. Young people in this country are less mature, less self-disciplined, and give less thought to their futures. (Not surprisingly, they also do less homework and register lower scores in academic skills.) True, there are cases where girls are forced into sex, or never wanted a child. In

PREGNANCIES EACH YEAR
(per 1,000 teenagers)

United States	
Black	186
White	93
England & Wales	45
Canada	44
France	43
Sweden	35
Netherlands	14

many parts of the United States, abortion facilities are not readily accessible, often because of local opposition. (There is only one clinic in the entire state of South Dakota.) Still, a disheartening number of young Americans of both races cannot be bothered with birth control, either because they find it too much trouble or because a child is desired. A survey of teenagers who had already become mothers, by the National Center for Health Statistics, found most admitting that they had engaged in sexual activity in hopes of becoming pregnant.

Such evidence as we have suggests that the forces propelling early parenthood cut across racial lines. One difference lies in the settings. Births among white teenagers tend to take place in depressed towns and rural areas, usually on the dreary side of the tracks where journalists seldom visit. Black out-of-wedlock births get much more attention, because more of them are clustered in central cities. Moreover, in low-income black areas, having babies outside of marriage is seldom seen as an act of rebellion, let alone defiance directed at parents or the larger society. Most black youthful parents are quite oblivious to whatever reactions they may be stirring elsewhere in the nation. For the young fathers, being able to point to a child they have sired is seen as tangible evidence of manhood, an important laurel for men unable to achieve recognition in other areas.

At the same time, it should be noted that there is far less promiscuity among black teenagers than critics like to suggest. In almost all cases, a girl has no difficulty identifying whomever it was who fathered her child, although the young man's interest will probably pall after learning of the pregnancy. In fact, teenaged mothers understand that the children will be their responsibility. They believe that having a baby to love will provide a focus for their lives. Given the surroundings so many of them have known, life offers few other options. So the act of reproduction becomes a way to validate yourself as a productive human being. Also, it offers a sphere of independence, including selecting its clothing and deciding how late it can stay up at night. Not least is the freedom to choose—or, even better, to make up—the baby's name. For many, discussing and comparing choices becomes a conversational staple in their early teens. Names like Equilla and Zanquisha are neither African nor Muslim, but schoolgirls' creations.

The real problem in our time is that more and more black infants are being born to mothers who are immature and poor. Compared with white women—most of whom are older and more comfortably off—black women are twice as likely to have anemic conditions during their pregnancy, twice as likely to have had no prenatal care, and twice as likely to give birth to low-weight babies. Twice as many of their children develop serious health problems, including asthma, deafness, retardation, and learning disabilities, as well as conditions stemming from their mother's use of drugs and alcohol during pregnancy. These conditions arise in part from a lack of clinics in rural towns and urban slums. But even when those facilities are available, younger mothers tend to be less conscientious about making and keeping scheduled appointments. Nor can they always find other sources of advice on matters like diet, their own during pregnancy and their baby's in its early years. Nor is poverty the full explanation. Federal figures show that women of Mexican ancestry have healthier babies, despite low incomes and less access to medical attention. One reason may be that more of their families have preserved a traditional structure, providing advice and authority from older members.

In the past, black families had their own support systems. These links had their origins partly in slavery, where relatives rallied round when parents were sold or sent away. After that, kinship was strengthened and sustained in the rural South. If a young woman found herself on her own with a baby, usually there was someone to take the two of them in. Nor was the assistance only economic; a new mother could count on guidance from relatives in the ways of parenthood. Also most extended families had several working members;

their earnings, however modest, ensured that there would be enough to go around.

Black families today still maintain deep and durable ties, often maintaining firmer roots than white households do. Yearly reunions are common, with relatives from all over the country returning to the setting they still regard as home. Black family members are also more willing to care for one another's children, sharing what they have. Still, the fact is that extended families can no longer take on these obligations in the ways they once did. For one thing, urban apartments are not as capacious as rural homesteads. In many cases, also, relatives have new burdens of their own. There is more unemployment, greater use of drugs, and a higher proportion of people in prison. But the key change has been in the balance of dependency. Instead of being the exception, single parents now outnumber conventional households. This helps to explain why so many young mothers end up in shelters for the homeless or derelict hotels and motels. Studies by social service agencies show that they usually began raising their babies at home, but had to move out when another sister arrived with an infant, making the crowding intolerable.

Since at least half of black women have no wish for an early baby, it remains to ask what distinguishes them from those who do. Income and education play a role, as can religious convictions and parental influence. Still, these kinds of factors tell only part of the story. Imagine, for a moment, two friends from similar surroundings, who move in the same circles in their school and neighborhood. And imagine, further, that each discovers she is pregnant. One of the two teenagers will decide to bear and keep her baby. She may have some more later on, with the possibility that she will spend a prolonged period on the welfare rolls. However, her friend will arrange to obtain an abortion, after which she will finish school and start on a promising job.

There are obviously many such twosomes. But why they take such divergent routes cannot be answered with any certainty. It could be argued that one lacked confidence in herself, whereas the other had greater inner strength and self-esteem. Perhaps one succumbed to the coaxing of friends who had already become mothers, while the other had an aunt who offered some timely advice. At the same time, it must be added that many who opt for early motherhood rearrange their lives later on and show they can support themselves. Still, explanations are elusive. As happens so frequently, we are watching the play of character and circumstance, the social and the personal, where the biography intersects with history. Neither psychology nor the social sciences can tell us much about why specific people pick the paths they do.

At this writing, the most recent figures, which cover 1988, report 14.9 percent of all white births as occurring outside of marriage, compared with 63.7 percent of black births. So as a multiple, the black proportion is 4.3 times that for whites. It will be recalled that the racial ratios for households headed by women have remained constant since such records were first compiled in 1950. However, the figures for out-of-wedlock births, displayed below, show that the black multiple has actually been declining, and is now less than half what it was in 1950. Put another way, even though the number of births to unwed black women has ascended to an all-time high, white births outside of marriage have been climbing at an even faster rate.

There is reason to suspect that in earlier years reports on white out-of-wedlock births were kept artificially low by indulgent physicians and health officials. Still, the chief explanation for the decline in the multiple has been the availability of legal abortion. While it is not something one would guess from watching "freedom of choice" rallies, black women have been availing themselves of abortion to a far greater extent than white women. While they comprise only 13 percent of women of childbearing age, they account for 31 percent of all the abortions performed.

PERCENTAGE OF BIRTHS OUT-OF-WEDLOCK
1950–1988

	Black	White	Multiple
1950	16.8%	1.7%	9.9
1960	21.6%	2.3%	9.4
1970	37.6%	5.7%	6.6
1980	56.4%	9.3%	6.1
1988	63.7%	14.9%	4.3

Hispanic births excluded after 1960.

Overall, white women have 274 abortions for every 1,000 babies they actually bear. For black women the ratio is 635 per 1,000, or 2.3 times the figure for whites. Among unmarried women—who account for about 80 percent of all abortions—white women are twice as likely to terminate their pregnancies, since more black single women want to bear their babies. After marriage, however, black women are almost three times as apt to seek abortions. The main reason is that black married couples are less regular users of birth control. Many black men disdain condoms for themselves, and often make it plain they do not want their partners using contraceptives either. So black women are more likely to return for subsequent abortions. In 1989, the year most recently studied, over half the black patients seeking abortions had had at least one previous termination.

Worth at least passing comment is that if the "right-to-life" movement achieves its goal of outlawing abortions, the impact will be felt most heavily by black women. As it happens, whites make up the great majority of those opposing abortion on principle. Their principal target seems to be professional women who want full and frequent sex lives, with abortion available as a fallback. Left unaddressed is whether right-to-life activists wish a steep rise in the black birthrate, which could very well happen were abortions to be made illegal.

Another sensitive issue has to do with the motives that lead so many whites to call for greater use of abortion and birth control by black Americans. Some say quite openly that all too many blacks should not be bearing children. Sometimes this reflects a feeling that they lack the resources to raise youngsters properly, so they should have fewer than they do, or in some cases none at all. The reasoning is that it is unfair to youngsters to bring them into a world of persisting poverty.

A good many black Americans discern other implications in these white concerns. As was noted earlier, black birthrates are not rising relative to those for whites, so it is not as if the black population is getting out of hand. In fact, indications are that Hispanics are on their way to becoming the country's principal minority. Therefore, efforts to induce blacks to limit their births is sometimes seen as a campaign to diminish the numbers of black Americans. To many blacks, the solution to social problems should not rest on curbing births, but in creating conditions that will enable those babies to have healthy and productive lives.

A further question involves variations within racial groups and among various parts of the country. The table on the next page gives figures for a selected group of states, showing how many of their births were to women who were not married. The figures for black births range all the way from 76.5 percent in Wisconsin to 15.3 percent for Hawaii. It could be argued that Honolulu does not have the kind of poverty and segregation that tends to be evident in Milwaukee. But if urban conditions make a difference, they do not explain why Michigan's rate of 62.0 percent is lower than Wisconsin's, since Detroit's problems are similar to Milwaukee's. Nor is it clear why states with relatively small black populations, like Iowa and Nebraska, have higher rates than Virginia and North Carolina. Mississippi and Minnesota would seem to have little in common, yet their rates are almost identical, as is also the case with Oregon and West Virginia. These variations and similarities suggest that black Americans live in settings which cannot be summarized in simple formulas.

White out-of-wedlock rates also vary from state to state, raising similar questions. Why, for example, should West Virginia differ so greatly from Georgia? The high rates for California and Arizona, as well as New Mexico and New York, can be at least partly attributed to the fact that their "white" category includes substantial numbers of Hispanics, who have a higher out-of-wedlock rate. But that does not tell us why Oregon, which has very few Hispanics, is also high on the list. Or why Texas, which is also largely Hispanic, has a much lower rate. It would appear to be the case that white women in the Southern states tend to wait until marriage before they have their babies, whereas black women in that region have a less constrained attitude toward motherhood. Indeed, comparing black and white rates within each of the states suggests that in both the South and the industrial Middle West, the two races have quite separate sexual cultures. On the other hand, in states like Hawaii and Maine, the racial ratios are much closer together.

However, the space between white and black America is not an empty void. The table on page 84 shows that the rates among ethnic groups span a spectrum, ranging from 3.8 percent for Americans of Chinese ancestry to 53.3 percent for Puerto Ricans. The fact that the

BIRTHS OUT-OF-WEDLOCK
(Selected States: 1988)

White Percentages		Black Percentages	
New Mexico	27.0%	Wisconsin	76.5%
California	26.9%	Illinois	75.3%
Arizona	24.3%	Iowa	69.1%
Oregon	22.4%	Nebraska	68.3%
West Virginia	21.0%	Minnesota	68.0%
New York	20.7%	Mississippi	66.5%
Maine	20.3%	Kentucky	64.8%
Rhode Island	19.4%	New York	63.9%
U.S.A.	**17.7%**	U.S.A.	63.5%
Kentucky	17.3%	Oregon	62.2%
Illinois	16.3%	West Virginia	62.2%
Iowa	16.0%	Michigan	62.0%
Wisconsin	15.9%	Georgia	61.5%
Minnesota	14.9%	North Carolina	59.5%
Montana	14.6%	California	59.3%
Texas	14.5%	Rhode Island	58.7%
Nebraska	14.0%	Virginia	57.3%
Idaho	13.7%	Arizona	54.4%
Virginia	13.2%	Texas	52.0%
Hawaii	12.9%	Utah	47.2%
Michigan	12.4%	New Mexico	46.0%
Georgia	11.9%	Montana	37.2%
North Carolina	11.7%	Idaho	22.5%
Mississippi	11.4%	Maine	20.0%
Utah	10.8%	Hawaii	15.3%

When Hispanic births are omitted from the nationwide figures, the white rate falls to 14.9% and the black rate rises to 63.7%. (Nationally, 34.0% of Hispanic births are to unmarried women.)

latter figure comes so close to that for blacks suggests that more than race is involved in such issues. After all, most Puerto Ricans identify themselves as white; they emigrated to the mainland voluntarily; and slavery played only a marginal role in their homeland's past.

In fact, Puerto Ricans, Hawaiians, Alaskans, and Native Americans share a common history in one crucial respect, which may help to explain their behavior concerning births among unmarried women. All four began as indigenous groups, either on the mainland or outlying islands, which were later overrun by conquerors or colo-

OUT-OF-WEDLOCK PERCENTAGES (11 AMERICAN GROUPS)	
Black	63.7%
Puerto Rican	53.3%
Native Alaskan	43.6%.
Native American	42.7%
Hawaiian	31.1%
Mexican	30.6%
Cuban	16.3%
White	14.9%
Filipino	10.4%
Japanese	6.5%
Chinese	3.8%

nizers from European powers, and then consigned to conditions of dependency. Of course, circumstances differed from group to group. Native Americans were subdued by military means, with the survivors consigned to reservations. Native Alaskans and Hawaiians were turned into exiles within their own homelands, so newcomers could exploit those territories. They were kept underemployed, allowed to addict themselves to alcohol, and subsist as tourist attractions or exotic relics. Puerto Rico was conquered first by Spain, after which it effectively became a colony of the United States, to which was added the option of easy migration to and from the mainland.

In the eyes of other Americans, all four of these groups continue to be viewed less as citizens than natives. While never slaves, they have been treated as subservient castes. Their conquerors prefer to keep them apart and quiescent, allowing them to sustain remnants of their cultures rather than become full citizens. Consequently, many of their men drop out of school and lead listless lives, while high percentages of their women end up as unwed mothers due to lack of other options.

Virtually everyone agrees that the Aid to Families with Dependent Children program—commonly called "welfare"—requires radical reform, if not outright abolition. In opinion polls, most Americans rate it a failure, if not a scandal and a shame. Among the most popular proposals is one that would compel the heads of the 3.7 million families now on welfare rolls to find jobs and go to work. Under current legislation, even mothers with young children will be forced to support themselves. Given this move toward compulsory labor, it is appropriate to examine some of the premises underlying this and other proposals.

Needless to say, race plays a role in this debate. Black and Hispanic women together account for over half of those receiving stipends. One reason why fewer white women need to apply for welfare is that the federal government has a less-publicized program, for which more of them are eligible, so its recipients escape scrutiny and criticism. Before considering the role of race, it would be well to look at how the welfare system works and some proposed alternatives.

Today, most Americans will say that women with young children should be free to take a job, if that is what they want to do. However, if married women decide they do not want to work, that too is viewed as a legitimate option. Indeed, many argue that at least during preschool years, youngsters need the full-time companionship of a parent for their proper development. The guilt that many working mothers feel stems, in some part, from their agreement with this position.

However, single mothers who wish to stay at home tend to be judged by rather different standards. (Exceptions are made for women who are independently wealthy or receive enough alimony to cover all their bills.) While under current AFDC rules, any single mother is allowed to apply for a public stipend, states vary in their readiness to make these grants and in the amounts they offer. In some states, more than three quarters of single mothers receive AFDC support; in others, fewer than 25 percent do.

In fact, the system has succeeded in ways that are seldom acknowledged. The nation contains millions of women who were once on welfare and who are now self-supporting. They simply needed time and financial help to get themselves together. Follow-up studies have shown that half of all recipients leave voluntarily before their third year. Many use their time on welfare to prepare themselves for work. Indeed, some states continue to pay stipends while recipients go to college.

Even so, most members of the public are persuaded that far too many women have made dependency a career. There are statistics to support that suspicion. Among all families with young children, close to one in eight is currently on the rolls. In 1960, the figure was one in thirty-three.

Most people prefer to think of an average welfare family as having half a dozen children, headed by a mother who has been in the program for at least a dozen years. But, as the next table shows, such households are far from typical. In fact, almost three quarters of AFDC households have only one or two children, while only one in ten has as many as four. Only a fourth of the parents have been receiving aid for five or more years; and fewer than 10 percent have been on AFDC for over a decade.

At the same time, the figures support the general view that most recipients are black or Hispanic. In a way, this is not surprising, since those minorities begin by having more households headed by women. Black and Hispanic women comprise about 45 percent of all single women who head households, and about 55 percent of those receiving AFDC. Stated another way, among black and Hispanic single mothers, somewhat over half are on welfare, while for white women the proportion is about 34 percent. Since the figure among whites is far from negligible, it suggests that single mothers of all races may have a good deal in common.

However, the figures confirm the common view that most mothers on AFDC have had their children out of wedlock. This is a major change compared with earlier years. In 1973, the largest single welfare category used to be women who were separated or divorced; now it consists of mothers who have never been married. In fact, the program was originally intended for women whose husbands were disabled or deceased, which were considered legitimate circumstances for public support. That rationale is now less easy to invoke.

There is no way to live well on welfare. Even in the most generous states, stipends fall below what the government defines as the poverty level. In 1989, annual cash allowances for families on AFDC ranged from $1,356 in Alabama to $7,692 in Massachusetts, with the national average at $4,644. All told, the typical AFDC stipend works out to one seventh of the average income enjoyed by American families. Recent years have seen cutbacks in federal contributions, while states let allowances lag behind inflation.

As was noted earlier, it is important to bear in mind that most single mothers are not on welfare, but in fact hold full-time jobs.

FAMILIES RECEIVING AID FOR DEPENDENT CHILDREN

Race		How Long on AFDC	
White	38.8%	Less Than 7 Months	18.2%
Black	39.8%	7 to 12 Months	13.2%
Hispanic	15.7%	1 to 2 Years	17.3%
Asian	2.4%	2 to 5 Years	26.3%
Other or Unknown	3.3%	Over 5 Years	25.0%

Children in Family		Mother's Age	
One	43.2%	21 or Younger	15.6%
Two	30.6%	22 to 29	39.5%
Three	16.1%	30 to 39	31.5%
Four or More	10.1%	40 or Older	13.4%

Fathers of the Children	1988	1973
Divorced or Separated	30.3%	46.5%
Deceased	1.7%	5.0%
Unemployed or Disabled	8.6%	14.3%
Not Married to Mother	54.6%	31.5%
Other or Unknown	4.8%	2.7%

Between 55 and 60 percent combine parenthood and employment. The fact that a quarter earn more than $25,000 shows how well they are coping as single parents, while caring for one or more younsters, a burden borne by few fathers. That another third earn between $10,000 and $25,000 tells us that they are not on welfare, since AFDC stipends seldom exceed $10,000. But because so many single mothers have shown that they can be self-supporting, the view has emerged that all the others should as well.

When marriages break up, the children almost always end up living with the mother. We seldom give this much thought, since people tend to assume that a woman will be a more natural parent. Few fathers ask for even partial custody, since they take it as given that they cannot handle the job, a sentiment their wives usually share. (In the rare cases where a mother asks the father to take over, she is seen as "walking out on the kids," an accusation we hardly hear nowadays when a father packs his bags.)

A further consequence of "men's liberation" is that fathers feel little obligation to support the children they have sired. In the Census Bureau's most recent report, 63 percent of single mothers received no payments at all. Among those who do get checks, the yearly figure averages $2,995, which must often be spread among several children. A California study found that men earning $45,000 were as likely to ignore court orders as those making $15,000.

Some of these financial strains might be eased if more single mothers married or remarried. In most cases, adding a man's earnings would more than double the family income. However, such statistics as we have show that after the age of thirty, women face dismaying odds in the remarriage market. Within the thirty-five to thirty-nine age group, only four in ten divorced women can expect to remarry. Among black women the prospects are markedly lower.

By far the fastest-growing group of AFDC families consists of women who were not married to the fathers when their babies were born and have not married anyone since. As the table on AFDC recipients noted, in recent years these mothers and their children have risen from less than a third of the welfare rolls to more than half. Breakdown by race shows that it is the black mothers who are less apt to have been married, while white mothers tend to be women who are now separated or divorced. As was noted earlier, most "never married mothers"—the official census designation—conceive and give birth without the expectation that the child's father will become a resident parent. In fact, census studies show that less than one in eight of unmarried fathers provide even token support payments.

New federal legislation orders government agencies to get tougher about making fathers pay. Since some men may try to deny paternity, the law allows states to require blood tests and genetic typing to make sure. States can also compel fathers to supply their Social Security numbers at the time a baby is born, to be used by agencies looking for delinquent dads. Unfortunately, many nonpaying fathers simply lack the cash. Large numbers are unemployed or have irregular work, and a considerable proportion are among the million men now in state and federal prisons or local jails. Others are drug addicts or homeless, or are youths who have yet to hold a steady job. While every dollar they pay will help, their prospects as providers are not very promising.

For this reason, federal legislation places greater emphasis on making women become self-supporting by getting them off the welfare rolls and onto payrolls. Mothers under twenty-two who have not graduated from high school may be obliged to return to their studies and obtain an equivalency diploma. After that, "mandatory participation" in job-training programs is specified for all women with children over the age of three. Upon completing such a course, a mother is presumed ready to go to work, and would be required to accept any "bona fide" offer of employment. The presumption is that such a job will give her wages at least equal to her welfare stipend, plus the value of food stamps and other benefits. If a mother refuses to accept the offer of a good faith job, she can be removed from the welfare rolls. To ensure that her children will not suffer, "protective payments" for them may be made to a "third party," presumably an official in a welfare bureau.

If women are compelled to leave welfare and enter employment, this raises the question of suitable care for their children. A recent U.S. Public Health Service survey found that among women who currently work, 31 percent leave their preschool-age children at home, 37 percent drop them off at someone else's house, and only 24 percent have them in child-care centers, nursery schools, or kindergartens. (The remaining 8 percent take them along to work.) But many feel that mothers now on AFDC should have more than custodial care for their children, which raises questions of quantity, quality, and cost. We hear that children from lower-income families need special attention to compensate for limitations at home. (This has always been the rationale for the Head Start program.) Many experts insist that child-care centers should have professional staffs, with one college-trained adult for every three or four children. Not surprisingly, the charge per child can run as high as $1,000 a month, as much as many mothers may earn, since a lot of them will have to start out doing unskilled work. Half of New York City's women on welfare have never held a job.

The beliefs that people hold about welfare are usually intensely felt, even when they seem to embrace conflicting principles. To start, there is the traditional tenet that a "good" mother should want to stay at home with her children while they are growing up. Even as they get older, she should want to be there in the afternoon when they return from school. Once the children are on their own, keeping house for her husband can be an honorable occupation. Nor are these married wives and mothers considered to be "dependent" in any invidious sense; what they do is seen as full-time, productive work. Moreover, many husbands are willing, even eager, to support this arrangement.

So why are so many people so adamant about wanting to get single mothers out of the home and into full-time jobs? (Among married mothers who work, only 27 percent are employed throughout the year in full-time positions.) The answer, in a pronouncement by a conservative research center, is that "no able adult should be allowed to voluntarily take from the common good without also contributing to it." Married women who stay at home are not seen as a cost to society, since they are supported by the incomes their spouses bring in. It has been argued as well that an attentive wife makes it easier for her husband to concentrate on his job. By this logic, only married women can be said to contribute to "the common good" by remaining at home with their children.

Under this reasoning, it would seem to follow that women who lack a resident husband have no claim to be subsidized by society. This stricture is most openly applied to those who have borne children without benefit of marriage, a higher proportion of whom are black. In a word, women who engage in irresponsible sex should not ask for a free ride. Indeed, giving them money will only increase their tendency to reproduce. More than that, there arise images of successions of sexual partners. So not only are they bankrupting society but they are also having a fine time while decent people toil.

In sum, mothers now on AFDC are seen as bad models for society as a whole and their own children in particular. If they will not marry or remain married, then they should redeem themselves by work. If most of the women on the welfare rolls are black or Hispanic, most of those who want to send them to work are white. Motives here are difficult to disentangle. One view is that too many blacks and Hispanics are on a course that has self-destructive consequences for themselves and their children. Some believe that if women are made to take jobs, it will improve their characters and deter them from having more babies.

Some states have already found that women will find work if admission to welfare is kept sufficiently stringent. As the figures in the next table suggest, many mothers who are now receiving AFDC in Ohio, Wisconsin, and Illinois would have managed to find jobs for

PERCENTAGE OF SINGLE MOTHERS RECEIVING AFDC	
Wisconsin	78.7%
Ohio	73.3%
Illinois	68.2%
Texas	33.9%
Idaho	28.6%
New Hampshire	21.6%

themselves had they been living in Texas, New Hampshire, or Idaho. One criticism of welfare is that it tends to cast its recipients as helpless individuals who would languish or even starve without public assistance. The sterner states take the view that the great majority of single mothers are resourceful human beings who can and will support themselves if this is made their only choice. Some take their model from the past, when there was no program that resembles today's public assistance. In 1940, for example, some 2.4 million women—most of them black—supported themselves and their families by working as domestic servants in other people's homes. While seldom explicitly stated, the hints are there that welfare mothers could do more of the kind of work their grandmothers did.

While people often mention money, the concern over welfare is not mainly financial. Most Americans find the presence of a supported class unseemly; it runs counter to the way we are supposed to organize our lives. Still, racial and class biases intrude. It is revealing that people who criticize middle-class career women because they see little of their children, have no compunctions about insisting that poorer women should leave their youngsters for the day and go off to work. The presumption seems to be that even if poorer mothers stayed at home, they would not do much good for their children.

As it happens, one group of single mothers has been exempted from rules requiring employment. These are widows with school-age children, whose husbands had held steady jobs, and contributed every payday to their Social Security account. Women in this position do not have to apply for welfare, nor are they expected to become self-supporting. Since they cannot be held responsible for the demise of their husbands, the Social Security law entitles them to full "survivor's" benefits. The presumption is that these stipends are not handouts, but were earned by dint of their husband's work. Currently, some 300,000 widows who have children are supported under this statute, and they can receive as much as $24,000 a year, more than four times the average AFDC award. If they choose to work, as many do, they still receive separate payments to assist their children. In short, they bear no stigma, nor do they have to apologize for living on public funds. Nor is this very surprising, since those receiving these Social Security benefits are overwhelmingly white.

CHAPTER SIX

THE RACIAL INCOME GAP

HOW MUCH IS DUE TO BIAS?

SINCE THEIR FIRST ARRIVAL, and continuing after they started receiving wages, black Americans have figured disproportionately among the nation's poor. Of course, differences in incomes can have explanations apart from race. After all, a lot of white people are poor, and a number of blacks are very visibly rich. Even so, after other factors have been accounted for, race still seems to play a role in how people fare financially. A recurrent theme of this and the following chapter will be how being black or white affects economic opportunities and outcomes.

Any discussion of incomes and earnings will depend strongly on statistics. While we cannot measure equity with precision, numerical disparities represent real facts about the races. Each year, the census asks a national sample of Americans to estimate their total incomes during the previous year. The next table gives some of the results from the 1990 survey, reported first as median incomes and then by how much blacks received for every $1,000 that went to whites. (This means of comparison will be used extensively throughout this chapter.)

The listings for families and for all men and women include every sort of income, ranging from pensions and welfare payments to disability benefits and capital gains. The figures for employed men and women reflect only the earnings of individuals who held full-time jobs throughout the year. The relative incomes for black families as a group and for black men are embarrassingly low, in particular when compared with those for the earnings of black women.

In 1990, the most recent figures available at this writing, personal income received by everyone living within the country added up to a grand total of $3.6 trillion. While black Americans made up 12.1 percent of the tabulated population, they ended up with only 7.8 percent of the monetary pie. Earnings by some 134 million gainfully employed persons accounted for $2.8 trillion of the income total. Black workers comprised 10.1 percent of that employment force, but received only 8.0 percent of all earnings. This chapter will focus on the conditions causing these gaps.

White households are more apt to have both a husband and wife present, which raises the likelihood of multiple incomes. In fact, 59 percent of white families have two or more earners, while only 47 percent of black families do. As it happens, among married couples, a smaller percentage of white wives work: 61 percent have jobs, compared with 68 percent of black married women. Since the earnings of black men tend to be lower, fewer of their families can afford the luxury of full-time housewives. When white wives work, they are more likely to take part-time jobs and their paychecks tend to be

INCOMES AND EARNINGS
(1990 Medians)

	White	Black	Ratio*
Families	$36,915	$21,423	$580
All Men	$21,170	$12,868	$608
All Women	$10,317	$ 8,328	$807
Employed Men	$30,598	$22,167	$725
Employed Women	$20,759	$18,838	$907

* Incomes of blacks per $1,000 for whites. Earnings for Year-Round Fulltime workers.

supplemental; Whereas among black families, the husbands' and wives' earnings are often of equal value. And since more black families are headed by single women, a higher proportion of their households must make do with only one income. Moreover, when black single mothers work—and the majority do—it is generally at a job paying relatively low wages.

So the question arises whether income ratios would change if black families had the same mixture of single parents and married couples as white households now do. If this became the case, then many more black homes would have someone bringing in a man's earnings. Were this change to occur, the income ratio for black families would only rise from $580 to $732, not exactly an impressive improvement. The reason is that while having more men's incomes would help, it would not accomplish very much since black men still make considerably less than white men. Moreover, even if more black households had a man in residence, some of the men would be unemployed or removed from the labor force for other reasons. So emulating the white family structure would close only about half of the income gap.

On the whole, increased education tends to bring in higher incomes. While we can always find exceptions, for most people most of the time, staying in school does pay off. The figures in the table below show how the rule works along a racial continuum. To make the comparisons as firm as possible, the table covers only individuals who worked full time throughout the entire year.

A steady economic progression is evident for all four groups: among black and white men and women, incomes ascend with added

EDUCATION AND EARNINGS
(Earnings of Blacks per $1,000 for Whites)

	Men	Women
High School Not Finished	$797	$974
4 Years of High School	$764	$942
1 to 3 Years of College	$825	$925
4 Years of College	$798	$1,002
5+ Years of College	$771	$973

years of school. The catch is that even when black men reach the same academic level as white men, their incomes stay several steps behind. Thus among men with four years of college, blacks still earn only $798 for each $1,000 going to whites in that educational stratum. Even worse, black college men end up just a few dollars ahead of whites who went no further than high school. When black men persevere to graduate school, they still receive only $771 compared with their white counterparts, even less than for black men who never finished college. Hence the advice so often offered to blacks, that they should stay in school, seems valid only insofar as it informs them that with additional education they will move ahead of others of their own race. There is little evidence that spending more years in school will improve their positions in relation to whites.

Of course, the table also shows that black women come much closer to parity, with their white counterparts making between $925 and $1,002 for each $1,000 earned by white women at their level. The greater equity among women results largely from the fact that few women of either race rise far in the earnings hierarchy. The comparative status of black women warrants only a muted cheer: achieving equality is easier within an underpaid cohort. Yet there remains the question of why black men are denied even the limited equity that black women enjoy.

If we want to find out how much income disparities result from racial bias, then we must do our best to compare similar groups, since additional elements like age and experience can distort comparisons. A census study that examined the earnings of male attorneys between the ages of thirty-five and forty-five found that black lawyers averaged $790 for every $1,000 made by their white counterparts. Given that these men are in the same age range and have the same level of education, it could be argued that race accounts for at least part of the $210 earnings gap. Of course, we would have to know a lot more about the individuals in question. Factors like talent, intelligence, and temperament could affect the equation. Or the variance in earnings might reflect different law schools the men attended and how well they did there. After all, it hardly needs mentioning that not all educations are comparable. If more of the white lawyers in the cohort went to Harvard, while the black lawyers were apt to have studied at Howard, then some people might want to argue that some part of the $210 difference is justified.

As it happens, black *women* lawyers in the same age group make $930 for every $1,000 going to their white colleagues. Moreover, this similarity holds even though black women attend the same spectrum of law schools as black men. So a question must arise: if black women in the legal profession are paid nearly as much as white women, then why don't black men make almost as much as white men? A suspicion cannot help but arise that some of the racial earnings spread among men stems from the fact that black men are given fewer opportunities to rise to better-paid positions.

Measured in economic terms, the last two decades have not been auspicious ones for Americans of any race. Between 1970 and 1990, the median income for white families, computed in constant dollars, rose from $34,481 to $36,915, an increase of 8.7 percent. During these decades, black family income barely changed at all going from $21,151 to $21,423. In relative terms, black incomes dropped from $613 to $580 for each $1,000 received by whites. As it happened, the incomes of white men dropped during this period, so if white families recorded a modest rise, it was because more of them had wives who could go to work.

However, medians—like averages—can conceal important variations. The four configurations on the next page show how incomes were distributed among black and white families in 1970 and 1990. The shapes for both races changed in revealing ways. In 1970, the black incomes depicted at the bottom left took the form of a classical pyramid, beginning with a fairly broad base and tapering at each subsequent level. Twenty years later, the base had become much wider, and families were arrayed more evenly among the higher brackets. This change reflects not only the much-heralded growth of a black middle class, but also a significant shift in black America's social structure, signaling a separation of better-off blacks from those at the lowest level.

In 1970, the white distribution shown at top left had the shape of a chunky column, with a heavy girth in the middle ranges. By 1990, aggregate income had moved toward the top. The figure had become an inverted pyramid, with more than half of the homes in the two top tiers. The rise in better-off households came in part from a growth in highly paid positions during the 1980s; but the principal reason was that by 1990 many more white homes had two earners. At the same

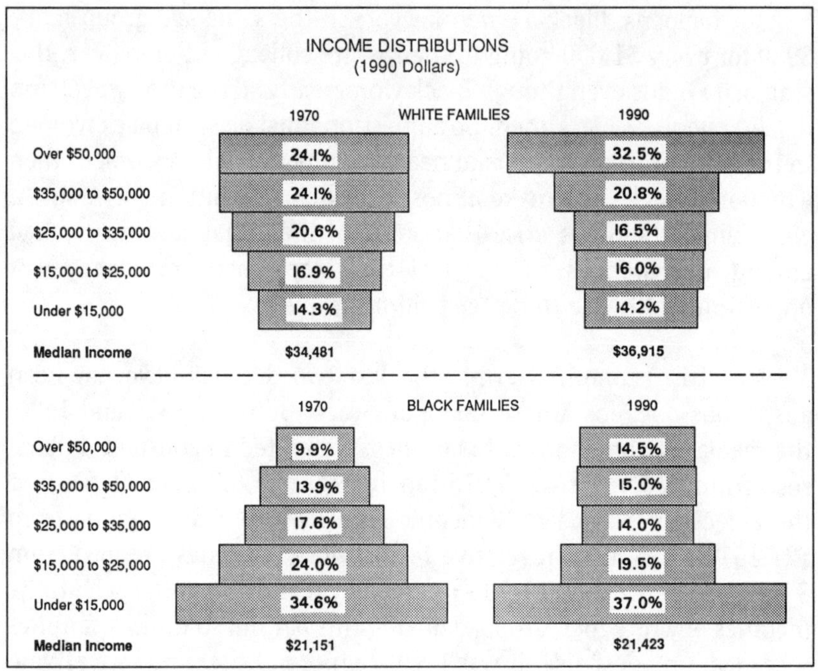

time, between 1970 and 1990, the size of the two bottom tiers had barely changed. However, there had been a shift in the composition of the white poor. In 1970, it consisted largely of the elderly, or employed persons working for very low wages. By 1990, low-income white households were more apt to be those headed by women.

During the two decades, the proportion of black households with incomes over $50,000 expanded by 46 percent, while the share of white homes at that level rose by only 35 percent. Even if whites were not advancing as fast, they were not falling behind; so it cannot be argued that blacks were replacing whites in better-paid positions.

Nor does the fact that more black families enjoy incomes of over $50,000 mean that many black men and women have jobs paying at that level. Indeed, only 3.4 percent of all black men make $50,000 or more; most $50,000 homes result from two or more sets of earnings. In contrast, 12.1 percent of white men receive over $50,000, and many more of them are the sole or dominant earners in their households. So while there is now a much larger black middle class, more typically, the husband is likely to be a bus driver earning $32,000, while his wife brings home $28,000 as a teacher or a nurse. A white middle-class family is three to four times more likely to contain a husband earning $75,000 in a managerial position, which allows him to support a nonworking wife. It is not easy to visualize these two couples living on the same block, let alone becoming acquainted with one another.

Some thirty years ago, federal officials devised a formula to designate which Americans could be considered poor. The poverty threshold is adjusted every year, to keep pace with the cost of living. In 1990, an older woman living by herself would fall in the poverty cohort if her income fell below $6,268. A single mother with two children was counted as poor if their income was lower than $10,530. In most parts of the United States, $6,268 spells not simply poverty, but a good chance of malnutrition. Nor is it possible to bring up, say, two teenagers on $10,530 a year. Even adding in the dollar value of school lunches, food stamps, and medical benefits, the formula understates the number of Americans who are truly poor. Another problem is that the figures ignore variations in living costs. A widow might manage on $6,268 in rural Arkansas, but that would barely pay her rent in Boston or Brooklyn. Still, if we make appropriate adjustments, the official poverty percentages can tell us a lot about who is poor and why.

As the table on the next page shows, 44.8 percent of black children live below the poverty line, compared with 15.9 percent of white youngsters. So black children are almost three times as likely as whites to grow up in poor surroundings. The ratio runs higher for all black families, and is somewhat similar for black people as a whole. However, the poverty figures have a much closer ratio (1.48) among households headed by women. Indeed, the proportion in poverty among white single mothers (37.9 percent) exceeds that for the black population as a whole. For women who must raise children on their own, being white loses much of its advantage.

The poverty figures also show that some two thirds of poor white Americans live in suburbs or rural areas. Anyone who has traveled along the back roads of outlying America has seen the homes of people who are white and poor. However, their homes are less likely to be clustered together in slum neighborhoods, unless one applies that description to decaying trailer parks. Among the poor white

POVERTY PERCENTAGES

	White	Black	Multiple
All Persons	8.8%	31.9%	3.63
All Children	15.9%	44.8%	2.82
All Families	8.1%	29.3%	3.62
Female Headed Households	37.9%	56.1%	1.48

WHERE POOR AMERICANS LIVE

	White	Black
Central Cities	32.7%	60.3%
Suburbs	35.2%	17.5%
Nonmetropolitan	32.1%	22.2%
	100.0%	100.0%

families who do live in urban areas, less than a quarter of them reside in low-income tracts. This suggests that there are relatively few white ghettos. Urban black families below the poverty line are more visibly segregated: no less than 70 percent of such households are concentrated in low-income neighborhoods.

Of course, there is a white underclass. Its members can be found among the addicted and the homeless, among men who have never held steady jobs, and women who have spent many years on welfare. The nation's prisons still have plenty of white criminals, some of whom are quite vicious and others who have made careers in small-time larcenies. Even so, neither sociologists nor journalists have shown much interest in depicting poor whites as a "class." In large measure, the reason is racial. For whites, poverty tends to be viewed as atypical or accidental. Among blacks, it comes close to being seen as a natural outgrowth of their history and culture. At times, it almost appears as if white poverty must be covered up, lest it blemish the reputation of the dominant race. This was not always the case. In the past, sociology textbooks dilated at length about families like the Jukes and the Kallikaks, who remained mired in squalor from generation to generation. In earlier days, too, white people could be "trash," whether along the tobacco roads or in pellagra-infested pine barrens. While class bias prompted these discursions, at least they granted that white people could occupy the lowest stratum of society.

Apart from people who are independently wealthy and those with generous pensions, enjoying the modest comforts of life requires having a decent job. Altogether, about 80 percent of Americans' personal income comes from wages and salaries or other gainful earnings.

Between 1939 and 1959, the earnings of black men relative to whites improved by over a third. Those who made the move to Northern cities relocated in search of employment. They were willing to take blue-collar positions once reserved for immigrants, but which newer generations of whites were beginning to spurn. This period saw the emergence of a stable black working class, underpinned by two-parent families and orderly neighborhoods. If many saw themselves as "poor," that status did not have the connotations conveyed by "poverty" today. The earnings of black women also grew during this period, as they turned from domestic employment to better-paid occupations.

However, during the past twenty years, as the accompanying table shows, the relative earnings of black men has tapered off. Between 1969 and 1989, their ratio in relation to whites has improved by only $22, and of that only a rise of a single dollar came during the second decade. (And this was a period when affirmative action supposedly gave blacks preferences in hirings and promotions.) The decline in blue-collar employment hit black men especially hard. Each year found the economy offering fewer factory jobs, while more were being created in the white-collar sector.

BLACK WORKERS' EARNINGS
(per $1,000 for Whites)

	Men	Women
1939	$450	$379
1949	$596	$434
1959	$612	$664
1969	$694	$819
1979	$715	$925
1989	$716	$919

If black women have fared better, it is because more of them have been seen as suitable for office positions. Professional and clerical occupations generally call for attitudes and aptitudes associated with the white world. For reasons that will be considered later, black women apparently satisfy employers on these counts more readily than black men. Even so, by 1979, it became clear that black women would still fall short of parity with their white female colleagues. While white women were later in entering the labor force in large numbers, their arrival on the scene brought pressures to move them into professional and supervisory positions, which has in turn increased the pay gap between white and black women.

Black men, women, and children were brought to this country for a singular purpose: to work. Indeed, the demand for their labor was so great that slaves continued to be smuggled in even after that traffic had been banned by the Constitution. In the years following emancipation, former slaves found that their services would not necessarily be needed. Their labor, like that of other Americans, would be subject to the vagaries of a market economy. The capitalist system has been frank in admitting that it cannot always create jobs for everyone who wants to work. This economic reality has certainly been a pervasive fact of black life. For as long as records have been kept, in good times and bad, white America has ensured that the unemployment imposed on blacks will be approximately double those experienced by whites. Stated very simply, if you are black in America, you will find it twice as hard to find or keep a job.

The ratios in the table on the next page make it clear that black Americans get jobs only after white applicants have been accommodated. In periods of prosperity, when the economy requires more workers, blacks who had been unemployed are offered vacant positions. But as last hired, they can expect to be the first fired. In bleak times, the jobless rate among blacks can approach 20 percent, as it did in 1983. Since 1974, unemployment rates for blacks have remained at double-digit levels, and they have not fallen below twice the white rate since 1976. Even more depressing, the gap between the black and white figures grew during the 1980s, suggesting that the economy has little interest in enlisting black contributions.

It is frequently remarked that many black men and women lack the kinds of skills that modern employment requires. However, these

UNEMPLOYMENT RATES

Year	White	Black	Multiple
1960	4.9	10.2	2.08
1961	6.0	12.4	2.07
1962	4.9	10.9	2.22
1963	5.0	10.8	2.16
1964	4.6	9.6	2.09
1965	4.1	8.1	1.98
1966	3.3	7.3	2.21
1967	3.4	7.4	2.18
1968	3.2	6.7	2.09
1969	3.1	6.4	2.06
1960s Average			**2.11**
1970	4.4	8.2	1.86
1971	5.4	9.9	1.83
1972	5.0	10.0	2.00
1973	4.3	8.9	2.07
1974	5.0	9.9	1.98
1975	7.8	14.8	1.90
1976	7.0	13.1	1.87
1977	6.2	13.1	2.11
1978	5.2	11.9	2.29
1979	5.1	11.3	2.22
1970s Average			**2.01**
1980	6.3	14.3	2.27
1981	6.7	14.2	2.12
1982	8.6	18.9	2.20
1983	8.4	19.5	2.32
1984	6.5	15.9	2.45
1985	6.2	15.1	2.44
1986	6.0	14.5	2.42
1987	5.3	13.0	2.45
1988	4.7	11.7	2.49
1989	4.5	11.4	2.53
1980s Average			**2.37**
1990	4.1	11.3	2.76

charges are hardly new. They were also common in the past, when blacks were shunted to the end of the line even for laboring jobs. And today, whites who barely make it through high school continue to get the first openings in the building trades. Moreover, blacks who do stay in school soon learn there is no assured payoff. Those who finish college have a jobless rate 2.24 times that for whites with diplomas, an even greater gap than that separating black and white high school graduates.

Exacerbating the situation today is the fact that millions of jobs are being filled by legal and illegal aliens, largely from Latin America and Asia. Few of the positions they take call for special skills, so the question arises as to why these places haven't been offered to native-born black Americans. This issue is not new, since it has long been argued that immigrant labor takes bread from the mouths of citizens. In most cases, though, aliens and immigrants acquiesce to wages and working conditions that black and white Americans are unwilling to accept. Indeed, newcomers often put up with what are essentially Third World terms of employment to gain a foothold in the American economy. And if these workers are exploited, it is often by employers or supervisors of their own origins who arrived here not much earlier. Nor is it likely that the pay for such jobs can be raised appreciably.

What black Americans want is no more nor less than what white Americans want: a fair chance for steady employment at decent pay. But this opportunity has been one that the nation's economy continues to withhold. To be black in America is to know that you remain last in line for so basic a requisite as the means for supporting yourself and your family. More than that, you have much less choice among jobs than workers who are white. As will be seen in the next chapter, entire occupations still remain substantially closed to people who were born black.

That black Americans are willing or required to do arduous work cannot be questioned. When a new hotel announces that it will be hiring porters and chambermaids, a line largely composed of black men and women can be seen curling around the block. Black youths sign on for the armed services in disproportionate numbers because it is the only promising job they can get. And other young men and women can be found on sordid streets in all hours and weathers, selling illicit services or merchandise. The baleful consequences aside, the fact remains that what they are doing is unquestionably *work*. For each one who sports a fancy car, dozens more serve as "stashers" or "spotters" in hopes of picking up a few dollars.

All in all, a greater proportion of black Americans lack regular employment than at any time since the 1930s Depression. Many of those who have jobs are needed for less than a full day's work or for only part of the year. And in addition to men and women who are officially recorded as unemployed, at least an equal number have given up the search. Because this is now a substantial group, the Bureau of Labor Statistics has created a category it calls "discouraged workers." These are individuals who say they would like to work, but have ceased looking because they have become convinced that they will never find a job. So they have been dropped from the "labor force" category and are no longer even counted among the unemployed.

On a typical day in 1990, the bureau was able to locate almost a million of these "discouraged workers." The true total has to be considerably higher, since many in this plight cannot be found for interviews or refuse to give out information about themselves. Of the recorded "discouraged workers," close to 30 percent are black, a much higher proportion than on the official list of the unemployed who say they are actively looking for work. As was just noted, some of these "nonworkers" support themselves on the streets by providing products and services in the underground economy. Others resort to theft, which means that sooner or later they will join yet another cohort of the nonemployed: the growing number of Americans who languish in this nation's prisons.

It is frequently proposed that the economy should create more semiskilled jobs at decent wages, which will be made available to black men. Just what kinds of positions they would be are seldom specified. As hardly needs mentioning, machines now perform many of the tasks once handled by human beings, while a lot of factory work once done within this country is being contracted overseas. Moreover, recent trends have expanded the sectors of the workforce open to women. Even if special jobs were devised, it is not clear how they could pay what today's men regard as a living wage. For at least a decade, newly created positions have been offering wages and salaries lower than those of the jobs they replaced. As a result, they are usually taken by women or teenagers or immigrants, who are willing to work at those rates because they have no other option. Put another way, many native-born men cannot see how they can work for such wages and still maintain a self-respect integral to their identity.

But the larger point is that this country cannot revert to a sweat-and-muscle economy of earlier eras. More than that, to contrive blue-collar jobs for black men would not only rouse charges of preferential treatment but accusations of racism as well, since it would imply that work requiring physical skills is all that black men can be expected to do.

CHAPTER SEVEN

EQUITY IN EMPLOYMENT

QUALIFICATIONS AND QUOTAS

BLACK MEN AND WOMEN number among the most highly paid people in the United States. Especially visible, at this time of writing, are Bill Cosby, Eddie Murphy, Mike Tyson, Dwight Gooden, Tina Turner, Darryl Strawberry, Whitney Houston, Earvin ("Magic") Johnson, Oprah Winfrey, Bryant Gumbel, and Michael Jordan as well as Janet and Michael Jackson. All have had annual earnings in the millions, often including ownership stakes in corporate enterprises.

Also, at this writing, a black physician serves as Secretary of Health and Human Services in the President's Cabinet, a black physicist heads the National Science Foundation, while a black military officer presides as Chairman of the Joint Chiefs of Staff. The Ford Foundation has had a black president for over a dozen years, while the National Baseball League is led by a black executive. A black man also heads the College Board, the nation's principal testing agency. Another has the top position at TIAA-CREF, one of the nation's largest pension funds. Black women are the chief officers at Planned Parenthood and several colleges and universities.

This, certainly, is the good news. At the same time, it is apparent that all the organizations just cited are governmental or in the public service sector. In fact, three black millionaires have been on *Forbes* magazine's rosters of America's 400 richest men and women. One is John Harold Johnson, who owns *Ebony* and *Jet;* and another was Berry Gordy of Motown Records. A recent addition is Reginald Lewis, who bought Beatrice Foods, and has a net worth of about $340 million. However, *Business Week's* 1991 listing of the chief executives of America's 1,000 largest corporations had only one black chairman: Erroll B. Davis, who heads a Wisconsin utility holding company and earns a comparatively modest $269,000. Unfortunately, there are no serious signs that the other 999 firms are grooming black executives for eventual top jobs.

The so-called "small business" sector can also be a route to wealth and social status. The Census Bureau keeps count of the number of firms owned by black men and women. Its most recent survey found 425,000 such enterprises, numbering about 2.4 percent of the country's corporations, partnerships, and sole proprietorships. By and large, the black businesses are local concerns, with annual receipts averaging around $50,000, and they deal largely in products or services oriented to black clienteles. Indeed, only 70,000 of the 425,000 have any paid employees. In other words, almost 85 percent are one-person enterprises or family-run firms.

Many arguments have been given for the paucity of black-owned enterprises. There is the difficulty of getting start-up loans and capital from banks and investors stemming from biased attitudes about blacks' business abilities. Nor is it easy for blacks to get experience in corporate management as a prelude to branching out on their own. Some blacks have done well providing products and services to their own community. Still, the real challenge is to build a wider clientele. In fact, some firms have been successful in this sphere. Most whites who have bought Park's Sausages and McCall's Patterns do not know that those companies are owned and managed by blacks.

It has occasionally been suggested that black Americans do not have a "culture" that encourages entrepreneurship. But it is best to be wary of such sweeping explanations, since they imply that the roots run very deep. There may be some validity to the view that youngsters who grow up in areas with few locally owned enterprises lack models for business careers. But even this need not be an obstacle, since the decision to start up on your own usually comes later in life. As it happens, in the generation following emancipation, many blacks set up businesses in Southern cities, just as others prospered in farming. Haitian and West Indian immigrants have brought entrepreneurial ambitions with them; and it will be interesting to see what becomes of the West African sidewalk vendors who have become a New York fixture.

Considering the advantages and opportunities open to white Americans, it is noteworthy that less than 8 percent of them operate enterprises of their own. The table below provides some census tabulations that suggest that other ethnic groups are well ahead of whites in embarking on entrepreneurship. For this reason, little will be gained by asking whether blacks have a "culture" that inhibits them from establishing their own businesses. Even if that answer is in the affirmative, it also applies to white Americans, 92.6 percent of whom spend their working hours on someone else's payroll.

Not so many years ago, entire spheres of employment were almost completely closed to blacks. As recently as 1980, the census could find only 254 black optometrists, 185 black actuaries, and 122 black auctioneers. In addition, blacks accounted for only 138 nuclear en-

PROPORTION OF MEN WHO ARE SELF-EMPLOYED IN 13 ETHNIC GROUPS

Korean	16.5%
Japanese	11.1%
Chinese	9.0%
Cuban	8.3%
White	7.4%
Asian Indian	6.6%
Mexican	4.4%
Hawaiian	3.9%
Eskimo	3.7%
Filipino	3.6%
Black	3.0%
Puerto Rican	2.9%
Vietnamese	2.1%

gineers, 89 theology professors, and 70 sheet metal apprentices. At present, it can be said that absolute barriers have been broken, and every occupation has some blacks among its practitioners. In many areas, however, the numbers remain exceedingly small. The table on the next page gives racial breakdowns for various areas of employment. Even now, blacks remain underrepresented in the professions of engineering, law, and medicine, as well as architecture and journalism. Until lately, black students felt little incentive to train for these fields, since there were few if any prospects of obtaining a job. (Paul Robeson turned to acting because no firm would hire him after he graduated from Columbia Law School.) While virtually all professions are saying they would like to have more blacks on their payrolls, it still remains to be seen whether they simply want a few faces for showcase purposes, or if they mean jobs with real responsibilities.

But moving beyond the professions, how are we to account for the low percentages of blacks when it comes to waiting on tables and tending bar? These are hardly elite occupations requiring sophisticated training. The suspicion arises that proprietors of restaurants and lounges may feel that their white clienteles do not want their food and drinks handled by black employees. Or it could stem from the belief that if a place has "too many" blacks on its staff, it will drop to a lower status. (Obviously, there are exceptions: for example, New Orleans dining rooms that affect the Old Retainer Tradition.) Perhaps most revealing of all is the small number of black dental hygienists. While white patients seem willing to be cared for by black nurses, they apparently draw the line at having black fingers in their mouths.

Occupations where black workers have the strongest showing are not necessarily menial. Still, they do more than their share of janitorial chores and cleaning up after others, which have been traditional "black" positions. As the tabulations show, the positions where blacks have greatest representation tend to be jobs that whites are reluctant to take (hotel maids and nursing aides) as well as some at lower civil service levels (correctional officers and postal clerks). Blacks now perform repetitive office chores (data keyers and telephone operators) and fill in at high-turnover occupations (security guards and taxicab drivers). In some cases, the fields offering more openings (bus drivers and social workers) are ones serving clienteles that have become disproportionately black.

BLACK OCCUPATIONAL REPRESENTATION
(Blacks = 10.1 % of Total Workforce)

Greatest Overrepresentation	
Nursing Aides & Orderlies	30.7%
Taxicab Drivers	25.5%
Postal Clerks	25.1%
Hotel Maids & Housemen	24.8%
Bus Drivers	23.4%
Vehicle Washers	23.0%
Correctional Officers	22.8%
Janitors & Cleaners	21.8%
Social Workers	21.8%
Security Guards	21.2%
Telephone Operators	19.7%
Data Entry Keyers	19.5%
Practical Nurses	17.6%
Closest to Parity	
Insurance Adjusters	12.1%
Bakers	12.0%
Garage Workers	11.3%
Chemical Technicians	10.8%
Dressmakers	9.9%
Elementary School Teachers	9.7%
Retail Salespersons	9.5%
Hotel Clerks	9.5%
Greatest Underrepresentation	
Waiters & Waitresses	4.7%
Editors & Reporters	3.8%
Bartenders	3.6%
Engineers	3.6%
Lawyers	3.2%
Physicians	3.0%
Realtors	3.0%
Photographers	2.9%
Speech Therapists	2.8%
Biologists	2.7%
Designers	2.6%
Dental Hygienists	2.5%
Architects	0.9%

How much "progress" recent years have seen depends on how one interprets percentage losses and gains. The listings on the next page show a greater black presence in some office positions and skilled blue-collar fields. There are now more black aircraft mechanics and firefighters, both decently paid occupations sought by high school graduates. However, not many people are lining up to become telephone operators and secretaries, jobs white women no longer find so attractive and which have consequently opened up to blacks. The picture is far from encouraging in some other fields. Three decades have passed since 1960, which presumably should have been enough time for increases among black librarians and college teachers and automobile mechanics. It would seem that even affirmative action programs have not done much to raise black representation in these areas.

That there are more black electricians is heartening. But what happened among structural metal workers, where the black share has actually dropped? One answer is that the bulk of construction work now takes place in suburbs or further flung locations, far from where most blacks live. So a real obstacle to workforce equity stems from the difficulties blacks have in finding housing in areas where jobs open up.

To find that the proportion of black physicians has actually declined makes dismaying reading. The same holds for black college professors, whose numbers have barely budged. As recently as 1960, most black students were still going to black colleges, which provided employment for black professors. By the same token, black physicians built up their practices from their offices in local neighborhoods.

The past generation has seen the medical and academic worlds enter new eras. Both have become highly specialized, as well as dependent on research and technologies. Since 1960, membership in both professions has experienced a threefold expansion. However, most of the beneficiaries in this increase have been white women, along with a growing proportion of Asians. While recruitment efforts have raised the number of black professors and physicians, their growth rate nevertheless remains smaller than for other groups. For this reason, they have retained the ratio they held three decades ago or have actually fallen behind.

* * *

BLACK REPRESENTATION WITHIN OCCUPATIONS
1960 to 1990

Representation More than Doubled	1960	1990
Telephone Operators	2.6%	19.7%
Aircraft Mechanics	4.6%	9.8%
Firefighters	2.5%	11.5%
Accountants & Auditors	1.6%	7.4%
Secretaries	2.0%	7.6%
Retail Salespersons	2.4%	9.5%
Electricians	2.2%	6.2%
Lawyers	1.3%	3.2%
Smaller Increases		
Painters	7.7%	9.5%
Librarians	5.1%	5.5%
Automobile Mechanics	7.4%	8.7%
College Teachers	4.4%	4.5%
Decreases		
Domestic Servants	54.3%	24.7%
Chefs and Cooks	24.9%	18.3%
Hairdressers	12.7%	9.2%
Structural Metal Workers	5.0%	3.7%
Physicians	4.4%	3.0%

Domestic service deserves special attention because of the real and symbolic role it has held for black Americans. Virtually every black adult can tell of mothers and grandmothers who cooked and cleaned and cared for children in white people's homes. This was one of the few forms of employment open to black women; indeed, it was so poorly paid that even lower-middle-class families could afford black "help." In 1940, there were 2.4 million household servants in a workforce of 52 million. In 1960, the ratio was still relatively high, 1.8 million out of 68 million. By 1990, however, the number of people working in other people's homes had dropped to 780,000 in a workforce that had risen to 118 million. Relative to the employed population, the country now has only a quarter as many servants as it did fifty years ago.

There are several messages here. In larger cities, women who are willing to work as servants—whether on an hourly basis or as full-time nannies for children—now demand higher wages, with the result that fewer households can afford domestic help. And in large stretches of the suburbs, it is difficult to find anyone available for this kind of work. One recourse has been to turn to immigrants and aliens, many of whom will settle for off-the-books arrangements.

Equally noteworthy is that between 1960 and 1990, the black proportion among household servants fell from over half to less than a quarter. One reason was the common one cited earlier: job possibilities are often in the suburbs, a long distance away. But there is a further consideration here, one having symbolic significance. In the memories of black women, domestic service represents not so much a job as something closer to servitude. Having to work within white homes recalls not only the smug condescension of employers, but having to feign gratitude and a cheerful demeanor. While black women continue to do much of the nation's arduous work, most prefer the option of a hotel or hospital rather than mopping and dusting for the mistress of a house.

White employers can sense racial tensions, and often seek to avoid them by hiring more acquiescent Filipinos or Hispanics. Some whites also worry lest having black servants will lower their status. Others of a more liberal bent fear that having blacks work in their homes may appear racist or exploitative. Families that once had black women look after their children now find it easier to work with—and converse about—their European au pairs.

Concerns over status may also explain the decline in black hairdressers and chefs. Sad to say, many white Americans feel uncomfortable in establishments that have a pronounced number of black employees. At best, they may go in once in a while, on a let's-try-it basis. By and large, however, they would rather not have black people taking charge of their hair or presiding over the kitchens where they dine. (This was not always the case in the past. In both Southern and Northern cities, for example, white men had their hair cut by barbers who were black.) One reason for the shift is that greater sophistication, including an international ambiance, has come to be associated with coiffure and cuisine. As a result, more whites have entered these fields, bringing about a displacement of blacks.

* * *

In recent years, black women have come to comprise a majority of the black workforce. The figures shown below give the proportions of the positions within various fields that are held by black and white women relative to men within each of their racial groups. Thus black women account for 63.8 percent of all black professionals, whereas white women represent 50.6 percent of the whites holding professional positions. In the technical and managerial groups, the black women are even further ahead, while among military officers the black figure is double that for whites.

One reason is necessity. More black women must manage on their own, since they are less likely to have a housemate who brings in a second income. But even when they are married or live with someone else, they must still make a serious work commitment, since it often takes two black incomes to match what one white breadwinner can bring in. This is especially true for the middle class, where one white executive can make $100,000, but a pair of black schoolteachers hardly reach that level.

But this describes only one element in the equation. Of at least equal importance are attitudes and decisions among white employers. If and when organizations feel compelled to hire more black workers, they generally prefer to take on black women rather than black men. Black women, like all women, are perceived as being less assertive and more accommodating. Thus there is the hope that black women will show less resentment or hostility, and will be less apt to present themselves as "black" in demeanor and appearance. A further concern of white employers, albeit not one openly stated, is that

POSITIONS HELD BY WOMEN

Women's Proportion	Among White Workers	Among Black Workers
Total Employment	44.7%	50.6%
Professional	50.6%	63.8%
Managerial	39.1%	55.0%
Technical	47.7%	62.6%
Blue Collar	24.5%	27.6%
Military Officers	10.1%	20.5%
Enlisted Personnel	8.9%	14.5%

having black men and white women work together might lead to familiar relationships that could either be misunderstood or have some grounding in fact.

In addition, black and white women tend to mingle more easily in workplace settings. This is partly because women tend to feel less tense about race. But there is also evidence that women can ignore racial lines in acknowledging common experiences, at least to a far greater extent than men are willing to do. At restaurants near their place of work, groups of black and white women can be seen enjoying lunch together. Far less frequently—if at all—does one encounter similar parties of men. Circumstances like these are not lost on employers, who may conclude that if they must have racially mixed workforces, things will go better if they consist largely of women.

As has been noted, public and nonprofit organizations have become havens for much of the black workforce. Over a third of all black lawyers work for government departments, as do almost 30 percent of black scientists. Blacks account for over 20 percent of the nation's armed services, twice their proportion in the civilian economy. They hold almost a fifth of all positions in the Postal Service, and have similar ratios in many urban agencies. Unfortunately, this makes middle-class blacks vulnerable to public budget cuts. Between 1979 and 1989, the average income of black college men declined by 11 percent, resulting largely from a drop in government hiring, which meant fewer opportunities for younger graduates. During this decade, however, incomes for white college men increased by 11 percent, since the private economy was expanding.

On the whole, then, the business world has not done much to expand black employment. White executives worry about how large a black presence they want to absorb within their firms. Obviously, these thoughts are not committed to paper, nor are they specified in percentage terms. At the same time, racial considerations often figure indirectly, as when companies decide to move operations to new locations or open facilities in new areas. When questioned, they usually allude to the lack of skilled people in urban areas rather than confess to racial prejudice.

Companies realize that too few black faces could lead to charges of bias, causing unpleasant publicity. At the same time, they worry lest they are seen as having "too many" black employees, or as promoting blacks too liberally. In this vein, they may fear that "too black" an appearance will jeopardize their image for competence and credibility. Firms also become uneasy if some of their products—a brand of cigarettes, for example, or a style of running shoes—seem to be attracting too large a black clientele. Perhaps projecting some of their own anxieties, they sense that white customers will shy away from items they feel have become associated with black preferences and tastes.

All the while, businesses can be expected to protest that they are "color blind" both in policy and practice, seeking only the best talent they can find, regardless of race or creed or gender. If there appear to be few black people on their payrolls, they will insist it is because hardly any have applied or not enough live near their facilities or have the necessary qualifications. What is not openly addressed is how far possessing a skin of a certain color might figure as one of those "qualifications."

Business has always been inherently conservative, waiting until other sectors take steps toward social change. In part, this attitude stems from anxieties about how their customers will react. Will they buy, or buy as much, from salespeople who are black? And can blacks join in the socializing so often needed to clinch a deal? Will users of your product feel confident that a black technician can work competently with complex equipment? Hence the tendency to play it safe, which usually means hiring as white a workforce as possible. (To combine competence and color, Asians serve as acceptable surrogates.) There is also the worry that blacks who are promoted to supervisory positions may not obtain the best performance from white subordinates, who may be resentful if not actually resistant. Chief executives may smile wanly and agree that the problem is one of prejudice. Not their own, of course, but those of customers and others who still cling to stereotypes.

In more secluded settings, white employees and supervisors may be heard to say that they find blacks hard to work with. ("We had one, but he didn't work out.") They will cite cases of coldness or hostility or chips-on-the-shoulder, compounded by a readiness to imagine racial insults. Or they will allude to an unwillingness of black men to relax in workplace relationships. Rather than inquire why this reluctance persists, or how it might be remedied, the tendency is to evade the issue by hiring and promoting as few blacks as possible. At that point, personal biases become transmuted into institutional racism.

Small wonder, then, that black Americans have always agreed among themselves that if they want to get ahead, they have to work harder and do better than white people. Given all the misgivings of white executives and supervisors, it would seem self-evident that blacks must put in a lot more effort simply to satisfy the standards their employers set. It is not as if they can simply walk in and start doing a job. All eyes are on them, as if a Great Experiment is underway.

It is not easy buckling down to a job when you have to expend so much of your energy contriving a "white" personality—or at least the appearance of one—so as to put your white workmates at ease. Nor is it easy to establish one's authority, since simply having a black face raises doubts in many white minds. Added to which is having to read nuances and allusions that whites recognize as a matter of course. All this demands much more from black workers than is ever asked of whites. If white people have any doubts on this score, they might imagine spending their entire careers with a foreign company, where they find that no matter how much they study its ways, it still refuses to grant that they can ever master the assignments at hand.

With employment, as in education, interests and emotions can cloud discussions of "affirmative action." Indeed, the phrase has become an epithet for our time. Simply hearing it mentioned causes individuals to raise defensive bulwarks, as if the most vital of principles are at stake. The issues and reactions to them are often similar in both employment and education. However, preferential policies have some different implications in educational settings, and these will be considered separately in the next chapter.

Most simply, affirmative action in employment proposes—or requires—changes in hiring or promotion policies. It aims at bringing more of certain categories of people into an organization, and then ensuring their representation at various levels. The intended beneficiaries may be women or persons with certain attributes or origins. However, the cases drawing the greatest attention have been those that focus on race.

Affirmative action is by no means new. It began in 1941, when President Franklin D. Roosevelt signed an Executive Order ordering defense plants to show that they were opening jobs to black workers.

Roosevelt also established a Fair Employment Practices Committee to ensure that his ruling would be enforced. This body was continued under Presidents Truman and Eisenhower, and later Congress expanded its authority and renamed it the Equal Employment Opportunity Commission. The Kennedy administration coined the actual phrase "affirmative action," in a ruling that directed firms with federal contracts to take "positive steps" to have a racially representative workforce. Under the Civil Rights Act of 1964, passed by a bipartisan majority, Title VII banned employment discrimination that might be based on race, religion, sex, or national origin. President Lyndon Johnson, shortly after signing the law, illustrated the thinking that led to racial preferences. Speaking at Howard University in 1965, he said:

> You do not take a person who for years has been hobbled by chains, and liberate him, bring him up to the starting line, and then say, "You are free to compete with all the others."

Martin Luther King, Jr., stated the position in similar terms, when he remarked that one cannot ask people who don't have boots to pull themselves up by their own bootstraps. It was President Richard Nixon, generally considered a conservative Republican, who took affirmative action a step further. In what his administration called "The Philadelphia Plan," companies were told that to keep federal contracts they would have to set numerical "goals" for hiring minorities. By 1972, Congress had amended Title VII so that courts could require affirmative action measures as a way of compensating for discriminatory practices.

Much has been made of whether affirmative action calls for setting "goals," which employers must make a good faith effort to reach, or if it imposes actual numerical "quotas." For many people, the latter term can have ominous overtones. President George Bush has used the word to frighten employers into believing they could be ordered to hire and promote precise percentages of black employees. In 1990, Senator Jesse Helms of North Carolina won reelection by stirring worries among whites that jobs they might have otherwise obtained would become unavailable to them. While it happened that his opponent was black, Helms's victory also sent a message to white candidates, alerting them to what could happen if they appear to favor quotas.

In fact, there have been cases where quotas were imposed. One of the first occurred in 1972, when a federal judge told Alabama officials that half of all new state troopers they hired would have to be black, and that order would remain in effect until blacks comprised one quarter of the force. Moreover, the Equal Employment Opportunity Commission has the power to file suit against private employers who do not appear to have enough black workers on their payrolls. In one case, the commission told a small Chicago firm that it had to hire eight more black employees, since statistical studies showed that it had an inadequate racial mix compared with other businesses in the area.

In increasing numbers of cases, however, employers do not wait for court orders or other official rulings. Rather, they take steps on their own to avoid litigation or bad publicity. In some instances, these moves arise from liberal motives, or at least a wish to appear progressive. Thus a law firm may decide that, no matter what, it will include at least one black graduate among its next intake of associates. (The producers of the television series "L.A. Law" took care to do just that.) Or the reasons can be semi-voluntary. A construction firm may move black applicants higher on its hiring list to secure or retain a government contract, since many local and federal agencies want evidence of a multiracial workforce. More than a few corporations have integrated affirmative action policies into their human resources systems. Not only have they been successful in changing their racial ratios, but they have sought to educate their staffs on how to make the new procedures work.

What have been the effects of affirmative action policies? At this point, no one can say for sure how many white Americans have been displaced or bypassed because preferences were given to blacks. The most carefully controlled survey yet done focused on some 68,000 firms that had government contracts, and were required by Executive Order to emphasize minority hiring. Within this group of companies, the employment of black men rose by 6.5 percent and that of black women by 11.0 percent, between 1974 and 1980, the period that was studied.

However, racial ratios can change for various reasons. As was seen earlier, there are more black telephone operators not because quotas were imposed but because fewer white people are applying for those jobs. Still, one can point to growing black representation in a number of positions that many people regard as desirable. For example:

BLACK EMPLOYMENT

1970		1990
23,796	Police Officers	63,855
14,145	Electricians	43,276
10,633	Bank Tellers	46,332
3,914	Health Officials	13,125
2,501	Pharmacists	7,011
2,227	Athletes	7,178

In all six of these fields, black employment rose between two and three times, while the black workforce as a whole grew by only 60 percent during this period. But how far these increases can be attributed to affirmative recruitment or preferential hiring remains a matter for speculation. There is reason to believe that traditionally white-dominated professions, like police officers and electricians, would not have made much of an effort to bring in more black men and women had they not been subjected to some kind of pressure or even legal compulsion.

An apparent exception might be professional athletes, all of whom are obviously hired on merit. After all, no one can force a team to sign up someone simply to redress a racial imbalance. Even so, there are signs that some sports that seem "too white" feel under pressure to add more black players to their rosters. (Ice hockey is one example.) Moreover, sports spectators seem to be thinking more "affirmatively," in that they want to watch the best athletes who are available. Thus they appear willing to have more blacks in the arenas, if that is what it takes to have the finest. And as can be seen with basketball, many white fans gladly root for teams that have mainly black rosters.

The purpose of affirmative action is not simply to avow good intentions, but to register results. Showing you have tried to find qualified people will not suffice. Rather, its aim is to achieve a visible increase in the number of black men or women at various levels on the nation's payrolls. Justifications for these policies can take several forms.

One is that blacks should figure disproportionately in hirings and promotions to compensate for past policies that excluded them from employment or allowed them entry only in token numbers. In these cases, those being hired will not necessarily be the same persons who suffered from discrimination in the past. So one presumption of affirmative action is that an entire race can deserve redress for unjust treatment. On this premise, at least some of the beneficiaries may come from later generations. An analogy might be that if a family's property was unfairly confiscated, restoration can go to descendants who were not even alive when the expropriation occurred. But not everyone accepts this view. Recent decisions by more conservative judges have declared that only specific individuals who can show that they were not hired or promoted due to racial bias can claim jobs or promotions or recover financial damages.

Another rationale for affirmative action suggests a broader basis for increasing the number of black physicians and professors, as well as structural metal workers and firefighters. Our society will be a better place if it has fairer racial representation in these and other occupations. If a country wants to vouchsafe that it has overcome discrimination and prejudice, visible evidence is necessary. Two hundred years ago, Alexander Hamilton said that the promise of America was to allow every individual to "find his proper element and call into activity the whole vigor of his nature." To make good on this principle would not require that the membership of all professions precisely mirror the population as a whole. Not everyone will want to go into every field or specialty. Even so, no group chooses to have most of its members remain below the norm in pay and prestige. Nor does affirmative action aim at eliminating gaps between the well-off and the poor. Indeed, it accepts the economic inequalities characteristic of America's economic system. Thus it seeks to redistribute status and rewards with more concern for racial equity.

A further justification for preferential policies relates to the "hobbles" Lyndon Johnson mentioned in his Howard University speech. If black people are to have a fair chance in the nation's economic competitions, they must amass enough training and experience to vie on an equal footing. To reach a higher status you must first get to the step immediately below. America will not have black chief executives unless contenders can learn the ropes at vice presidential levels. In this view, affirmative action promotions are temporary expedients, which may lapse once black representation becomes evident in all sectors of the system.

A variant of this view may be found in "set aside" provisions, under which public contracts are awarded to firms owned by blacks and other minorities. In some instances, exact quotas for such contracts have been set by public agencies, but this has now been questioned by the courts. Until recently, under this system, minority-owned firms that put in bids have had a better chance of securing a contract. Here, too, the idea has been that once they begin to gain experience in construction or manufacturing or providing financial services, they will be able to compete without special subventions. The Federal Communications Commission also makes it easier for minority owners to obtain radio and television frequencies. Nor should it be forgotten that government help for private firms is by no means new. Military contractors have been given quite costly subsidies, on the ground that they need to build up the expertise to provide products or services the government requires.

Thus far, few minority firms can be said to have graduated from dependence on their "'set aside" cushion. If the aim of the program is to get them to the point where they can compete with other businesses on an unassisted basis, it still has a long way to go. An additional concern is that some companies seeking "set aside" contracts have not in fact been owned by blacks or other minority entrepreneurs. As successive prosecutions have shown, firms have frequently been underwritten by white businessmen, with some black or other minority executives displayed as figureheads. In one egregious case, a white contractor won an award because he claimed he had a Native American great-grandmother.

The debate over affirmative action raises some basic questions about how people are selected for positions and promotions. Methods will obviously vary among industries and occupations. In some cases, personality plays a major role; in others, more formal criteria hold sway. Increasingly, however, credentials like degrees and diplomas are expected at the outset, simply if you want to have your name considered. In public employment, standardized tests can be critical for civil service positions, and rules may specify that openings can go only to the persons with the highest scores. Many private firms now administer similar examinations to job applicants.

The problem is that most such tests have had "a disparate impact" when their results are broken down by race. Generally, blacks as a group do not do as well as whites on multiple-choice tests. In 1971, the Supreme Court confronted the impact of testing in *Griggs* v. *Duke Power Co.* The company had kept black employees in lower-level jobs, arguing that their test scores showed they were not "qualified" for better positions. The Court rejected this explanation, ruling that employers who hired and promoted on the basis of tests had to show that those examinations in fact provided good forecasts of how well people would do at their jobs.

Thereafter, companies could continue to use tests that disparate numbers of black applicants failed to pass only if they could demonstrate that those examinations served a "business necessity." That is, they had to show that only by using these tests could they find the best people, who were needed for the firm to perform profitably. Under this logic, even if test results display some racial bias, a business is still entitled to hire the people who will best benefit its balance sheet. Affirmative action proposals would then have to argue that considerations other than profits should also play a role.

Legal phrases like "disparate impact" and "business necessity" recur in the debate over affirmative action. Another term is "bona fide occupational qualification." In some professions, employers may ask that all candidates have an advanced degree, since that attainment stands as evidence that they have the "skills and aptitudes essential to the job." A good example is academic employment. As was seen earlier, black professors continue to hold only 4.5 percent of all faculty positions, even after twenty years of affirmative intentions by college administrations. The most common reason given is that the "pool" of qualified blacks is very small, and those who already meet its standards have a multitude of offers. As is well known, the basic qualification for college teaching is the Ph.D. degree. Colleges argue that having it is their equivalent of a "business necessity."

In 1990, a total of 25,831 doctoral degrees were awarded to American citizens and aliens who intend to remain in this country. Of those doctorates, 904–or 3.5 percent—went to black men and women. Even if all 904 joined college faculties, it would not do much to improve the existing percentage rate. As it turns out, the largest single field for black doctorates is education, and most of the recipients were school administrators averaging over forty years of age. Altogether, only 34 black candidates received Ph.D.s in engineering, 25 were in physics and chemistry, and altogether eleven won degrees in business administration. Given the small size of these "pools," it seems that a lot of college departments will not have much success in their search for black colleagues.

But need a Ph.D. be mandated as a "bona fide occupational qualification" for everyone in college teaching? Most institutions do not place much emphasis on research. In fact, many professors cease being productive scholars or writers after they get tenure. Moreover, in fields like business and engineering, practical experience and an ability to communicate may actually make for better teaching than an advanced degree. Law is another practical calling, yet many law schools continue to limit their hiring only to candidates who have published articles in professional reviews. This limitation led the Reverend Jesse Jackson to call on law schools to abandon these and other "archaic rules" and cease defining "who is qualified in the most narrow, vertical, academic terms." A lawyer experienced in defending an inner-city clientele could have a lot to teach apprentice attorneys.

Not all occupations have such formal requirements. Decisions concerning who gets jobs are often made informally by individuals or committees. When law firms hire new associates, they obviously expect all candidates to have a legal degree. But another question the partners ask themselves—although not always aloud—is whether the individual they are interviewing seems to be the kind of person who "will fit in here." In many personnel decisions, personal judgments come into play. Seasoned interviewers say they can sense when a person has the traits and attributes their organization requires. Nor can these intuitions always be detailed in written reports. Hence the difficulty of presenting—or obtaining—the real "reasons" why someone has been passed over for a position or a promotion.

Suppose we discover that a law firm with fifty attorneys has not even one black associate. Its senior partners may insist that they have been looking, but they have yet to find black candidates who have the qualities they look for in colleagues. If that is their reply, they are issuing a very disturbing statement, since they are suggesting that not a *single* one of the black law school graduates they have interviewed has measured up to the standards they invariably set.

In actual fact, many job requirements are artificial or overly rigid, and bar people of real talent from professions where they could do a lot of good. In medicine we want physicians who have an intuitive flair for diagnosing maladies. Others may have personalities that put patients at ease, obviously an important element in treatment. Yet many of these potential healers may not score well on tests designed to assess abstract reasoning. Even if they are admitted to medical schools under special provisions, they may fall behind since the first years stress not clinical treatment, but lectures on scientific subjects. (One study of black medical students found that one in six had to take their first-year courses a second time.)

While everyone supports standards associated with "quality," the term can also conceal vested interests and biases. Why not say that an orchestra or a law school or a medical center should accept incorporating new people as a challenge? After all, there are literally dozens of fields where blacks have come to excel once opportunities started to open. (The military is an obvious case in point.) There is no reason why a more representative workforce could not be brought to match, if not surpass, standards set in more segregated days.

Public employment has been a prominent target in affirmative action cases, partly because it relies more heavily on tests and also because government is held to higher standards than enterprises committed to pursuing profits. Also, official agencies cannot use the defense of "business necessity" when their hiring practices are challenged. Of course, we all want public bureaus to do their jobs efficiently, and most of us believe they should provide better service than they currently do. Still, they are not businesses, and do not usually have to vie against competitors for customers and revenues.

In 1979, in *United Steelworkers* v. *Weber*, the Supreme Court renewed its early support for affirmative action by approving plans that intended to "remove manifest racial imbalance" in hirings, placement, and promotions. This principle was applied two years later in New York City, where a lower court agreed that not enough black police officers were passing the test for promotion to the rank of sergeant. The question arose whether something about the test itself might have been racially biased. Certainly, the results showed a "disparate impact." It was not an easy test, and only 10.6 percent of the whites taking it received passing grades. However, among the black candidates, the passing proportion was a dismaying 1.6 percent. So the court ordered the police department to come up with a new examination, to be revised in ways that would enable more blacks to get passing grades.

The new test put less emphasis on reading and interpreting paragraphs of prose. Instead, the officers taking it watched situations acted out on video tapes. Even so, they had to fill in answer sheets that required them to know the meaning of words like "relevant," "disposition," "unsubstantiated," and "tactfully." When the results were computed, the number of passing black candidates was about as low as it had been before.

But this raises an issue similar to those considered with medical schools and college faculties: whether existing tests really have "a significant relationship to job performance." So far as policework is concerned, everyone agrees that we need more officers who can communicate with people in poorer and rougher neighborhoods. One could well argue that the knowledge and skills black candidates bring to law enforcement would more than make up for the lower scores they tend to receive on standardized tests.

At the same time, we now expect even officers on patrol to be well informed about complex constitutional matters. Investigations must be conducted to hold up later in court, where terms such as "disposition" and "unsubstantiated" inevitably figure. Officers are also expected to write reports with sufficient precision so they can withstand scrutiny if the case comes to trial. These arguments have been used to defend the need for literacy skills among police officers.

Despite huge investments in research, even the experts have yet to devise tests that will be "race-neutral" in their results. In theory, such tests would give all candidates the same chance to reveal their skills and intelligence, regardless of their racial origins or cultural backgrounds. But another expectation for "neutural" tests is that satisfactory numbers of black candidates will achieve passing scores. Since this has yet to happen, New York City resolved the problem by setting a lower passing grade for black police officers. This issue will be explored further in the next chapter, with regard to college admissions.

As has been noted, a frequent argument for affirmative action is that it will serve the nation's interests to have more black men and women serving as physicians and police officers and teachers, as well as in other professional fields. For one thing, they will be role models for youngsters: living evidence that hard work can be rewarded. Moreover, in the occupations just cited, they can provide more effective service to patients, students, and citizens of their own race. To the extent that black Americans have their own culture, vocabulary, and styles, white practitioners may fail to grasp important nuances and meanings. Even with good will and careful training, it is unlikely that a white—or Asian or Hispanic—psychiatrist will be able to offer a full diagnosis of a black patient's mental state. And one reason why so many white policemen harass so many black youths is that they cannot catch the clues that distinguish law-abiding young men from those who are up to no good. One could hope that even black felons would see more fairness in the justice system, if they were tried and sentenced by black judges.

But such a defense of preferential hiring comes close to suggesting that the skills of black professionals hinge on their ability to serve clienteles of their own race. If that is why they should be hired, then the question arises whether they can also serve the more general population. If black police officers are hired primarily for patrolling—and controlling—black neighborhoods, they will soon begin to wonder whether they will be considered for promotions and broader assignments. It will be revealing to see, as more black physicians open practices, how many white patients come to them for treatment.

Interestingly, an obverse argument is less often heard. That is, that white students and patients and criminals would gain by being taught or treated or tried by black teachers and physicians and judges. Given the everyday advantages that come with being white, having to face black people with power may awaken whites to realities about themselves and their society they have failed to recognize.

A further concern with affirmative action is that colleagues and patients and clients will wonder whether people promoted under these programs made it on their merits, or if they got where they are due to race-based preferences. Similar reactions have been expressed about those benefiting from the programs. How, it is asked, can people go through life, knowing that they have been hired not on their inherent talents, but to fill some quota or to satisfy appearances?

Not surprisingly, white people seem to do most of the worrying about this apparent harm to black self-esteem. In fact, there is little evidence that those who have been aided by affirmative action feel many doubts or misgivings. For one thing, most of them believe they are entitled to whatever opportunities they have received. The experience of being black in America cannot help but stir suspicions that in most cases you were never given a fair chance. So if preferential treatment comes your way, your response may be that it makes up for at least some of the inequities you have faced throughout your life.

Nor should it be forgotten that feelings of unworthiness seldom plague white Americans who have profited from more traditional forms of preferment. For years, so-called selective colleges have set less demanding standards for admitting children of alumni. (This by itself should show that affirmative action has a venerable history.) These privileged offspring know full well that other applicants with better records received rejection letters. Yet few of them are seen slouching around the campus, their heads bowed in shame. Worries about the mental and moral health of persons labeled as undeserving can underestimate the readiness of individuals to justify good fortune. If nothing else, one can always rationalize: for years others have been favored; now it's our turn.

In its 1979 *Weber* decision, one reason the Supreme Court gave for permitting an affirmative action plan was that it did "not require the discharge of white workers and their replacement with new black hirees." The judges seemed to be saying that whites should not suffer in order to bring about benefits for blacks. This principle has generally prevailed. According to the Court, white workers who hold jobs should not have to worry that they will be let go and replaced by blacks simply to change a racial ratio.

In fact, there have been such cases, although care is often taken to blur the connection. Thus, a white college instructor whose contract is not renewed may have these suspicions when he discovers that his successor is to be a black assistant professor. By and large, though, white fears focus less on losing their jobs. A more pervasive concern has to do with not getting a position they may be applying for or being passed over for promotions. This worry is what gave rise to the case of Allan Bakke, a rejected medical school applicant, which came before the Supreme Court in 1978. He had sued the University of California, claiming that although his record entitled him to a place, it was given to a less-qualified black candidate. He was rejected, he argued, simply because he was white. While Bakke did not use the phrase, his position was that he had suffered from "reverse discrimination." In other words, he argued that whites can also encounter bias; and in such cases, courts should find in their favor.*

No one can say with certainty how many white Americans may have been bypassed or displaced because preferences have been given to blacks. As was noted earlier, whites have not lost ground in medicine and college teaching, despite considerable efforts to open up those fields. Some answers can be suggested by returning to a group of occupations examined earlier in this chapter. Those tabulations showed the actual numerical increase among black police officers, electricians, bank tellers, health administrators, pharmacists, and professional athletes between 1970 and 1990. However, that analysis did not take into account that even more whites may have entered those occupations during these years. If that turned out to be the case, then even allowing for black advances, whites as a group would not have lost out.

As might be expected, the picture is mixed. Blacks obviously accounted for a high proportion of new police hirings. Yet this was probably to be expected, given the public profile of the profession,

* The Court allowed California to continue preferential admissions for blacks, on the ground that colleges have always been allowed to select diverse student bodies. But it also told the medical school that it had to admit Bakke.

EXPANSION IN EMPLOYMENT: 1970–1990

Positions	New Positions	Black Share
Police Officers	97,506	41.1%
Athletes	25,507	19.4%
Bank Tellers	218,757	16.3%
Electricians	229,541	12.7%
Health Officials	90,861	10.1%
Pharmacists	61,358	7.4%

along with the fact that a growing proportion of the people the police deal with are black. And, as was remarked upon earlier, professional sports have come a long way in recognizing the talents of black athletes. The 16.3 percent gain for black bank tellers is more ambiguous. While it ranks as a white-collar job, it is not particularly well paid and the turnover tends to be high. As with telephone operators, there is reason to believe that more blacks are being hired because fewer whites are applying. (In higher bank positions, there are still very few black faces.) The figures for electricians, health administrators, and pharmacists indicate that over the twenty-year period, black representation increased only by a point or two, remained static, or actually fell.

Still, it would be disingenuous to deny that some white men—and perhaps even some white women—did not get jobs that, in the absence of affirmative action, might otherwise have gone to them. Some of these individuals may be quite bitter about having been kept from positions they feel they worked for and deserved. So long as there are a limited number of desirable jobs and fewer avenues for promotions, there are going to be disappointed people. In some cases, they may be young men who had always aspired to police careers or the building trades, perhaps following in their fathers' footsteps. In other instances, they may be administrators in public service organizations, who believe that they did not get a promotion because those higher up felt it timely to have someone black in a visible position.

But given the disappointments that so often accompany having a black skin, it could be argued that whites could give way just a little. Even so, few white Americans feel that they should be held personally responsible for racial discrimination, either now or in the past. Thus they resent policies that would allow others to move ahead of them, and most of them sincerely feel that they have been subjected to "reverse discrimination."

In actual fact, talented advertising executives and successful surgeons have little to fear from minority preference. The whites who lose out are more generally blue-collar workers or persons at lower administrative levels, whose skills are not greatly in demand. One of the chief effects of affirmative action has been to pit whites with modest aspiritions against blacks who want better lives for themselves.

* * *

A few concluding comments are in order. The first is that such evidence as we have shows that white women have benefited more from recent workforce changes than have black men. And among blacks, women have gained more than have black men. Perhaps if the movement of women toward work and careers had come at another time, progress relating to race would have been given greater priority.

If some of the changes in racial ratios can be ascribed to affirmative action, the programs themselves were never intended to create new jobs. Rather, they focus on the allocation of jobs that already exist. Expanded employment ultimately depends on a flourishing economy, plus new kinds of positions the society is willing to pay for. (In the latter category are jobs like prison guards and nursing home attendants.) Where racial preference has played a role, black workers with middle-class credentials were more apt to be the ones who benefited, especially in more visible public service professions. So what needs to be stressed is that despite all the controversies surrounding affirmative action, fewer blacks now have steady jobs of any kind and their unemployment rates have been growing progressively worse relative to those recorded for whites.

Much has been heard about the need to improve Americans' work skills, if only to maintain the nation's living standards and keep the country competitive in the world economy. Increasing numbers of companies have found they have to educate their own employees, often in collaboration with urban schools and community colleges. Firms like Motorola and Monsanto and Corning Glass have made extra efforts to place black workers and other minorities in such programs. Nor is this always in response to official prodding or threats of litigation, let alone pressure to fill "'quotas." In many cases, companies are finding that not enough whites entering the workforce are willing to consider blue-collar jobs. Benefits for employers include improved morale, retaining skilled people, and better company-community relations. Insofar as this is so, self-interest may force more businesses to devise their own variants of affirmative action.

But this may be wishful thinking. Companies that do not wish to pay the wages Americans expect have been turning elsewhere. In 1990, for example, Nike managed to sell $1.7 billion worth of footwear with a payroll of only 3,500 people. The reason is that it has no manufacturing operations within this country; all of its sneakers are made abroad. And rather than trying to teach white-collar skills to a local labor force, some insurance companies are flying their paperwork to Ireland, where operators key it into computer systems. Indeed, architectural specifications can be sent by satellite, with the drafting done as far away as Bombay.

Here in the United States, many employers are quite open about preferring immigrants to native-born black workers. Apartment houses are more apt to choose Hispanics or West Indians for their service staffs, while retail shops look for Asians. A black owner of several fast-food restaurants in and around Harlem confessed that he confined his hiring to foreign-born applicants.

And, as has been noted, firms opening new facilities make a point of selecting sites with minimal black populations. This is especially true of foreign-owned corporations, an increasing source of American employment. Thus Toyota located an assembly plant in Kentucky's Harlan county, in which 95 percent of the residents are white, while Honda settled on a stretch of rural Ohio, where the white figure exceeded 97 percent.

CHAPTER EIGHT

EDUCATION

ETHNICITY AND ACHIEVEMENT

IF AFFIRMATIVE ACTION has had a mixed record in employment, it remains alive and well on the nation's campuses. Until a decade or so ago, conflicts could be construed largely in black and white terms. Now there are more players in the field, with Hispanics and Asians, and women and other groups also making claims. Decisions about college admissions are based on varied views of merit and equity. Two cases illustrate some of the issues that are involved.

- In recent years, the University of Virginia has moved to double its admissions of black students, while cutting back on white enrollments. Recently, it accepted over half the blacks who had applied, but only a quarter of the whites, even though the Scholastic Aptitude Test scores for the black group averaged 240 points lower. An admissions dean admitted, "We take in more in the groups with weaker credentials and make it harder for those with stronger credentials."

- In California, about 33 percent of high school seniors with Asian backgrounds have academic records that qualify them for the state's university system. However, in 1988 they were allotted only 26 percent of the places at the Berkeley campus, and 18 percent at UCLA. Many Asians complained that a ceiling had been set to limit their presence on some campuses, despite their records and qualifications.

Virginia's admission policy for black students is an example of *affirmative action* at work. The Asians objecting to California's plan were asking for an *equal opportunity* to compete fairly with other applicants. The two principles may sound similar, but they can actually be in opposition.

Today, every college and university says it is committed to "equal opportunity" in faculty hiring and student admissions. On its face, the principle would seem unassailable: all applicants should be given full and fair consideration, regardless of age or race or sex, or other characteristics and conditions, including physical disabilities. Under equal opportunity, standards would be set and all would stand the same chance in the competition. If this seems a commonplace now, it was not always the case. In the past, colleges turned down qualified candidates because they were Catholic or Jewish, and in many cases would not even consider blacks. Now, as has been noted, some Asians are protesting that while they have satisfied admissions standards, they are not getting their fair share of college places. In a similar vein, some whites have complained that blacks with lower test results are given places sought by higher-scoring whites.

"Affirmative action" is rather different from "equal opportunity." No colleges today turn down black applicants who meet their academic criteria. Virtually all schools say they would like to attract even more black students, since small black enrollments have become a matter of embarrassment. At last report, only 3.2 percent of the students at Smith College were black. Bates College in Maine could manage only 2.1 percent, and at the main University of Wisconsin campus at Madison the black proportion was only 1.7 percent. Few schools simply wait for black candidates to apply; almost all mount recruiting drives.

The difficulty has been to find candidates the schools believe are qualified. Not only elite private schools but many state universities want to maintain minimal standards for the people they admit. Hence their quandary when too few black applicants meet those requisites.*

* Of course, black students are not the only group "protected" (the official term) by affirmative action. Most programs also provide for Hispanics and Native Americans. Berkeley has added Filipinos, as well as applicants from low-income families and persons with physical disabilities. The City University of New York, having decided it should have more Italian-Americans on its faculty, is allowed to judge candidates from that group by less stringent standards.

To solve this problem, affirmative action programs have moved beyond recruiting drives and offers of financial aid. In other words "action" must mean more than "opportunity"; it has to be able to point to results. To ensure that entering classes will display a certain racial composition, applications from black students are judged by a separate set of standards.

Separate standards can be rationalized in several ways. One argument is that preferential treatment is hardly new. For years, Ivy League colleges acted "affirmatively" by giving places to mediocre students from fashionable prep schools. Or, to cite a current example, since the Massachusetts Institute of Technology wants its classes to have a certain ratio of women, it admits some who have lower mathematics scores than male applicants. It can also be argued that reserving places for athletes is a variant of affirmative action, as is greater indulgence toward candidates from distant states. The most common practice involves giving favored consideration to the offspring of alumni, even if their records are less impressive than those of other applicants. A recent study of Harvard, for example, found that about 40 percent of alumni children were admitted, compared with 14 percent from less well-connected homes. To be sure, "reasons" can be marshaled to support alumni preference or athletic scholarships or applicants from Alaska.*

Presumably everyone approves of diversity. In the *Bakke* case, which upheld a medical school's affirmative action program, Justice Lewis Powell wrote that institutions should be allowed to assemble a varied student body. In this vein, a report by the Faculty Senate at Berkeley has suggested that the possession of certain ethnic backgrounds could be seen as a "qualification" for admission. The diversity that such students would bring to the campus would, it was argued, make for "a more dynamic intellectual environment and a richer undergraduate experience."

Indeed, one of the most graphic examples of how affirmative action works has been on the Berkeley campus. It is an intricate story, involving at least four ethnic groups. In 1973, an official plan recommended that "each segment of California public higher education shall strive to approximate by 1980 the general ethnic, sexual, and

* In response to inquiries from the U.S. Department of Education, Harvard officials said that alumni whose children were admitted gave more generously to the university. However, they later confessed that they had no figures to support this supposition.

economic composition of the recent high school graduates." Despite this goal, a count taken in 1981 found that only 3.8 percent of Berkeley's students were black and only 4.4 percent were Hispanic, whereas students from those two groups together made up 27.2 percent of California's statewide pool of high school graduates. Black and Hispanic enrollments at Berkeley were still two-thirds short of the target set eight years earlier.

The reason for this shortfall was not overt discrimination, but the prevailing standards for admission. To be accepted at Berkeley and seven other selective campuses, applicants had to rank in the top 12.5 percent of California's high school graduates, determined by an index combining grades and Scholastic Aptitude Test scores. Unfortunately, few blacks and Hispanics were in that 12.5 percent.

As the table on this page shows, by 1988 only 5 percent of the Hispanics and even fewer of the blacks were eligible for Berkeley. Using these and other figures, the Faculty Senate found that a class admitted solely on academic grounds would be less than 4 percent black and Hispanic. The chief reason was that Berkeley, enjoying its status as the most selective campus, took only the very top scorers within the group of students eligible for the statewide system. To raise its ratio of Hispanic and black students, it would be necessary to change the admission procedures to allow applicants from these groups to come to Berkeley regardless of where they ranked in the

ETHNICITY AND ADMISSIONS AT BERKELEY (1988–1989)

Blacks	Hispanics		Whites	Asians
7.9%	19.3%	Ethnicity of California's High School Graduates*	61.1%	8.7%
4.5%	5.0%	Proportion of Each Group Eligible for University	15.8%	32.8%
11.4%	19.6%	Ethnicity of Students Accepted by Berkeley*	38.9%	27.5%
37.5%	43.5%	Graduation Rate for Students in Each Group	71.5%	67.3%

* Totals run across and omit other ethnic groups.

state pool. As a result, in the 1988 entering class, black and Hispanic applicants together were given 31 percent of the places. This was achieved by admitting almost all the black and Hispanic candidates who met the minimal standard. In the past, as many as two thirds of those entrants would have been sent to other colleges in the system, which have lower admission standards.

The total enrollment at Berkeley has remained fairly stable over the past dozen years; so if some groups receive more places, others will get fewer. Of those admitted to the 1988 freshman class, 27.5 percent were Asian, three times their proportion among high school graduates. Even more striking, only 38.9 percent of its places went to whites, who numbered 61.1 percent of the state's high school graduates, and who had received two-thirds of the freshman places just seven years earlier.

Yet it was not easy for white Californians to complain, since their overall scholastic records were not very auspicious; only 15.8 percent of white high school graduates met Berkeley's academic standards. Asians might have been content since, as was noted, their share of the entering class worked out to three times their representation among high school graduates. However, they were not, because a large number of Asians who had suitable academic scores were still rejected by Berkeley. Many claimed in newspaper and television interviews that they had been subjected to a quota system. Equally disturbing to Asian applicants, the number of places based solely on academic criteria, which they had worked to satisfy, had been substantially reduced. The fear of having "too many" Asians seemed to many a replay of policies colleges once had concerning Jews.

Complicating the equation is the fact that most Asians wanted to

AVERAGE SAT SCORES OF STUDENTS FROM LOW-INCOME FAMILIES (1990)

	Number	Score
White	65,599	881
Asian	18,729	832
Hispanic	21,291	738
Black	32,738	692

attend Berkeley or UCLA, rather than less metropolitan campuses like Davis or Santa Cruz. One reason is that many of them have part-time jobs in family businesses and must remain close to their homes. Given their good records and the large numbers applying, there is a likelihood that those campuses could become overwhelmingly Asian. Indeed, in the UCLA class admitted for the fall of 1990, Asian freshmen in fact outnumbered whites.

Since the system is not expanding its enrollment, if more Asians are admitted, then fewer whites or blacks or Hispanics can be let in. Most Asians say that they have no quarrel with affirmative action for those who need it. For their own part, however, they would rather be judged by regular admissions criteria, which ends up pitting them against whites. And that has been happening not only at Berkeley and UCLA. Yale and Harvard, which draw on national pools, now have entering classes which are 13 percent and 15 percent Asian respectively. At Stanford, the figure is close to 20 percent, while at MIT it is close to a quarter.

It will be interesting to see how white applicants will react as they find fewer college places open to them. At selective undergraduate and professional schools, more will no longer get their first choice. Of course, this need not doom their college plans. Someone who in the past might have got into Berkeley or UCLA can still enroll at Riverside or Santa Barbara, where the competition is less stringent.

White students may grumble about being denied admissions they feel should have been theirs. By and large, however, few have gone public with their complaints. To start, one can't easily object to facing Asian competitors, since they play by the regular rules. (So far there haven't been complaints about recent immigrants' being subsidized by taxes and contributions from native citizens.) At all events, whites still tend to make up the majority of those admitted to competitive schools, so those who find themselves rejected tend to have less impressive records. So they resign themselves to attending Lehigh instead of Amherst, or going to law school at the University of Michigan rather than at Yale.

It remains to be seen how Berkeley's new student body will function in practice. In introductory courses, on one side of the room will be Asians admitted on the academic track. Across from them will be blacks and Hispanics with classroom skills at a rather lower level. It is almost as if two dissimilar colleges were sharing the same campus. Indeed, an earlier Berkeley study of freshmen calculus courses found that whereas only 5 percent of the Asian students failed, half of the black students did.

The real test is how many actually make it to graduation. Even before affirmative action, minority attrition was a cause for concern. Also included in the Berkeley table are the graduation outcomes for students who started as freshmen in 1983. As can be seen, 71.5 percent of the whites and 67.3 percent of the Asians received degrees by 1988. The figures for Hispanics and blacks were 43.5 percent and 37.5 percent.

Studies of attrition suggest that affirmative action programs may do some students a disservice, by placing them in colleges for which they are not properly prepared. Pennsylvania State University has even tried cash incentives to stem the dropout and failure rates. Black students who manage a C+ average have been given awards of $550; higher grades can win them double that. These grants have stirred some controversy, since they are confined to students of one race. Harvard has sought to avoid the attrition problem by ensuring that most of its black students will come from middle-class homes and have attended predominantly white schools. As an admissions officer explained, "It is right for Harvard and better for the students, because there is better adjustment and less desperate alienation."

Most colleges remain committed to their affirmative action programs. Smith College, which now has a 3.2 percent black enrollment, has pledged to double that proportion over the next ten years. Since this step will almost inevitably bring in students who will have difficulty keeping up with their classmates, it seems appropriate to ask why Smith and other schools persist in this kind of effort. The candid answer is that many professors and quite a few students regard the paucity of black faces on their campuses as a cause for shame. To raise the minority presence eases a lot of academic guilt. The fact that the newly admitted students themselves may bear an unfair burden is hardly ever mentioned in campus discussions. Even with intensive remedial programs, teenagers from inner-city high schools are unlikely to be lofted to Ivy League levels.

The question frequently arises why affirmative action must specify race. After all, it can be argued, the whole intent of the civil rights drive was to remove race as a factor, since it was long used to bar blacks from enrolling in many colleges. Yet today, preferential policies for blacks mean that some whites are being shunted aside, simply because they are white.

Hence the argument has been made that if a college wants a diverse student body, it could gear preferential admissions and aid to *all* low-income students, regardless of their ethnic origins. And because a higher proportion of black applicants come from families of modest means, they should get more than their share of low-income places and scholarships.

There is only one problem with this proposal. Among the black, white, Asian, and Hispanic school seniors who took the Scholastic Aptitude Test in 1990, a total of 138,357 came from families having incomes under $20,000. The table on page 138 shows how they divided by ethnicity and average SAT scores. Since all 138,357 have similar economic backgrounds, presumably admissions and aid would be allocated according to academic merit. But gauged by SAT scores, low-income whites and Asians would end up with almost all of the "race-blind" awards, since they obviously have better records from a strictly scholastic standpoint. This is why affirmative action that aims at helping blacks must take race into account.

The kinds of abilities the SAT actually evaluates has been the subject of much debate, and some of those issues will be considered momentarily. At this point, it can simply be said that doing well on the SAT shows how well students have prepared themselves—and been prepared—for the admissions competition as it currently exists.

The next table gives SAT scores for the four groups, along with some background information about those taking the test. The gap between the average scores of black and white students—almost 200 points—has received a great deal of attention, and need not be belabored here. Further insights can be obtained if the black and white groups are compared not with each other, but with two other cohorts. This approach makes sense, since in terms of parental income and education, the Hispanic and black students taking the SAT have fairly comparable backgrounds. The Asians and whites are also quite similar so far as parental education is concerned.

Yet Hispanics average 66 points higher than blacks, which might be considered surprising since two thirds of the Hispanic students

STUDENTS TAKING THE SAT (1990)

Blacks	Hispanics		Whites	Asians
737	803	Average Scores*	933	938
150	176	Point-Gain: Low to High Income	119	211
40.4%	37.5%	Parents Attended College	60.5%	55.5%
8.0%	67.8%	English Not First Language	5.8%	70.0%
23.3%	25.8%	Family Income over $40,000	56.0%	39.5%
37.9%	37.4%	Family Income under $20,000	10.3%	28.3%

* SAT scores run from a low of 400 to a high of 1,600.

come from families in which English is not the primary language and may not be spoken at all. So it is impressive that they score as well as they do, as their parents are often new to this country or live in Spanish-speaking neighborhoods. That Asians do five points better than whites is at least equally striking, since English is not the principal language in most of their homes and their economic status is relatively modest. And, as is apparent from the depiction on the next page they move further ahead of whites as their economic standing improves.

This is not the first time that immigrants and their offspring have surpassed native residents. Hard work and ambition still pay off, as they have in the past. However, there is another factor at work. While today's newly arrived immigrants tend to start out with lower incomes, many of them belonged to the middle class in their countries of origin, and they bring those values with them. Over half of the Asian students taking the SAT have parents who attended college, as do more than a third of the Hispanics. Also, immigrants who arrive today are less beset by culture shock. In the global village of an electronic age, most are prepared for American ways.

The Scholastic Aptitude Test has become the closest thing we have to a national IQ test. So it is best that we be clear about what this three-hour examination measures. Clearly, it does not gauge "intelligence" or "aptitude" in a broad sense. At best, it rates a narrow range of academic-oriented skills. Some have argued that, as much as

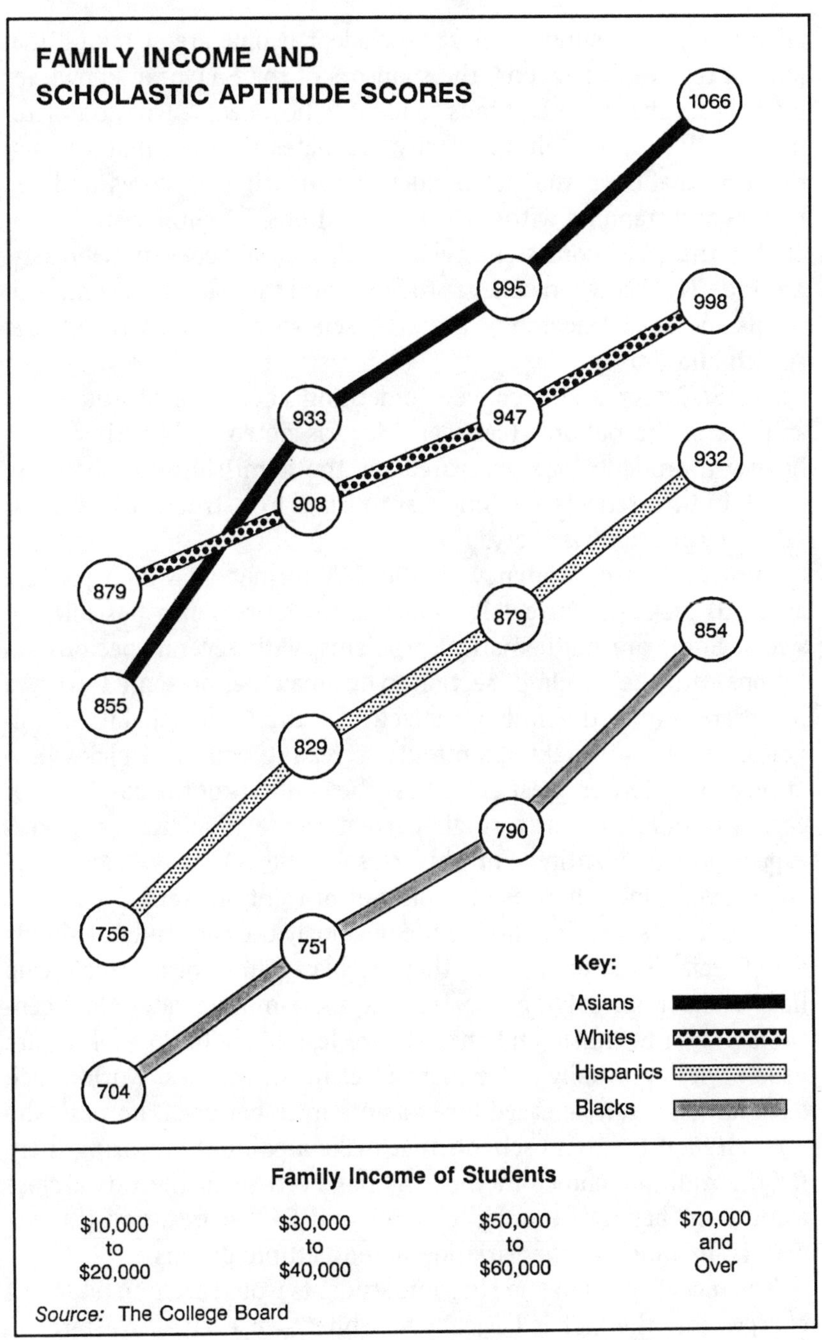
FAMILY INCOME AND
SCHOLASTIC APTITUDE SCORES
1066
995
998
933
947
932
908
879
879
854
855
829
790
756
751
704
Key:
Asians
Whites
Hispanics
Blacks
Family Income of Students
$10,000
to
$20,000
$30,000
to
$40,000
$50,000
to
$60,000
$70,000
and
Over
Source: The College Board

anything, scores simply reflect how adept people are at taking that kind of test. As it happens, the sponsors of the SAT have known for many years that their test fails to identify how people will do in later life. A follow-up of Yale University graduates revealed that "no significant relation could be found between original scores and . . . honors and standing within their occupations." A similar study concluded that "no consistent relationships exist between Scholastic Aptitude Test scores in college students, and their actual accomplishments in social leadership, the arts, sciences, music, writing, and speech and drama."

Yet SAT scores still convey something about the attitudes and abilities of the nation's teenagers. As was noted earlier, they show how well students have prepared for the admissions competition, which in turn reflects a willingness to adapt to a structure of success set up by the adult society.

Most of us are familiar with the SAT format, in which you are asked to pick the correct responses from four or five possible answers. Some are mathematical problems, with several specious solutions. In the reading section, you may be presented with a paragraph on an unfamiliar subject, say, the feeding habits of migratory birds. After taking a minute to read it, you must pick which of several sentences "best describes" the contents of the passage. For each question, there is a single correct answer that the testmakers expect you to identify. For this reason, the SAT has been called "objective," since there is only one set of right answers.

Do the tests discriminate? Quite obviously they do, and not simply along racial lines. First of all, they are biased in favor of people who have a knack for solving puzzles at a one-a-minute rate. Also teenagers drawn to music and the arts are less likely to do well, as are people who eventually prove themselves in the business world. Such disadvantages can be eased for students from better-off homes, who are more apt to attend schools that make a point of preparing them for the multiple-choice method. As has been seen, there is a close association between economic status and SAT scores, and this accounts for much of the variation among ethnic groups.

The record of Asian and Hispanic students would seem to undercut charges that the SAT is basically a "white"—or even a "Western"—test. Of course, it does have a class bias, since much in the verbal portion alludes to information or experiences with which middle-class children are more likely to be familiar. One question once asked which of the following options was most analogous to "runner . . . marathon":

(a) envoy . . . embassy
(b) martyr . . . massacre
(c) oarsman . . . regatta
(d) referee . . . tournament
(e) horse . . . stable

Still, a presumption of American life has been that those at lower social levels will come to know about how people above them live, an awareness presumably to be derived from movies and television which depict embassies and regattas. That so many young Asians and Hispanics have shown themselves able to master the SAT would suggest that they have adapted to this "white" world. Nor is it simply that they cram for the tests. Asian high school students have been found twice as likely as whites to take the full academic program recommended by the National Council on Excellence in Education, which includes intensive work in American history and literature.

So it may be more accurate to say that tests like the SAT now reflect not a racial or national corpus of knowledge, but a wider "modern" consciousness. In the past, the word "modern" tended to have white and Western connotations. Today, however, the term has a far broader range. Much of Asia and Latin America have become modernized, to degrees few would have predicted a generation ago. Taiwanese and Costa Rican teenagers arrive in the United States already schooled in advanced mathematics and the multiple-choice method. So "modern" now stands for the mental and structural modes that characterize the developed world. It calls for a commitment to science and technology, as well as skills needed for managing administrative systems. The modern world rests on a framework of communication and finance, increasingly linked by common discourse and rules of rationality. Indeed, evidence from the educational scene suggests that even within this country, young people from immigrant backgrounds are showing themselves to be more "modern" in these commitments and skills than many of their native-born classmates. Between 1982 and 1988, over half of the top sixty Westinghouse science competition winners were immigrants or the children of immigrants.

Aspiring middle-class Hispanics have outlooks similar to those found among Asians. In fact, the term "Hispanic" underscores the European element in their origins, rather than aboriginal American links or ties to Africa. (An alternative, "Latino," carries Mediterranean connotations.) In common with Asians, many young Hispanics can pass what someone once called the "telephone test": you cannot identify their ancestry from their accent, something not as easily said for black Americans. For these and related reasons, white Americans are considerably less averse to having Hispanics and Asians as neighbors, or as classmates for their children.

It is striking that black students from better-off homes do not do particularly well on the SAT. Indeed, those whose parents earn between $50,000 and $60,000 barely match Asians from families in the $10,000 to $20,000 range.

Surveys of neighborhoods and schools show that black Americans spend more of their lives in segregated settings than even recent immigrants. One outcome of this isolation is that black Americans have less sustained exposure to the "modern" world than have many members of immigrant groups. Blacks with middle-class jobs and incomes may have greater opportunities to meet and mingle in this world, but those contacts are seldom allowed to develop to the fullest extent. The fact that black modes of perception and expression, which are largely products of segregation, become impediments to performing well on tests like the SAT reveals that racial bias remains latent not only in the multiple-choice method, but in the broader expectations set by the modern world.

CHAPTER NINE

SEGREGATED SCHOOLING

VOLUNTARY AND IMPOSED

A HALF-CENTURY AGO, virtually all black students who attended college enrolled in all-black institutions. In part, this was because most of them then lived in Southern or border states, where higher education was strictly segregated. Even private colleges banned black undergraduates. And since schools elsewhere in the country accepted only token numbers of black applicants, many Northern blacks traveled to segregated colleges in the South. Limited admissions continued into the postwar period. Amherst College, reputedly a "liberal" institution, could display only two black faces among the 258 seniors at its 1951 graduation.

Today, close to half of all black Americans live in the North, and what had once been all-white Southern institutions now take in applicants of all races. As a result, four out of five black undergraduates now attend schools that can be described as "integrated," if by that is meant having student bodies that are predominantly white. Nor is this surprising, since whites still make up the majority at most colleges. It is only at inner-city campuses that black students begin to reach 10 percent of the enrollments.

At most colleges, black students are relatively few in number and continually aware of their minority status. All too often, when they enter a classroom, they discover that they will be the only one of their race in the course. Even after official welcomes and overtures expressing good will, they soon sense that they are seen as an alien presence at what still remain essentially "white" institutions.

Given the struggle to enter schools that once barred them, all indications are that black students are far from happy once they get there. A study entitled *Blacks in College* surveyed several thousand black undergraduates in both Northern and Southern states. According to its author, Jacqueline Fleming, most of those attending integrated colleges said they felt "abandoned by the institution, rebuffed by fellow students, and inhibited from taking part in any but all-black organizational activities." It was also found that the majority of those who stayed to the senior year showed signs of "intellectual stagnation" and "frustrated academic drives." Many diverted their disappointment "into less constructive outlets," including attacking the school's administration or its curriculum.

More than many whites might assume, black students view "white" colleges as hostile terrain. Unfortunately, whites tend to hear of only the most vivid episodes that attract media attention. A group calling itself the National Institute Against Prejudice and Violence reported on a wave of "campus ethnoviolence," citing some 200 events involving ethnic or sexual bigotry over a two-year period. Despite a disturbing number of incidents that involved physical and verbal harassment of Jews and homosexuals, black students at predominantly white colleges suffered most of the harassment. Moreover, the episodes occurred not simply at provincial schools, but also at well-known institutions like Stanford, Columbia, and Smith.

The incidents varied in extent and gravity. At least two colleges had crosses set on fire in front of black residence halls. Elsewhere, a white fraternity gave a "ghetto party" with demeaning decorations; while on another campus, sorority members put on blackface for a musical program. The list also includes threats to individuals. A black undergraduate at the University of Texas reported that he was confronted at gunpoint by two white students who, he said, wore Ronald Reagan masks. A black library employee charged that his white supervisor "intentionally pushed a door into his back." The report also recounts an argument in which a white man shouted a racial slur at a black woman who had taken a parking space he had been waiting for. At another school, a student claimed that a professor called her a "black bitch" after she had charged him with racism for not passing her in a class.

Obviously, we have to be careful before characterizing these incidents as atypical episodes. Clearly, there is cause for concern when an entire fraternity sponsors a party with a racist theme. All in all, the study concluded that bigotry suffuses even sophisticated campuses. After a complaint that a Wesleyan University dean had used the word "nigger" while chairing a job interview, an outside investigator—a dean from Yale, as it happened—felt obliged to conclude that the Wesleyan campus as a whole was suffused with "a pattern of subtle institutional racism."

Many of us would like to feel that colleges should show more civility than the workaday world. At the same time, it must be borne in mind that most undergraduates are teenagers, not a group notable for tact or immune from displays of bravado. They are at an age where they try to impress one another, often with heavy-handed humor and ill-considered pranks. There are still plenty of beer brawls, especially along fraternity row. While undergraduates often express liberal sentiments on social issues, many come to college never having known black people their age. Nor should this be surprising, since most attended schools that were almost or wholly white, or where the races tended to go their own ways.

There is something about a college setting that makes race a visible issue. Campuses tend to be closed-off communities, where professors and students have a lot of free time, much of which they spend inflating the meanings of local events. It often turns out that colleges with liberal reputations receive the most recriminations, not least because protesters know how to play on the feelings of faculty and students, many of whom need little prompting to plead guilty to racism.

Colleges also care more about the principles of free speech, which is certainly to their credit. But because they are compacted settings, it takes only one statement or expression to ignite an entire campus. Moreover, the freedoms in question seldom involve a "speech" in the sense of an extended presentation. True, there can be debates over whether a Louis Farrakhan or a David Duke should be invited to give a lecture, or about what they may say if they actually come. Even so, speakers like Farrakhan and Duke are more ideological symbols than expositors of intellectual positions. Still, no one has ever said that to be counted as "speech," talk must be reasoned or profound or, for that matter, even truthful. What can be said, though, is that if a Farrakhan or a Duke appears on a campus, the event is unlikely to improve comity between the races.

Even today's Supreme Court has agreed that "speech" can also include expressive action, such as burning a flag or printing a slogan on a shirt. In 1991, some Harvard undergraduates hung Confederate flags inside their dormitory windows, which were visible to passersby. This also was defended as "speech," since it was a message aimed at arousing reactions. Not surprisingly, some observers saw the flag as defending slavery, perhaps even proposing its return. They felt that this display hardly helped interracial relations at Harvard, which they saw as a more important goal than the freedom to hang a piece of cloth in a window.

Brown University, another Ivy League citadel, actually expelled an undergraduate for shouting "nigger" and several other slurs in a well-trafficked part of the campus. The administration reasoned that his words were not a "speech," but rather an "action" that impaired the college atmosphere. To black people, certainly, to be called a "nigger" barely differs from an actual slap across the face. And all the more so on a predominantly white campus, where blacks are never sure of their welcome. Nor can it be argued that shouting "nigger" constitutes an argument or an idea, although one can sense the general sentiment, which is essentially one of hatred. Of course, the student had his defenders, who argued that even insulting shouts must be tolerated, lest we open the door to censoring more coherent expressions.

Perhaps the greatest problem is that legal determinations focus on balancing personal freedoms with preserving public order. What the law cannot readily do is deal with the subtler sensibilities that make for social relationships. If colleges that are mainly white wish to become amicable interracial communities, they will have a hard time achieving that end if some of their students insist on hanging flags in their windows or giving vent to their hatreds. To point this out is not to argue against free speech, but simply to note some of its effects. As matters now stand, the First Amendment covers a very wide area. It could be used, for example, to protect some students on a predominantly white campus who decide to set up a table, and then spend the day shouting "gorilla!" or "nigger!" at whatever black students happen to pass. Whether this will ever occur is not the point. But there is hardly a black student who cannot visualize such a scene.

As a matter of fact, college enrollments are more multiracial than at any time in the past. Some 80 percent of college-bound blacks go to integrated schools, where they make up 7.4 percent of the overall student body. (When those at predominantly black schools are added in, blacks account for nine percent of all college enrollments.)

Until relatively recently, black undergraduates who chose white campuses knew they would find few classmates of their own race. Most spent a lonely four years, whether in the classroom or residence halls. Any misgivings they might have had about the curriculum were usually kept to themselves. Things are now very different, due to the trebling of black undergraduates on integrated campuses. At many schools, there is now a large enough pool of black students to create their own organizations and social centers. At some colleges, black freshmen come early for their own orientation sessions. This more pronounced presence has had practical consequences, leading to calls for more black professors and programs that focus on their racial experience.

Black students are frequently berated for sticking closely together, especially at campus dining tables. Whites who talk this way seldom think about how they too have a circle of white companions. Indeed, they almost invariably sit at "white tables." But, it may be replied, there are many kinds of white people, and white students select their friends on the basis of shared temperaments or interests, not simply because they belong to one's own race. If white students cared to look, they would see that blacks do not simply sit down alongside any other blacks. They also have preferences based on outlooks and affinities. At the same time, they do have a shared experience of belonging to a black minority on a largely white campus. Compounding this sense of isolation is the fact that the communities surrounding most campuses tend to be virtually all white. Black students who seek to do a little shopping in Ithaca or Palo Alto find themselves objects of wary attention. As the figures on the next page show, very few "integrated" colleges have black enrollments that are at or even near the 10 percent figure.

* * *

But why an apparent upsurge in "ethnoviolence"? Here the attitudes of white students need to be examined. To start, they no longer dominate the college world as they did in the past. As was noted earlier, at UCLA the Asian freshmen now surpass the white percentage. But while whites cannot easily cavil when Asians with better records receive college places, they can and do grumble if black students get special scholarships or preferential admissions.

Bigoted behavior among white students also comes as a reaction to the more assertive attitudes of some black classmates. To describe the interchange this way is not meant to justify white calumnies. Still, if we want to know why students put up Confederate flags or set fire to crosses, one explanation is that these are ways of telling black undergraduates that they have been making themselves too pronounced a campus presence. While no one says so explicitly, many white students still believe that blacks should be grateful simply for having been admitted, and that they have no business criticizing the structure or the system.

BLACK ENROLLMENTS (1988)

Private Institutions		Public Institutions	
Amherst	5.4%	California	
Bates	2.2%	Santa Barbara	2.9%
Bowdoin	2.9%	Santa Cruz	2.8%
Chicago	4.0%	Michigan	
Columbia	4.2%	Ann Arbor	6.2%
Dartmouth	5.4%	Wayne State	23.0%
Emory	6.9%	Montana	0.5%
Harvard	5.4%	New Hampshire	0.3%
Reed	1.4%	New York City	
Smith	3.4%	Brooklyn	19.2%
Stanford	6.3%	Queens	11.1%
Vanderbilt	3.9%	Oregon	1.3%
Vassar	7.5%	Utah	0.6%
Wesleyan	6.8%	West Virginia	2.7%
Yale	5.8%	Wyoming	0.8%

There is another route by which black students come to white campuses. Here the schools involved are less likely to be liberal arts colleges or Ivy League universities, but rather institutions intent on having winning athletic teams. These colleges, which make sports a money-making business, have been shameless in recruiting black players, many of whom have barely made it through high school. One survey of the member institutions of the National Collegiate Athletic Association with the biggest sports budgets found that 56 percent of their basketball players were black, as were 37 percent of those on their football rosters. But apart from athletes, these colleges do not seem particularly committed to recruiting black students for regular courses of study. Among the 291 schools in the NCAA's Division I, blacks average only 4 percent of their student bodies. At more isolated institutions like the University of Wyoming and Western New Mexico, these athletes may be virtually the only members of their race on the campus.

Few do well at their studies. Another NCAA study showed that almost 75 percent of black Division I athletes failed to graduate. This is hardly surprising, since most tend to lack the level of preparation that ordinary college work requires. There are also the long hours of practice, trips to distant games, and the sheer exhaustion from an all-but-professional regimen. Nor are the demands only physical. Today's athletes are expected to memorize, analyze, and apply the voluminous play-books compiled by their coaches, assignments easily as arduous as those in many college courses. The system uses student-athletes for as many seasons as possible, abetted by cynical interpretations of eligibility and academic standing.

From time to time, the NCAA decides to crack down on colleges that give financial aid to athletes with academic deficiencies. In a recent year, over 90 percent of the students barred from playing for academic failings were black. One reform proposal would require an SAT score of 700 to participate in intercollegiate athletics. This might not seem like a stringent requirement: it means picking only 40 correct answers out of some 150 questions. Still, among the black players currently on NCAA rosters, less than half have done that well. The rule might make athletics more intellectually acceptable, but its effect would also be to remove even more blacks from the college scene. And at predominantly black colleges, demanding a 700 SAT could lead to curtailing many of their athletic programs.

With few exceptions, these semiprofessionals have never really been "students," nor do the colleges view them as such. They were not admitted on an academic basis, nor were they given financial support to encourage their studies. It has been contended that regardless of the reasons for their admission, once they have been officially enrolled, the institution has a duty to such students to foster their education. However, the magnitude of such an effort should not be understated; it would call for scholastic tutelage at least as demanding as the athletic coaching they currently receive. At this point only a few schools, like Georgetown and Notre Dame, take such commitments seriously.

Many coaches reply that these teenagers take up athletic offers of their own free will. They have few illusions about their options, and believe this is the best chance they have to make something of themselves. They may have been raised in segregated surroundings, but they know enough about the real world to realize the odds they face, whether at home or on a campus. So there is probably not much point in telling them that they are unlikely to get a degree, let alone be chosen by a professional team. Hope springs eternal, and that as much as anything sustains this insalubrious offshoot of higher education.

The nation has a group of ninety-nine colleges and universities that describe themselves as "historically black" institutions. Within this group, fifty-six are under private control and forty-three are branches of public systems, and all but four are located in Southern or border states. (The exceptions are Central State and Wilberforce in Ohio and Pennsylvania's Lincoln and Cheyney.) All of them began as segregated schools, either by law or by choice. Their purpose was to offer further education at a time when public and private colleges took hardly any black students or barred them altogether. That is their history. Of more than passing interest are the roles that they still serve, augmented by arguments over whether states should be allowed to sponsor schools intended for members of only one race.

Jacqueline Fleming's study, *Blacks in College* also interviewed students who had chosen to attend predominantly black colleges. Their responses were much more heartening. By and large, she found, "black students in black schools show more academic progress than their counterparts in white colleges." Not least, their rates of retention tended to be higher. Her report makes only modest intellectual claims for these institutions. At Morehouse in Atlanta, widely known as a selective black school, the SAT scores of its incoming freshmen averaged 980, while the figure for Pennsylvania's Cheyney University was 671, lower than the 700 that the NCAA proposed for scholarship athletes. At none of the ninety-nine historically black schools do the average scores approach those at comparable white institutions.

But Fleming's study adds that the strength of black colleges rests on their "unique experience in providing higher education to students from inadequate secondary schools." In other words, they take their applicants as they find them, and then help them move along from there. In an all-black setting, undergraduates have a more relaxed social life, and a wider range of extracurricular activities. A strong case can also be made that black colleges "impart the orientation and skills that allow black students to function well in the larger society." Having achieved academic success, they graduate with fewer feelings of resentment or emotional strain. At the fifty-six predominantly black private colleges, attrition rates are lower than for black students at integrated schools. Moreover, studies of alumni suggest that black colleges do as well as racially mixed schools in preparing their students for graduate study and careers in a dominantly white society. Thus over half of the black professors now teaching in white universities did their own undergraduate work at black schools.

There should not be any objections to a private college calling itself a "historically black" school, just as Brigham Young University can refer to itself as a "historically Mormon" institution. If such schools are in any way segregated, they are so by choice and not imposition. But what of the forty-three "historically black" campuses that remain parts of state systems? Their persistence would seem to betoken governmental sponsorship of racial segregation. It is true that in some cities, many public schools have all-black enrollments. But this is because they are located in neighborhoods where virtually all the children are black. However, this isolation does not usually hold for state colleges, which draw their undergraduates from many parts of the state.

While predominantly black state colleges were originally set up in the years when segregation was mandated, they now continue with predominantly black enrollments on a voluntary basis. The table below gives the racial breakdowns for eighteen public colleges in nine states. While all of these states have sizable black populations, their flagship campuses still have quite modest black enrollments. On the other hand, all have maintained one or more campuses that are predominantly black, and these schools would seem to have loyal clienteles. Indeed, there is reason to believe that a fair number of the students at, say, Maryland's Morgan State would have been accepted at the College Park campus had they chosen to apply.

Schools like Morgan State and Fort Valley State have become embroiled in controversy, over whether their high black enrollments make them "segregated," and hence in violation of the 1964 Civil Rights Act. True, they and others like them are not legally required to be blacks-only institutions, as they had been in the past. In varying proportions, some whites can and do attend.

North Carolina's public system offers a good example of how self-segregation works. It is a state with a considerable black population: according to the 1990 census, 21.9 percent of the total. This is one reason why it maintains five "historically black" colleges, plus eleven others that once barred blacks but are now deemed to be integrated. Altogether, black students represent about 18 percent of the 140,000 students in the system.

As the table on the next page shows, none of the schools is solely of one race. At even the historically black colleges, nonblack enroll-

BLACK ENROLLMENTS IN EIGHTEEN STATE CAMPUSES (1988)

Flagship Campuses		Predominantly Black Campuses	
Mississippi	7.0%	Mississippi Valley	99.3%
Georgia	4.7%	Fort Valley State	92.1%
Alabama	8.5%	Alabama State	97.1%
Maryland	8.6%	Morgan State	91.7%
North Carolina	7.8%	Winston-Salem State	84.6%
Tennessee	4.5%	Tennessee State	62.8%
Florida	5.8%	Florida A&M	83.1%
Texas	3.6%	Prairie View	83.1%
Pennsylvania	3.9%	Cheyney University	92.0%

ments range from 15.4 percent at Winston-Salem to 30.0 percent at Fayetteville. Black enrollments at the integrated schools go from 3.5 at Asheville to 12.1 percent at Pembroke. Still, a gap exists between the two groups, and the two sets of schools can be said to have quite distinctive enrollments.

All told, a clear majority—59.5 percent—of the black students attending the state system chose its five historically black schools. And because so many black students avoid the eleven "integrated" branches, the black ratios at the latter are seen as embarrassingly low. After all, in a heavily black state like North Carolina, even a 10 percent black enrollment would fall below the goal of true integration, prompting the conclusion that public higher education in the

THE NORTH CAROLINA STATE SYSTEM

Predominantly Black Campuses	Percentage Black
Winston-Salem	84.6%
North Carolina A&T	83.8%
North Carolina Central	82.6%
Elizabeth City	81.5%
Fayetteville	70.0%

These five campuses account for 13.1% of all enrollments in the state system and 59.5% of all black enrollments.

Predominantly White Campuses	Percentage Black
Pembroke	12.1%
School of the Arts	11.1%
East Carolina	10.4%
Charlotte	9.7%
Greensboro	9.7%
North Carolina State	9.3%
Chapel Hill	7.8%
Wilmington	7.3%
Western Carolina	4.7%
Appalachian	4.5%
Asheville	3.5%

These eleven campuses account for 86.9% of all enrollments in the state system and 40.5% of all black enrollments.

state remains basically segregated. Indeed, it could be argued that for all practical purposes there are two systems, one for each race.

For many people who believe in integration, separate racial systems signify more than self-segregation by choice. The largely black schools receive less funding, have fewer academic programs, and rank lower in prestige. (Although apart from the Chapel Hill campus, faculty salaries are now roughly comparable.) So it can be contended that the states are still sustaining an arrangement where the colleges for whites are superior to those attended largely by blacks. In Louisiana and several other states, steps have been taken to merge black public colleges with nearby white institutions. As it happens, these moves are being protested by many black students and faculty members. In the case of professors and administrators, careers are at stake. Most know they would not get equivalent positions if transferred to predominantly white schools. In the students' view, if these colleges are segregated, it is not because apartheid has been imposed from the outside. As has been noted, these undergraduates have opted for black colleges over integrated schools. Moreover, these and other historically black colleges do not aim to keep whites out. Legally, anyone is free to apply and attend, even if whites may sense that they are not particularly wanted. Still, at the predominantly black Alabama A&M, white students now account for 13.2 percent of the enrollment, while at Georgia's Albany State and Arkansas's Pine Bluff, white attendance reaches 16.8 percent and 17.3 percent.

If many black students choose predominantly black schools, it may be a very rational choice. As has been noted, some make this choice because they wish to avoid the racism and alienation they may encounter at largely white campuses. And given the level of high school preparation many black students have received, they will probably do better by enrolling, say, at a school like North Carolina Central than by applying to the flagship campus at Chapel Hill.

There are several analogies here. Some women argue that even today they cannot receive full intellectual encouragement at sexually "integrated" schools. The very presence of men, they say, inhibits women's participation in classroom discussions and extracurricular activities. Women's colleges that are under private control can still legally refuse to admit men, even if the schools receive some public funding. The same freedom applies to private all-male schools. The law also allows colleges to affirm their religious auspices, or to let it be known that they stress Chicano culture or have "historically black" antecedents.

However there is one American group that is not allowed to announce that a college it sponsors is intended mainly for its own members. Nor can it make such an announcement even if it adds that it is willing to admit persons who do not belong to its group. Nor may this group point to the institution's history as a way of describing its identity and orientation. All of which is a roundabout way of saying that not even private institutions can depict themselves as being "historically white," even if that happens to be an accurate description.

Are double standards being tolerated here? When blacks or women or Mormons say they prefer being educated among people of their own backgrounds, they are generally seen as having that right. But if whites express similar sentiments, they can and should be charged with discriminating on racial grounds.

The differences have to do less with logical consistency than with the consequences of exclusion. When people who have dominant power set up organizations that keep others out, they do so to exclude those they have barred from sharing their advantages. That is why businesswomen wish to break down barriers that deny them admission to men's clubs. It is why, in earlier generations, Jews and blacks sought more equitable admissions to Ivy League colleges. No one will deny that persons with less power also on occasion wish to associate among themselves. That is a major reason why black colleges persist. Even so, it cannot be shown that the existence of all-black colleges causes harm to whites in the way that whites-only policies have injured blacks.

That many blacks wish to attend "their own" colleges lifts a burden from many white consciences. Most white Americans feel uneasy in the presence of blacks, unsure of what to say, and uncertain about what overtures to make. So if blacks want to go off on their own, not many white persons will complain.* One reason is that most whites

* But some will, citing constitutional consistency. At Syracuse University, the Black Student Union had a policy of not accepting white undergraduates as members. University officials objected, on the ground that any group using campus facilities had to admit anyone enrolled at the university. The black students replied that their cultural consensus would be undercut if outsiders could attend their meeting.

would like black Americans to "be happy." So if blacks say they are happier among themselves, that would be a double benefit.

By and large, whites prefer not to inquire what goes on in black colleges, so long as the students seem satisfied there. For this reason, racial self-segregation is supported by many whites. For one thing, it reduces pressure for affirmative action. The University of Texas's flagship campus at Austin can say that it has tried to attract more black applicants, but they seem to prefer Prairie View. For another, it means less attention need be given to improving conditions for blacks on white campuses, whether with remedial programs or simply by striving to create a more hospitable atmosphere. What is barely acknowledged is that it is the racial mood at so many white schools that prompts large numbers of black students to choose predominantly black schools.

CHAPTER TEN

WHAT'S BEST FOR BLACK CHILDREN?

IN 1954—ALMOST FOUR DECADES AGO —the Supreme Court handed down its *Brown* v. *Board of Education* decision, telling states and localities they could no longer maintain school systems that separated pupils by race. The Court's reasoning, simply stated, was that the schools set aside for blacks would always be inferior. This did not result from deficient facilities, although that was usually the case. Even if separate schools for blacks were well-financed showcases, that would not solve the problem. The crucial fact, as the Court saw it, was that segregation based on race sent the message to black children that whites did not want them in their schools. And that exclusion, the justices concluded, "generates a feeling of inferiority as to their status in the community that may affect their hearts and minds in a way unlikely ever to be undone."

Brown was the most sweeping of a series of decisions affirming that if black Americans are to feel that the United States is truly their country, doors cannot be shut to them simply because of their color. Since that time, courts have ordered that everything legally possible must be done to ensure that white and black children will share the same schools and classrooms.

While state and local laws requiring segregation have been nullified, the goal of racial integration has not been achieved. According to studies by the National School Boards Association, upward of two thirds of all black youngsters—63.3 percent—still attend segregated schools. In part, the failure has stemmed from a lack of political leadership. But the crucial determinants have been the attitudes and actions of white parents, who have made it clear that they will accept integration only on the most minimal of terms. In consequence, the United States has few genuinely integrated schools.

Usually the reason is residential. There are few if any neighborhoods with populations that reflect the nation's ethnic makeup. Black households are not spread around the country evenly; indeed, such dispersion is less likely in their case than for any other group. To the extent that schools draw their students from local communities or officially defined districts, enrollments mirror racial demography. Many large cities and a growing number of suburbs no longer have enough white families to give their systems a white majority. Nor, in most cases, will parents or authorities send suburban children in to integrate city schools.

The National School Boards Association measures segregation by computing the number of the black youngsters in a state or locality who are enrolled in schools where they, or Hispanics, make up a majority of the pupils. (Apparently, mixing Hispanics and blacks does not rate as "integration.") According to this formula, a racially integrated school is one with *some* black students, but one where whites comprise a majority of the pupils.

The table on the next page shows how many black students are enrolled in segregated schools in the thirty-two states that contain 98.2 percent of America's black population. As it turns out, the extent of segregation is not necessarily related to the number of blacks in the public schools. Illinois and New York top the segregation list even though they rank fourteenth and sixteenth among the states in black enrollments. Similarly, only 9.0 percent of California's pupils are black, as are 8.9 percent of Wisconsin's. Nevertheless, over 70 percent of their youngsters attend segregated schools. The major reason, of course, is that black children are often concentrated in segregated sections of larger cities. The 70.4 percent figure for Wisconsin really represents Milwaukee, while Illinois's 83.2 percent speaks for Chicago. However, these are not universal patterns. Kentucky, whose

BLACK STUDENTS: SCHOOL SHARE AND SEGREGATION

	Share of Statewide Enrollments	Attending Segregated Schools
Illinois	18.7%	83.2%
New York	16.5%	80.8%
Mississippi	55.5%	80.3%
Michigan	19.8%	76.7%
California	9.0%	76.6%
New Jersey	17.4%	72.8%
Maryland	35.3%	72.3%
Wisconsin	8.9%	70.4%
Ohio	15.0%	67.6%
Alabama	37.0%	63.8%
Texas	14.4%	63.3%
Pennsylvania	12.6%	62.1%
Louisiana	41.3%	61.6%
Missouri	14.9%	61.0%
Connecticut	12.1%	60.2%
South Carolina	44.5%	60.0%
Tennessee	22.6%	59.7%
Georgia	37.9%	59.3%
Massachusetts	7.4%	58.5%
Arkansas	24.2%	53.8%
Virginia	23.7%	49.5%
Indiana	9.0%	46.8%
Rhode Island	5.6%	45.6%
Florida	23.7%	45.1%
Colorado	4.5%	44.9%
Oklahoma	7.8%	40.8%
North Carolina	28.9%	37.5%
Kansas	7.6%	32.0%
Washington	4.4%	29.6%
Nevada	9.6%	20.0%
Delaware	27.7%	8.9%
Kentucky	10.2%	6.6%

10.2 percent black enrollment exceeds California's, has been able to ensure that 93.4 percent of those students do not attend segregated schools. (The chief reason is that Kentucky's cities and suburbs form single school districts.) Moreover, among the Southern states, the degrees of segregation vary quite considerably.

Segregation statistics tell us about racial enrollments for individual schools, but not about what happens within those buildings. For example, while black pupils represents 16 percent of all public school students, they make up almost 40 percent of those who are classed as mentally retarded, disabled, or otherwise deficient. As a result, many more black youngsters are consigned to "special education" classes, which all but guarantee that they will fall behind their grade levels. Even if their diagnoses are couched in clinical terms, too often the message is that their behavior fails to mirror middle-class demeanor. Slower tracks also become repositories for pupils whose conduct teachers find bothersome or inappropriate.

If a community cannot have all-white schools—although many towns and suburbs clearly do—white parents and officials strive for segregation within the buildings. The most common method is "tracking," which is always defended on scholastic grounds, with race never mentioned. At the elementary level, schools that have two or more classes for each grade often separate children according to their presumed potential. In some cases, teachers' reports play a part in tracking decisions; but as often as not the key factor will be how pupils have scored on standardized tests. High schools have even more elaborate divisions, ranging from courses at the college level to sections for students deemed to be barely literate. Once put in lower tracks, even pupils who show promise tend to stay there throughout their school careers. Not surprisingly, black students are more likely to end up on lower—and slower—academic tracks.

The arguments for scholastic segregation are familiar. How, it will be asked, can students prepare properly for Princeton, if they must share lessons with classmates who hold them back? The idea of integrating students having varied levels of preparation ("mixed ability grouping") no longer has an avid following. In reply, one could note that many Americans were once educated in smaller untracked schools and went on to impressive careers. Some educators contend that brighter students will do even better if they are asked to explain materials and methods to less sophisticated classmates. However, parents anxious about college are unlikely to volunteer their offspring for such assignments. So even in an arithmetically integrated school, whites prefer to minimize their children's contacts with black classmates. (In fairness, it should be added that many black middle-class parents feel much the same way, although they see the issue as one of class rather than race.) Perhaps the last word should go to an Alabama legislator. "Before the 1960s," he remarked, "we had separate and segregated schools. Then came tracking, so while black and white students now walk through the same school door, they get segregated once they are inside."

In some communities, integration is possible because blacks form a small portion of the population and their presence does not stir white anxieties. In other settings, however, integration can be achieved only if some children are sent to schools outside their neighborhoods. This was the aim of what came to be called "forced busing." By and large, it has only operated in one direction. That is, officials have been reluctant to transport white children to schools in black neighborhoods, or to schools that have appreciable black enrollments. Indeed, even suggesting such assignments can spur a white exodus out of the school district.

In some cases, the use of buses has been effective. Sometimes, a few black pupils travel to schools in dominantly white districts. In Hartford, for example, some inner-city youngsters arise early for trips to the suburbs. Of course there can be selectivity here, since they are usually put in the program by aspiring parents. In another use of busing, white parents will let their children travel some distance to attend "magnet schools," where programs and facilities promise high-quality education. At the same time, such special schools succeed only if parents are assured that they will limit their black enrollments. On the whole, these variants of voluntary busing have not done much to reduce the number of schools that are basically all black or all white.

One unresolved debate concerns the effect of integrated learning on black pupils who do enroll in predominantly white schools. What some psychologists call a "transmission-of-values" hypothesis underlay the original *Brown* decision. It was argued that if black students were placed in classrooms where they would be outnumbered by whites, they would absorb and emulate the values of academically inclined classmates. And since teachers would gear their lessons to the white majority, black pupils would be motivated to use their best abilities. Also, once released from segregated settings, black children would begin to view themselves in a more positive light, since they were now integrated into the "white" system. According to some scholars, this has in fact been the experience of black students. One study concluded:

> Children who have attended desegregated schools tend to have more friends who are of another race, to work in higher-status jobs, to attend and graduate from multiracial colleges and universities, and to live in integrated neighborhoods.

Other scholars, who also observed black children in integrated schools, found "no systematic evidence supporting the idea that the majority can change deep-seated values held by the minority." In fact, there is "little meaningful contact, let alone contact that would permit learning about each other as individuals." Even worse:

> Thrusting the black child into a predominantly white status-oriented classroom does nothing to enhance the black child's self-esteem. Instead, we find that self-esteem diminishes after desegregation.

There are real contradictions here. One problem is that the studies seldom tell us how the black students in question had come to attend white schools; if their parents had expressly asked for such transfers; or whether their families had moved to or near white neighborhoods to take advantage of schools there. What we do know is that proportions play a role. If the school is heavily white, then the few blacks may feel isolated. Only those willing to adapt to white expectations will succeed, and not all want to move in that direction. According to some research, optimal achievement can be expected when black pupils make up about 20 percent of the school's enrollment. That level provides a sufficient pool for friends and support groups, as well as whatever advantages accrue from attending a school with a racially balanced student body.

This is a good place to inquire how far feelings of alienation have a racial basis. A study of high school drop-out rates in New York City, released in 1990, found that while 25 percent of black students were failing to graduate, this was also the case with 32 percent of Hispanic students and 21 percent of those having Italian-American backgrounds. The high attrition for Italian-Americans suggest that white students can also be turned off by the ambiance and expectations of secondary education. Sitting for much of the day in classrooms is not something they particularly enjoy or at least not as that regimen is imposed in New York City's schools. Since the proportion of black students who drop out exceeded the Italian-American figure by only four percentage points, it would appear that factors related to culture and class have at least as great an impact as those associated with race.

In recent years, the United States has become less white, less "European," and less bound by a single language. As the 1990 census has made clear, the country now has a greater variety of cultures than at any time in its history. This has resulted largely from the rise in immigration, mainly from Latin America and Asia, but also from Eastern Europe and the Middle East. In addition, some native-born Americans are saying they can no longer identify with prevailing cultural perspectives.

One reaction has been calls for recognition of heritages beyond the western world. Much of the controversy has centered on classrooms and campuses, and particularly on the content of curriculums and the makeup of college faculties. As in all such debates, advocates often claim they represent ignored and inarticulate constituencies.

Black Americans, in particular, have objected to what some call the "Eurocentric" orientation to life and knowledge that has been imposed on their children. In a report submitted to the Commissioner of Education in New York State, several black educators advanced the view that minority pupils have "been the victims of an intellectual and educational oppression," due to the "Euro-American monocultural perspective" that dominates most school curriculums. This insensitivity, they asserted, has had a "terribly damaging effect on the psyches of young people," whose native "cultures are alienated and devalued."

Many white Americans have been put off by epithets like "monocultural" and "Euro-American" and "educational oppression." Some have replied that Europe itself is a varied continent, stretching from Inverness to Istanbul, just as the "Euro-American" immigrants came from Spitsbergen and Salonika and many points in between. Even so, it can be replied that whether they are Christians or Jews, or from Poland or Portugal, persons of European origin have shared a common culture and civilization. Moreover, this country's schools have always reflected the literary and scientific side of that tradition, which came with the first English settlers and has essentially endured.

Until now, that hegemony has been accepted, or at least not occasioned wide protests. In past generations, immigrants who arrived from the rural reaches of Ireland or Sicily found that the school systems felt no obligation to acknowledge their customs. Nor did educators devise special curriculums when they set up separate schools for liberated slaves or on Indian reservations. Black youngsters in Alabama and Cherokee children learned essentially the same lessons as were taught in white schools. The schools were to stoke the proverbial melting pot, which meant accepting the society as it had been shaped by those who came before you. Few thought to ask if this might have, as the New York educators now claim, "a terribly damaging effect on the psyche of young people," because their ancestral cultures were "distorted, marginalized, or omitted" in lessons and textbooks.

Ours is much more an age of psychology and social science, as well as expressly ethnic politics. We also have a minor industry of ethnic writers, eager to tell of injuries they suffered from having to conform to the dominant culture. Along with loss of language and tradition have been strains between immigrant parents and assimilating children. There is a real issue here, and it should not be minimized. To some observers, the erosion of older values explains much of the aimlessness and self-indulgence so common in this country. We may now be paying a heavy price for marginalizing so many cultures.

At the same time, the promise of America has been the chance to make it on one's own, which often calls for loosening older ties. Moreover, the United States cannot be accused of false labeling, at least so far as voluntary immigrants have been concerned. All came here freely, aware of the pressures they would face. However, not everyone's ancestors came here by their own choice. Many were brought in chains, while others were overrun and conquered in the name of a "Euro-American" manifest destiny.

The New York report warrants mention, because similar efforts have begun in many parts of the country, including calls for new courses to be required at the college level. As might be expected, these proposals call for expanding the curriculum to give major attention to cultures outside the European sphere. In particular, pupils would learn much more about the customs and contributions of blacks and Hispanics, as well as Asians and Native Americans. Nor will short summaries suffice. Under the Asian umbrella are Chinese, Koreans, Filipinos, and at least half a dozen other nationalities that differ in significant ways. The same holds for the Hispanic grouping, within which Mexicans, Cubans, Puerto Ricans, and many others have distinctive histories and cultures. Nor can justice be done to Native Americans with some well-meant generalities. Rather, the New York report insists, "curricular materials must be developed so there is equity in the coverage of . . . Mohawks, Oneidas, Cayugas, Onondagas, Senecas, and Tuscaroras."

Presumably, then, a full menu of ethnic studies will be offered in all schools. After all, given the premise that the United States is a multiracial and multicultural country, children should be imbued with an appreciation and understanding of all its constituent groups. For this reason, black history and African culture will also be taught to white children, including in suburbs and towns where no blacks reside. Similarly, Hispanics should learn about the contributions of Asians. Whether whites will be compressed into a single "European" culture, or if each country will get separate treatment, has yet to be decided. Some educators seem to feel that because white children are already privileged, their separate stories do not need special recognition.

At the same time, it is not entirely clear how the self-esteem of youngsters from, say, Haiti might be enhanced by learning about the culture and customs of Korea. Such study could well broaden their horizons and stir intellectual interests. But that is rather different from the aim of strengthening confidence and character. Moreover, there are schools in New York and California that have pupils from upward of twenty different countries. If all their cultures are to be covered, each cannot get more than several minutes in a busy syllabus.

At this point, too, a sensitive issue arises. This has to do with the "contributions" various groups have made to this country's development. The traditional teaching of history has tended to focus on those who exercised power and formulated policy. In this reading, most major decisions have been made by white Christian men. It may be worthwhile to tell children from Chinese origins that laborers of their ancestry laid the tracks for the Central Pacific Railroad. But they should also learn how Leland Stanford and Collis Huntington conceived of the project and supervised its completion. Is wielding a pickax as significant a contribution as syndicating debentures? This is not simply an academic question, but has ideological overtones as well.

We can all agree that minority groups have done their bit. At the same time, since Americans of European origin got here first, they have tended to be the ones in influential positions. Students will hardly understand how this country evolved to its current shape—or, indeed, how power works—if they are taught that all ethnic groups have played equally important roles.

Established scholars worry lest lessons may be turned into ethnic cheerleading, laced with indictments of Europe's culpability for slavery, colonization, and the decimation of native populations. At the same time, most scholars are willing to admit that there can be no such thing as an "objective" history or "neutral" social science. All depictions bolster some interests; all interpretations support some preset views. Even such praiseworthy precepts as "individuality" and "freedom" arise and are sustained in specific settings. And those contexts often embody systems of privilege.

Certainly, schools at all levels can and should be doing more about teaching black history, African culture, and the contributions of black Americans in the nation's life.* After all, white children have been learning about their own race's history, and its culture and contributions, for a very long time. Most educators will grant that having a pride in one's people plays a vital role in building self-respect, and this can translate into academic achievement. As one scholar put it, youngsters "do better academically when they see themselves in the curriculum." That does not happen often for black children. The chief message they still get, in school as elsewhere, is that this is a white country, to which they do not fully belong.

That black children have not been well served by the schools hardly needs recounting. In the view of growing numbers of black educa-

* One challenge for such a curriculum, and for scholarship in general, deserves specific notice. More strenuous efforts could be made to show how "white" character and culture have been shaped by the presence of African-Americans. Older literature on the South stressed this theme. But more recent interpretations have not gone much beyond the incorporation of black music and athletic styles, plus a few hesitant forays on dress and sex.

tors, the reasons are inherently racial. In all parts of the country, as they see it, school systems are organized and administered by white officials who have little understanding of the needs of black children. Even in schools that have black principals and are staffed largely by black teachers, state rules shape most of the curriculum, often limiting the choice of books and imposing uniform testing. To a casual visitor, such a school may seem "all black." Yet further observation reveals the influence of white power and authority. Saddest of all, abilities and aspirations of black children often remain unrecognized, if not discouraged or destroyed.

Some proposals are quite modest and should not give rise to debate. One group of black educators has pointed out that "it takes nothing away from Shakespeare or Emily Dickinson to include the dramas of August Wilson and the poetry of Langston Hughes as an integral part of the school curriculum." These educators also stress that many black children learn a distinctive language in their homes, one with rules and expressions of its own. White teachers, they point out, must come to realize that "black English possesses a grammar, a system of deep cultural meaning, and a linguistic integrity on a par with that of standard English." Among those supporting this position have been such well-known figures as Roger Wilkins, Eleanor Holmes Norton, and John Hope Franklin. While they do not urge classroom lessons in black English, they want teachers to be conversant with it and draw on its usages when necessary, much as happens in bilingual programs for children new to this country. Still, black pupils must come to show proficiency in standard English. In later life, they can decide for themselves which speech they will use in varied circumstances and settings.

A related question concerns whether black and white children have different "learning styles." This, too, has become a sensitive subject, with education and ideology very much entwined. Many black educators have proposed that white teachers should be taught to recognize the strengths—and enthusiasms—black youngsters bring to school. In the early years, for example, black pupils should be given more opportunities for expressive talking, since black culture gives as much attention to style as to the substance of speech. Here, too, it has been found that black youngsters apply themselves more readily to lessons involving actual people than to more abstract situations. Similarly, teachers should be tolerant of more casual approaches to syntax, time, and measurement. Professor Asa Hilliard of Georgia State University has found that white children tend to tell stories in a "linear" fashion, while black children are more apt to employ a "spiral" style. When given an assignment, they frequently "skip around to several apparently irrelevant topics before they come back to the theme, and then they begin to work on it."

Black children are also more attuned to their bodies and physical needs. So, some educators argue, they should be allowed more leeway for moving around the classroom. "Michael Jackson, Michael Jordan, Bill Cosby, and Eddie Murphy would be a kindergarten teacher's worst nightmare," one black professor noted. "She would wind up telling Michael Jackson to sit still, Michael Jordan to sit down, and Bill Cosby and Eddie Murphy to shut up." Similarly, it has been found that black pupils are more apt to work to full potential if their teachers identify with them in a caring and solicitous way. For this reason, they may perform best with teachers of their own race.

From nursery school through graduate school, most black students have most of their classes with white teachers. Due to seniority and union rules, even schools in all-black neighborhoods can still have a majority of white faculty members. Everyone agrees on the need for more black teachers, partly to serve as role models and also because they understand the needs of black pupils. In recent years, sad to say, their proportion in faculty positions has actually been declining. To make matters worse, black undergraduates currently account for fewer than 5 percent of the college students who are majoring in education. In common with many of their white classmates, a lot are choosing better-paid fields, or those with more prestige. Another reason has been that most states have introduced so-called "competency examinations" not only for beginning teachers but also to recertify those with classroom experience. As the table on the next page shows, the pass rates for black candidates have not been impressive. An awareness of these results may have signaled at least some students away from careers in education.

In 1990, school systems in several cities—most notably, Milwaukee, Detroit, and New York—began making plans to set up separate schools for black pupils. In actual fact, this is hardly new, since many schools in those cities already have wholly black enrollments. Even so, there are legal obstacles to declaring that only blacks will be

TEACHER COMPETENCY EXAMS: PASS RATES

	White	Black
Alabama	86%	43%
Arizona	80%	44%
Arkansas	88%	33%
California	76%	30%
Connecticut	54%	18%
Georgia	94%	54%
Louisiana	78%	15%
Mississippi	70%	40%
New York	85%	50%
North Carolina	94%	54%
Virginia	98%	69%

States use different tests and scoring methods, which accounts for some of the variance in the pass rates.

enrolled, as that would suggest a refusal to admit persons of other races. Clearly, a bit of playacting is going on here. As was seen in the previous chapter, colleges that choose to call themselves "historically black" say they would be pleased to consider applicants of any race. At the same time, they let it be known that they don't really welcome such applications, since they wish to maintain their distinctive atmosphere. The same message could be sent by high schools having similar aims.*

Elsewhere in the country, new curriculums have been developed for classes composed of black students. Here the emphasis is on African history and cultures, as well as the accomplishments of black Americans and peoples of African descent throughout the world. Here are some sample lessons:

- The fact that some Pre-Columbian sculptures have what could be seen as Negroid features strengthens the supposition that it was Africans who first sailed across the Atlantic to America.
- The draftsman Lewis Howard Latimer, who worked closely with

* New York City has a Harvey Milk High School in Greenwich Village for homosexual teenagers. While in theory it is open to everyone, thus far no heterosexual youngsters have applied.

Alexander Graham Bell, should be recognized as the coequal inventor of the telephone.

- In 1879, an African surgeon performed successful Caesarean sections, a procedure European physicians had yet to perfect at that time.
- Vaccination against smallpox was introduced into the United States in 1721, by a slave who brought the method over from Africa.
- Carbon steel was manufactured in blast furnaces in Tanzania before the birth of Christ. Early Africans also built ships that could carry as much as eighty tons, one of which transported a cargo of elephants from Kenya to China in the thirteenth century.

Attention to the African heritage pervades all lesson plans. Instead of having black children dress up as Pilgrims for Thanksgiving pageants, they would celebrate Kwanza, the simulation of an African harvest festival. Given the richness and variety of tribal customs, there should be no shortage of source materials, ranging from coming-of-age rituals and herbal healing, to the role of Islam in modern Africa. In some schools, students might be invited to adopt African names, following the lead of Molefi Kete Asante of Temple University, a prominent curriculum consultant, who started life as Arthur L. Smith in Valdosta, Georgia.

There may be a conflict between the multicultural approach described earlier and the curriculums proposed for racially separate schools. Some black educators see attention to other cultures as a tactic to deflect black students' attention from their unique heritage. One professor has gone so far as to attack the whole multicultural idea as "mental genocide."

In 1954, the Supreme Court outlawed officially segregated schools on the ground that they generated in black students "a feeling of inferiority as to their status in the community." Now, a generation later, it is being argued that blacks who go to schools with predominantly white enrollments can end up with the same inferior feelings. There is no inconsistency here. Today, the people proposing separate schools want those who enroll to sign up voluntarily. And, at least as important, these schools should be under black control.

The question black Americans will deal with for themselves is how much attention they wish to give to African and African-American history and culture, and how much to mastering the skills needed to succeed in a highly technical world. In theory, this need not be a difficult choice. In a history class students can learn about how slaves resisted their masters; and then, in the next period, work in a computer lab where they study mathematical models. This already happens in Orthodox yeshivas, some of which have sophisticated scientific programs; pupils study the Talmud in the morning, and spend the afternoon mastering biochemistry.

Insofar as black Americans want their fair share of what a modern world has to offer, it will be for them to decide how far they can retain the fruits of their heritage and also prepare themselves for the tests the impending era will set. Some may, of course, conclude that they do not wish to adapt to a world dominated by technology, administration, and corporate priorities. (Many whites make similar decisions, but most of them still possess—and rely on—modern skills more than they may admit.) Still, the number of purely "black" careers that are available will depend on the number of such positions that white society is willing to underwrite. While black men and women can and do succeed on their own, they also realize that white America largely decides how many black people will be promoted and rewarded. And here white motives run across a spectrum, ranging from a desire for entertainment, to a wish to pay off moral debts, or the hope of buying social peace.

The accent on African identities comes at a time that finds growing numbers of white Americans less engaged with their European origins. The causes are not difficult to discern. As the passage of years dims memories of forebears, so the increasing incidence of intermarriage has diluted single-country ancestries. More white Americans now live and work and play in ethnically heterogeneous settings, where national origins are seldom if ever mentioned. Indeed, with each passing year, more and more white Americans are becoming "nonethnic" in character and culture. A recent study of Americans of Irish, Italian, and Polish origins found that insofar as they displayed an "ethnic" demeanor, this tended to take place "in private rather than public realms." Fewer than one in three had occasion to use "words or phrases from their ancestral language" or expressed an intention to "teach their children about their ethnic background." The most common "ethnic experience" was an affinity for "special foods or dishes," and this was volunteered by less than half of the respondents. Moreover, this affirmation came mainly from Italians, whose cuisine is well established in America. And even with cheap airfares and chartered tours, only one in ten had visited their ancestral region on a European trip.

At the same time, there persists what could be called an "ethnic industry," which has political motives for stressing the immigrant origins of certain white citizens. Hence we hear frequent references to "white ethnics," often accompanied by allusions to "ethnic neighborhoods." This emphasis can be useful for politicians who seek to divert attention from economic issues, an end which can often be achieved by sharpening racial divisions. In particular, "white ethnics" are cast as the chief victims of affirmative action, as well as the first to be affected by the changing compositions of schools and neighborhoods. This has been a favored strategy of the right. It has been deployed with unusual success in the presidential campaigns of Ronald Reagan and George Bush, and will be explored further in this book's closing chapter.

Still, it is by no means clear how far persons described as "white ethnics" actually perceive themselves that way. Individuals who are identified by their ethnicity may in fact see themselves more as working-class or middle-income householders who are concerned about the education of their children and the safety and security of the areas where they live. A lot of "nonethnic" Americans share these sentiments, which have little or nothing to do with the countries one's grandparents came from.

Of course, the United States is becoming host to new clusters of immigrants, who bring their languages, customs, and cultures with them. Undoubtedly, many older adults in these groups will retain much of their personal past. But it should not be assumed that younger immigrants and their children intend to retain their parents' ways. Indeed, there is not much evidence that immigrant parents are entranced with proposals for "multicultural" lessons: most want their children to learn about their new homeland and the modern world it represents. Evidence of this emerges in the number who object to having their offspring assigned to separate "bilingual" classes. So the United States need not necessarily become more "multicultural." Rather, the process of assimilation adhered to by earlier arrivals is once again getting underway. Of course, the culture and society to which new arrivals adapt itself changes with each era. But, as has been noted, the format remains essentially Anglo-European, even after generations of mutations and transfusions.

* * *

Several of the cities that have begun planning all-black schools have also proposed limiting their enrollments to boys and young men. The reasoning is that they need more special attention than girls and young women. A study by the American Council of Education has pronounced that "black men are disproportionately at risk in American society." All too many black men, it added, "begin life in circumstances that diminish their chances of educational attainment." By now the litany of causes is familiar, ranging from a misplaced bravado to drugs and death at an early age. The report also points out that "educational institutions tend to have low expectations of black males," while "the dominance of elementary and secondary education by women diminishes the number of role models in the schools."

Among those who do complete high school, many enlist in the armed services instead of applying to college. In fact, this can be a very sensible choice, since in the military they can upgrade their educational and vocational skills, as well as get their lives together, and then decide whether to remain in uniform or pursue careers in the civilian sector. Rather less heartening is the fact that the country now has more of its black men locked in prisons and jails than are attending classes on college campuses.

In the early 1960s, black women began to outnumber black men at institutions of higher education. This trend has continued, with each autumn finding fewer black men continuing beyond high school. As it happens, however, it is not only black men who are dropping away. Between 1976 and 1989, white and Hispanic men also lost their majority status among enrolled undergraduates and degree recipients. If current trends continue, Asians will also have a majority of women. So it would seem that young men generally are an endangered gender, since whatever forces are at work cut across racial and ethnic lines. In fact, between 1973 and 1988, the proportion of white youths who finished high school fell from 79.7 percent to 75.3 percent.

Studies by the National Center for Education Statistics have found that high school girls have better academic records than boys, even allowing for their slower starts in mathematics and science. Teachers at all levels report that many more women now volunteer in class. At the same time, girls submit more readily to classroom discipline, where they take better notes and turn in assignments to their teach-

WOMEN'S SHARE OF BACHELOR'S DEGREES WITHIN FOUR ETHNIC GROUPS

	1976	1989
White	45.2%	52.5%
Black	56.7%	61.5%
Hispanic	43.4%	53.3%
Asian	43.5%	48.9%

ers' liking. They also put in more time doing homework at both the school and college levels. Unfortunately, fewer boys have a makeup suited for twelve or more years of sustained sitting. Perhaps that was always the case, but in the past more of them endured the regimen.

The general success of women in education helps to explain why more are moving into occupations once the preserves of men. The other side of the equation is that each year finds more young men—white as well as black—lacking the diplomas and degrees expected in a modern economy.

CHAPTER ELEVEN

CRIME

THE ROLE RACE PLAYS

TWO BLACK AMERICANS played critical roles in George Bush's 1988 presidential victory. One was Jesse Jackson, who became a major contender for the Democratic nomination. The other was a man named Willie Horton, a convicted murderer from the state of Massachusetts.

Jesse Jackson will be considered in a later chapter. Willie Horton was made part of the campaign by Republican strategists, who cited him as a casebook study of what is wrong with the criminal justice system. Even though he had been sentenced to a lengthy term for murder, Horton still qualified for a furlough program, which allowed him to leave the prison for specified periods. During one such sojourn, he took off for Maryland, where he broke into a home of a white couple, and then proceeded to tie up the man and brutally rape the woman.

All this happened while Michael Dukakis, the 1988 Democratic candidate, was serving as governor of Massachusetts. Of course, Dukakis had not been directly aware of Horton's eligibility for a furlough. Even so, those managing the Bush campaign took care to have Willie Horton mentioned in speeches and advertisements. They knew that few voters supported furloughs, and that most would be aghast to learn they were awarded to murderers. That one ended with a rape was not only reprehensible; some might add it was quite predictable. It would be hard to find a better case for portraying a politician as soft on crime and solicitous toward criminals.

But there was also the racial aspect. Willie Horton was black; his Maryland victims were white. That racial nexus would have roused emotions had he simply got hold of a gun and robbed a liquor store. However, Horton used his grant of freedom to rape a white woman. Of all the offenses black men may commit, a sexual assault on a white victim stirs deeply primal fears.

What most Americans regard as "black crime" has become a preoccupation of public and private life. Black men, and the offenses they commit, are viewed differently from other felons and felonies. Of course, this kind of characterization is not altogether unique. While no one speaks of "white crime," since it would have too broad a compass, the phrase "Italian crime" has meaning for most people, implying the involvement of "the Mafia." After all, men of Italian ancestry seem to figure disproportionately in certain illegal activities, especially those involving extortion. The same might be said of "Colombian crime," insofar as it centers on cocaine importation. Even so, the damage done by Colombian and Italian criminals causes less public concern than the prospect of being accosted by someone like Willie Horton. If movies have rendered murders by Italian mobsters as comedy, it is hard to imagine scenes of "black crime" evoking many chuckles.

Such information as we have about crime can be calculated in several ways. The starting point is that black Americans make up between 12 and 13 percent of the general population, depending on estimates of the census undercount. In virtually all spheres—offenders, victims, prisoners, and arrests by the police—the rates for blacks are disproportionate to their share of the population. Thus black men and women account for 47.0 percent of the individuals awaiting trial in local jails or serving short terms there. They also comprise 40.1 percent of the prisoners currently under sentence of death. And they make up 45.3 percent of the inmates in state and federal prisons. Overall, more than a million black Americans are currently behind bars or could be returned there for violating probation or parole.

ARREST RATES BY RACE (1990)

Crimes	Black Share of all Arrests	Disproportion of Black Arrests
Robbery	61.2%	5.1
Murder and Manslaughter	54.7%	4.5
Gambling	47.5%	3.9
Rape	43.2%	3.6
Receiving Stolen Property	41.2%	3.4
Vagrancy	40.8%	3.4
Drug Violations	40.7%	3.4
Weapons Possession	39.8%	3.3
Prostitution	38.9%	3.2
Motor Vehicle Theft	38.4%	3.2
Aggravated Assault	38.4%	3.2
Forgery and Counterfeiting	34.0%	2.8
Disorderly Conduct	32.4%	2.7
Embezzlement	32.1%	2.7
Domestic Violence	30.3%	2.5
Burglary	30.1%	2.5
Vandalism	22.6%	1.9
Curfew and Loitering	17.7%	1.5
Driving While Intoxicated	8.7%	0.9

Another set of figures enumerates annual arrests, which the Federal Bureau of Investigation collects from local law enforcement agencies. In 1990, more than 10 million criminal counts were logged, ranging from embezzlement and counterfeiting to vandalism and vagrancy. Within these and other categories, the suspects are identified by race. The table on this page shows how many of the persons arrested on various charges were black, and the relation of those figures to the black share of the general population. (Unfortunately, the FBI does not classify suspects by their economic status or other ethnic origins. So we have no measures for, say, Jews and Italians, or savings-and-loan executives and investment bankers.)

Quite clearly, the phrase "black crime" does not make people think of tax evasion or embezzling from brokerage firms. Rather, the offenses generally associated with blacks are those that carry the threat or actuality of bodily injury. In a word, crimes involving violence: most particularly, murder, robbery, and rape. As the table shows, while blacks comprise only about 12 percent of the population, they account for a high proportion—61.2 percent—of all robbery arrests. And they include over half of the suspects arrested for wrongful deaths, and close to half in cases of rape. Overall, black arrest rates are disproportionate for every offense except drunken driving.

Still, figures based on arrests may have a built-in bias, since police may be more apt to stop and detain black suspects. This certainly seems the case with violations like gambling and prostitution, since blacks in those trades tend to do so in the open, where they can be more easily apprehended. Whites, on the other hand, apparently perpetrate more of their felonies in offices or behind other doors.

A good check on FBI reports is the annual "victimization" survey conducted by the Census Bureau. This study polls a cross-section of the nation's households, asking if any of their members had been a victim of a crime during the preceding year. If they were, they are asked to indicate their own race and that of the criminal. One purpose of the survey is to measure the extent of crime, since by no means all offenses are reported to the police and not all of those that are reported eventuate in arrests. As it happens, the figures for murder and manslaughter show a similarity between the two sets of records. In instances where the races of the assailants were known, blacks perpetrated 53.1 percent of all criminal deaths, and accounted for 56.4 percent of the arrests.

All together, 69.3 percent of the people who reported they had been robbed during the previous year also said their assailants had been black. While this is higher than the 61.2 percent figure for black robbery arrests, it still allows the conclusion that blacks do commit most of the nation's robberies. That more of the black suspects end up getting arrested suggests that white robbers find it easier to elude the police.

On the other hand, the census reports on rape victimization differ quite markedly from rape arrest records. In all, 33.2 percent of the women who said they had been raped identified their attackers as black. However, among the men arrested for that offense, 43.2 percent were black. This disparity suggests either that assaults by white rapists are less likely to be reported to the police; or, if they are, they are less apt to lead to arrests.

MURDERS (1990)

	Assailants	Victims
White	46.1%	49.2%
Black	53.9%	50.8%
	100.0%	100.0%

Race of Assailant and Victim

Both White	43.2%
Both Black	47.9%
Black and White	6.0%
White and Black	2.9%
	100.0%

ROBBERIES (1989)

	Assailants	Victims
White	36.1%	69.2%
Black	63.9%	30.8%
	100.0%	100.0%

Race of Assailant and Victim

Both White	34.0%
Both Black	28.7%
Black and White	35.2%
White and Black	2.1%
	100.0%

RAPES (1989)

	Assailants	Victims
White	75.7%	66.8%
Black	24.3%	33.2%
	100.0%	100.0%

Race of Assailant and Victim

Both White	66.5%
Both Black	24.0%
Black and White	9.2%
White and Black	0.3%
	100.0%

Based on reports where the victims and assailants were identified as white or black.

The most obvious question is why blacks are responsible for so large a ratio of crimes entailing threats or acts of violence. One explanation is economic: those most drawn to violent crimes tend to be poorer members of society. That blacks account for a high proportion of the nation's poor needs no reiterating here. The contrast is especially vivid among young men between the ages of twenty-five and thirty, a group most likely to run afoul of the law. The most recent census reports show that white men in this group have a median income of $20,153, whereas for black men, the amount is $14,333, close to one-third lower. Among white men in their middle and late twenties, the 1990 unemployment rate averaged 5.5 percent. Among black men of that age, the rate was 13.0 percent, more than double the white rate. Clearly, there is a considerable pool of black men who feel they have few opportunities in the legal economy. That could cause them to turn to crime.

Yet despite some initial plausibility, this explanation needs further scrutiny. For one thing, most poor people of all races labor honestly, even for a small return. By the same token, persons who do choose to break the law come from every tier in the social structure. What can be said, then, is that class positions facilitate—or circumscribe—individuals' options. If poorer prostitutes walk the streets rather than meet customers by prearrangement, so poorer men who decide to steal find they must resort to open-air robberies. Thieves who work in offices have a wider and less easily detected choice of larcenies, ranging from rigging computers to fixing prices in private dining rooms. If more black felons end up in prison cells, not the least reason is that they lacked office-based opportunities.

In the minds of most people, rape is one of mankind's most brutal crimes. That it persists, even flourishes in our time, undercuts such claims as we have to being a civilized society. Men do not rape for sexual pleasure. Rather, rape is a malicious assault, intending physical and psychic harm. And it is clearly a violent crime. Rapists cannot carry out their acts unless they are prepared to beat their victims into submission or threaten them with injury or death. Even if victims submit, they may still be maimed or killed, since sexual conquest does not always satiate the rapist.

Not all men are potential rapists, if by that is meant that they are prepared to use the violence associated with the act. Even so, not all men can be sure just how they might behave in a situation that might awaken passions they never knew they had. On this entangled question, we have little objective information, but no shortage of speculation. While most men may protest that they have never considered rape, some analysts will say that what happens in men's fantasies and dreams tells another story. Indeed, studies have found more than a few men admitting to rape fantasies, in which they take women against their will. Some feminist writers have argued that the men who actually commit rape are acting not only on their own, but also on behalf of other men who do not dare to take the step. Note how many men, on hearing reports of rape, wonder whether the victim did something to lure her assailant on.

Men who rape hate women. They see them as haughty, castrating creatures, who must be put in their place. Many pick their victims pretty much at random: so long as she is a woman, she represents her sex. Others may vent their anger on particular women, whom they feel need an indelible punishment. In these cases, the victims are often persons they know: acquaintances or dates or even wives. The rapist's aim is to inflict a grievous wound, a humiliation that will haunt the victim forever.* (This is why so many rapes involve sodomy.) So rape is also a political act. And beyond politics, it is war: a campaign whose purpose it is to pacify, indeed destroy, a historic enemy.

Where race is concerned, several observations are in order. First, such studies as we have suggest that black and white women are equally willing—or unwilling—to report having been raped, whether to enforcement authorities or survey interviewers. In addition, the race of the rapist does not seem to affect whether a report will be forthcoming. Because of this, it is not easy to argue that there are more assaults by white men that do not come to public attention.

Several statistics stand out. One is that three quarters of the black men who perpetrate rapes have black women as their victims. A second is that regardless of the race of the victims, black men commit this crime at a three to four times greater rate than white men. These findings suggest that black rapists regard women of their own race as war-

* Men are raped every day, usually within the walls of prisons. But it is not "homosexual" sex in a literal sense. Most of the assailants regard themselves as fully heterosexual, which is how they conducted themselves prior to going to prison and will after they get out. Still, the aim of prison rape is much the same as when the victims are women. It is an overpowering act, designed to show new convicts whom their masters will be.

ranting intimidation and humiliation as much as white women. And given the segregated spheres in which the races move, black women are more readily available for black men seeking a victim.

Still, there remains the question of whether black men feel more hostility toward women than occurs among white men. About the most we can say is that some lower-class black men have been more candid on this score. Insofar as rap lyrics echo some ghetto attitudes, we hear women referred to as "bitches" and "whores" with a bitterness seldom heard in even cruder white circles. In reply, it can be argued that expletives do not constitute evidence. White manners may mask quite similar enmities. Yet as was mentioned earlier, more black women are achieving higher status in education and occupations, which can create class divisions and stir sexual tensions. Men have always sought to bring down women whose ambitions or achievements threaten male esteem.

Yet the fact remains that a high proportion of black rapists take the trouble—and the risk—of assaulting white women. And they do this with the realization that if they are caught they will be more severely punished. Given the purposes of rape, choosing a white victim compounds defiance with the thrill of danger. Eldridge Cleaver once claimed that violating white women has political intentions as well. Each such act brings further demoralization of the dominant race, exposing its inability to protect its own women from the worst kind of depredation.

Certainly, the conditions black men face in the United States generate far more anger and rage than is ever experienced by white men. To be a man is made doubly difficult, since our age continues to associate "manliness" with worldly success. If black men vent their frustrations on women, it is partly because the women are more available as targets, compared with the real centers of power, which remain so inchoate and remote.

Robbery is also a personal encounter, in which the assailant is usually armed and threatens to use deadly force. Unlike rape, the reasons why people rob are relatively simple: to obtain money or articles of value. It is also the crime in which blacks are most heavily represented. They account for more than 65 percent of all reported robberies and subsequent arrests, which works out to a rate five times greater than for whites.

Robbery is also the crime where blacks are most likely to pick whites as their victims. One reason, obviously, is that they can be expected to carry more cash or items of worth. Each year, several hundred thousand white and black Americans find themselves accosted by black thieves. In fact, more blacks than whites are victimized by black robbers. Indeed, black crime rates would be dramatically lower if blacks did not prey so frequently on members of their own race.

For white victims caught in interracial robberies the loss of cash or valuables is seldom their chief concern. Rather, the racial character of the encounter defines the experience. In the social scheme of things, the tables have been turned. For the present, a black man has the upper hand. Hence the added dread that your assailant will not be satisfied simply with your money, but may take another moment to inflict retribution for the injustices done to his race.

Some white Americans might agree that they owe blacks some form of repayment, although they would prefer not to proffer it in this way. Given the choice, white people would far rather be confronted by a thief of their own race. Indeed, they would be happy to lose considerably more money, rather than face the prospect of racial revenge.

Reactions like these show that white Americans in fact acknowledge that the crimes blacks commit are in some part expressions of resistance. Given the disproportionate violations of the nation's laws by black Americans, it may to some degree be because they feel they never consented to the content of those statutes or the ways they are enforced. In the words of Bruce Wright, a black New York City judge, they are simply breaking "a social contract that was not of their making in the first place." Viewed this way, engaging in crime becomes a form of rebellion, not dissimilar to the banditry of earlier eras. Very many blacks who are young and poor feel they have never had a fair chance, nor is that prospect likely. In light of the insults and discrimination they have faced throughout their lives, it is not surprising that as many as do vent their resentment in violence. Through crime, blacks are paying whites back, in the most ominous way they can. That they harm themselves as much if not more compounds the tragedy.

The dread whites feel of black crime goes beyond actual risks or probabilities. The visage of Willie Horton stirred fears in parts of the country where black faces are seldom seen. Violent acts by blacks have weakened the self-assurance and morale of white America. The feeling is not simply that crime is out of control. Far more troubling is the realization that white citizens can be held in thrall by a race meant to be subservient.

In the antebellum South, an abiding fear of slave owners was that their chattels might rise in revolt. Any night, they could enter the manor house, and slay their masters and mistresses in their beds. Hence the recourse to whips and other tortures to break rebellious spirits, and show the price of defiance. Historians differ on the frequency of slave risings, or on how often they were contemplated. Still, it would take only a few sullen glances to stir fears in every owner that his turn could come next.

After the ending of slavery, the nation found it expedient to continue blacks as a subordinate caste. But given their admission to citizenship, new controls had to be devised to keep them in place. One was to give the police a long leash, devising ways to absolve them if they went too far with their powers. The 1991 videotaping of Los Angeles policemen mauling a young black man made it clear that they felt such impunity. Even today, in most parts of the country, black men who stir suspicions cannot count on being accorded a presumption of innocence. Despite constitutional safeguards, police and prosecutors and judges still find it relatively easy to ensure that one out of every five black men will spend some part of his life behind bars.

Much of what has been said about robbery and rape applies to murder as well. With most homicides, as with other assaults, the assailant and victim are of the same race. In the past, most such slayings involved relatives or acquaintances, which meant they were usually followed by arrests and convictions. Today, many more murders occur during robberies, which means more people are dying at the hands of strangers, so that fewer slayings are being solved. In racial terms, the most striking development has been the sharp rise in black youths killing one another, so that homicide has become this group's leading cause of death.

This self-inflicted genocide, reflecting both bravado and despair, causes a great deal of grief. There is hardly a black teenager who cannot cite a friend or schoolmate who died on a nearby street. Yet it often appears that black Americans express even more concern over cases where persons of their race have been killed by policemen, or much-publicized occasions where a black youth has been slain by a white gang. One reason is a reluctance to talk about black-against-black crimes within white hearing. But another is that deaths at white hands bring home their race's minority status.

Here the statistics tell only part of the story. Between 1976 and 1987, the most recent period studied, some 1,800 black persons and about 3,000 whites were killed by law enforcement officers. So given their proportion of the population, black Americans have a three times greater chance than whites of dying from a policeman's bullet. As it happens, a disproportionately high number of these killings of blacks are by black policemen, which suggests that departments tend to give black officers assignments where they encounter suspects of their own race. (This is especially the case with undercover drug work.) For many years, police forces hired few if any blacks; now there is a tendency to use blacks to control blacks.

Black Americans know as well as anyone that there are felons of their own race, not a few of whom are armed and prepared to use their weapons. Why, then, the readiness to defend even offenders who fall afoul of the police, rather than side with officers whose job it is to preserve safety and order?

The first answer is that by no means is every black person slain by the police a criminal. Most law enforcement officers are white, and many lack the intuition or experience to distinguish a law-abiding citizen from a dangerous offender. As a result, tragic "mistakes" are often made. Quite enough incidents have made the news to suggest that blacks are more likely than whites to be killed in error. Indeed, in many cases no weapon was found on the suspect's body; or, in some instances with youngsters, it was only a toy gun. Most blacks can recite a litany of names, to be memorialized as victims of official white force. Here are just a few from the New York City area: Arthur Miller, Marian Johnson, Elizabeth Mangum, Peter Funches, Jay Parker, Michael Stewart, Eleanor Bumpurs, Nicholas Bartlett, Yvonne Smallwood, Stephen Kelly, Kevin Thorpe, Phillip Pannell. White New Yorkers would be hard-pressed to cite even a single police victim of their own race.

And even if the police do not draw their guns, most black Americans can recall encounters where they were treated with discourtesy, hostility, or worse. At issue is a proclivity of police personnel to judge individuals first by their color. Perhaps day-to-day experience has jaundiced so many officers that they see even law-abiding blacks as belonging to the "other side." Compounding these stereotypes is the fact that the typical police officer is a high school graduate, from a working-class background, who had never previously set foot in the areas he now patrols. (In many cities, officers commute from the suburbs.) And it would appear that at least a few police officers still move in circles where no censure attaches to using the word "nigger."

These issues crystallized in a 1987 court case in New York, arising from an episode that occurred in a poorer section of the Bronx. A black drug dealer named Larry Davis, who was being sought for several felonies, escaped through a window when a group of police officers arrived at his home. A tip revealed where Davis was hiding, and a heavily armed squad was dispatched to bring him in. As they entered the apartment, shots rang out. Witnesses differed about whether it was Davis or the police who fired first. As might be expected, the officers swore they came in peacefully and then used their guns only in response. Davis certainly fired, since he wounded some members of the squad.

While Davis's attorneys conceded that he had shot back, they quickly added that it was only after the police had opened fire on him. Thus they contended that Davis had used his gun in self-defense. He sincerely believed that the police meant to kill him then and there, that they had no intention of bringing him out alive. Davis's case was that he was not trying to kill any officers; he was simply defending his life.

It is not unusual for a defendant to claim that a weapon was used in self-defense. But, until the Davis case, that plea had not been employed to justify firing at the police. After all, it will be replied, citizens should have no need to draw arms when confronted by the law. We should presume that the police want to bring their suspects in alive; that they are professionals, trained to use their weapons only as a last resort. This may be the view of most whites. It is not commonly shared by black Americans.

The Bronx jury, composed of black and Hispanic householders, voted unanimously to acquit Davis of the charge of attempted murder. They later told reporters that they had accepted his explanation that he used the gun only to protect his life. It should be added that these jurors were law-abiding citizens, all of whom held steady jobs. But due to segregation, they lived in or near risky neighborhoods, and they needed no reminding about what life is like in a high-crime area. If asked, they would certainly say that their own blocks needed more and better police protection. At the same time, they could also understand Davis's perception of the police as a hostile force.

Indeed, when black citizens become victims of crimes, they tend to find scant attention from the police for their plight. Underlying this official unconcern seems to be the notion that if you are a black person in the United States, you should not be surprised if you happen to be robbed or raped or even lose your life. Hence, too, the greater solicitude by the police for white victims, who are seen as more shaken when violence intrudes on their lives. Indeed, white citizens complain more stridently about crime, even though their likelihood of becoming victims is far lower than for blacks. From this race-based reasoning flows the corollary that less is lost when black persons die, whether they are slain by the police or a criminal. And since black lives are viewed as having lesser value, the act of taking them warrants a lighter censure.*

Given their greater vulnerability to crime, black Americans have a legitimate claim for effective police protection. Their problem is that when the police do display zeal, innocent blacks are likely to be rounded up and arrested. This concern arose in the notorious "jogger" case, involving a gang attack on a white woman in New York's Central Park. Most black New Yorkers could privately agree that a group of black youths had assaulted the young investment banker and left her on the edge of death. Why then did so many have ambiguous feelings about the subsequent trial? One reason was that all six of the teenaged defendants were charged with rape and attempted murder, the heaviest possible counts. But it was not abundantly clear that all six of them had taken part in the sexual and physical attack. Even so, the prosecution was demanding full guilty verdicts, even for some who might have been bystanders. It is one

* A study prepared in 1987 for a Supreme Court appeal found that murderers who killed white people faced a ten times greater chance of a death sentence compared with murderers who had black victims. When circumstances such as the ferocity of the crime and the social status of the victim were held constant, the prospect for the death penalty was still four times higher than when the victim was white.

thing to demand appropriate punishment for rapists and murderers. It is another to automatically accept that the police have caught the guilty parties. If blacks frequently find themselves identifying with defendants, it is because they realize how easily their own sons could be caught in such a net.

The case of Bernhard Goetz brought these and other racial issues to the fore. Goetz was an electronics expert, slight and unassuming in appearance. He had been previously attacked by a band of black men in a New York subway station, who robbed him and inflicted some serious injuries. The felons were never caught, a not uncommon occurrence. So Goetz concluded that he could not count on official protection. Thereafter, he carried a gun of his own, albeit without a permit.

On a December afternoon in 1984, in a half-empty subway car, he found himself accosted again, by another group of black youths, who demanded some money. (They later claimed they had merely "asked him" for a few dollars.) Goetz responded by pulling out his gun. And then, without uttering a word, he proceeded to fire away, wounding all four of the young men. As an afterthought, he again shot at one of them who lay bleeding on the floor, saying, "You seem to need another." Goetz fled into a subway tunnel, and a few weeks later turned himself in at a police station in Concord, New Hampshire.

The young men survived, although the one who received the extra shot would be paralyzed for life. It soon emerged that three of the four had extensive criminal records. When charged with attempted murder, Goetz argued that he believed his life was in danger and he therefore had fired in self-defense.

The Manhattan jury, which had two black members, apparently accepted Goetz's assessment of the threat. Even though he might have killed all four, and had maimed one of the group, it acquitted him of all charges save the smallest: carrying an unauthorized firearm. By most reckonings, it was a popular verdict. A local newspaper poll found that Goetz's exoneration was supported by 90 percent of white New Yorkers, as well as 83 percent of the Hispanics who were interviewed, and over half—52 percent—of the black respondents.

This support for Goetz's vigilantism was notable, considering New York's reputation as a liberal city. In the eyes of the jury, and much of the public, he had let loose an overdue salvo in an ongoing racial war. It was about time, they seemed to be saying, that a white victim struck back at these gangs of marauders. That those who had confronted him were young and black was taken as presumptive evidence that they intended to rob him or worse. Goetz was sending a message on behalf of many citizens who were tired of feeling terrorized in the city's subways and streets.

Most revealing—and ambiguous—was the fact that slightly more than half of the black New Yorkers who were polled were willing to defend a white man who had gunned down four youths of their own race. In other words, in answering the question "Do you approve or disapprove of the jury's decision in the Goetz case?" the black respondents divided almost equally between those who supported the verdict and those who would have voted the other way.

But what such a survey could not show was the intersection of feelings *within* each of these black New Yorkers. There seems little doubt that all of them reached their final response only after painful deliberation. For one thing, black Americans hold no brief for ruffians of their own race. As has been noted, they are more apt than whites to suffer victimization at the hands of other blacks. At the same time, the fact that approval for Goetz went as high as 52 percent is significant, given a reluctance to condemn fellow blacks in public polls. And while the youths Goetz shot were far from model citizens, the worry remains that the next vigilante may gun down someone close to them, since not all whites can distinguish between a reprobate and a dean's list student.

Most American cities have neighborhoods whose residents are largely working class and almost exclusively white. Most of these enclaves have made efforts to preserve their character, which means doing whatever they feel is necessary to ensure that black families will not move in. In occasional cases, arson and gunfire have been used to get that message across. Some areas have also let it be known that blacks should not expect a warm welcome if they stroll on their streets.

Howard Beach in New York's borough of Queens and Bensonhurst in Brooklyn are two such neighborhoods. Toward the end of the 1980s both made national news as the scenes of fatal racial incidents. In the Howard Beach episode, a car carrying three black men broke down, and they got out to find a garage or at least a telephone. They had the ill-fortune to encounter a dozen or so local youths, who told them they had no business being in the area. Words were exchanged, after which one of the black men was severely beaten, while another managed to escape. The third tried to get away by running across a busy highway, where he was killed in the speeding traffic. Under law this was murder: it was fleeing for his life that led to his death.

In Bensonhurst, a rumor was making the rounds that a band of blacks would be entering the neighborhood, intent on making trouble. A group of young men armed themselves to repel the incursion. As it turned out, four black teenagers were already walking through Bensonhurst, having come to inspect a car that had been advertised for sale. They happened to pass by the assembled whites, who assumed the young men were part of the impending invasion. A shot rang out from the back of the group, and one of the black youths fell dead. His friends escaped unharmed.

Both events were patently racial. White strangers entering these areas would not have been set upon this way, let alone deprived of their lives. In neither case, moreover, could the violence be described as a response to anything these specific blacks had done. In both cases, several of the white youths were tried, convicted, and sentenced to prison, although on lesser counts than premeditated murder.

For blacks, the events in Howard Beach and Bensonhurst had profound significance. In subsequent years, Michael Griffith and Yusuf Hawkins—the two black youths—would be mourned as the victims of white lynching parties. Yet few whites understood the depth of black concern over what could be seen as two isolated incidents. Indeed, what happened to Griffith and Hawkins were rather unusual occurrences; black youths in New York and other cities are not ordinarily attacked by gangs of whites. In fact, statistics cited earlier in this chapter confirm the impression that more whites are killed by blacks—usually in the course of robberies—than the other way around. So what did these two deaths symbolize?

What Howard Beach and Bensonhurst made vivid for black Americans was that there remain whole stretches of this country that they enter only at their peril. In most places the danger is not so much physical assault as hostile glances and attitudes. Not only do most white communities not want blacks on their streets; many shops and restaurants make it clear that they would be happier without their patronage at all. As was noted in an earlier chapter, white Americans can drive across the continent, stopping for gas and meals and lodging without a second thought. For black Americans, the prospect of humiliation or worse will haunt every mile of the trip.

Nor do blacks care to hear that whites harbor a justified fear of crime. Prior to World War II, when lawbreaking by blacks was relatively rare, communities still posted these signs:

NIGGER, DON'T LET THE SUN SET ON YOU IN THIS TOWN!

Throughout most of this country's history, bands of whites could decide it was time to bring blacks into line. Sometimes victims were simply picked at random, to let black people as a group know that any of them could be next. There might be beatings or maimings, or murder by blowtorch, or dismemberment. On other occasions, local judges would oblige by imposing chain-gang sentences on blacks identified as troublemakers. And black women had scant defenses against sexual assaults, since white men were seldom prosecuted for such crimes.

So the reactions stirred by Howard Beach and Bensonhurst go to the heart of what it means to be black in America. The incidents in the two New York neighborhoods reminded black Americans of how vulnerable they are in a country where they are a minority in numbers and power. Blacks do not consider it paranoid to wonder whether they might someday find themselves behind barbed-wire enclosures, as happened to Americans of Japanese descent during the Second World War. The white race, after all, has had a long history of dealing harshly with human beings it has considered its inferiors.

As was remarked early in this chapter, all social and ethnic groups, including the very rich, include men and women who show a propensity for larceny. For reasons we only dimly understand, some individuals are prone to steal money or articles of worth that do not belong to them. Among the middle and upper classes, thieves are in less danger of getting caught, since the kinds of crimes they commit may be difficult to detect. (In many cases, victims never realize they have been swindled.) Such crimes tend to be job-related, since many white-collar jobs offer opportunities for embezzlement or fraud. There is also plenty of "blue-collar" crime, at factories and warehouses or on building sites, where it is not hard to make away with equipment or materials. Department stores suffer more from thefts by their employees than they do from shoplifters.

So there is no reason to presume that poor people have a greater proclivity for larceny compared with persons of other classes. However, as was also noted, their alternatives are much more limited. Among young black men who choose to steal, even breaking into private homes is less of an option. As the tabulations for arrests showed (see page 181), black rates for burglary are less than half of those for robbery. If nothing else, their visibility makes it harder for black criminals to move surreptitiously in better-off neighborhoods. This is why so many black people who do decide on crime end up stealing from people on the streets or robbing small shops.

As it happens, the thieves who prowl the streets do not enjoy what they do. Most would prefer safer and more rewarding kinds of theft. Even if only a small fraction of all robberies are solved, the eventual odds of a petty thief getting caught are relatively high: after all, one in five black men ultimately spends time behind bars, almost seven times the rate for whites. (And the "white" rate is even lower if Hispanics are excluded.)

If as many whites faced as many social and visual barriers as blacks, there would be a more equitable distribution among the various kinds of crimes. In fact, across small-town America, there are white men who have been raised in an atmosphere of firearms and violence, who are apt to use both. They are not the sort of people one would want to cross on a steamy Saturday night. The prisons of West Virginia, or Oregon and Idaho, have inmate populations that are overwhelmingly white, most of whom were convicted for crimes that in other states tend to be associated with blacks.

Moreover, while black inmates now outnumber whites in America's penal institutions, this was not always the case. Indeed, during the last half-century, there has been a discernible shift in the racial composition of the prison population.

These figures tell several stories. For one thing, it is noteworthy that so few blacks were behind bars in 1930. This would suggest they were really very law-abiding, since most blacks lived in the South, where they could have been imprisoned with relative ease. At the same time, the dramatic drop in the white proportion does not necessarily mean that white people have become more honest. A more

BEHIND BARS IN AMERICA
(Inmate Populations)

	White	Black	Other
1930	76.7%	22.4%	0.9%
1950	69.1%	29.7%	1.2%
1970	60.5%	35.8%	3.7%
1986*	39.6%	45.3%	15.1%

* In 1986, the most recent figures, Hispanic inmates were removed from the white and black groupings and were listed in the "other" column.

accurate explanation is that over the last half-century most white Americans have moved upward on the social scale, so that fewer of them remain among the class of people who tend to receive prison terms. In the United States and elsewhere, people who are poor and have sporadic employment end up filling most of the cells. Most of this group used to be white; now the largest number are black.

Given the crimes black Americans commit, the proceeds tend to be small. The typical armed robbery involves relieving someone of a wallet rather than commandeering an armored car. Most who are caught do not usually have enough cash to raise bail; so they languish in jail cells until their trial dates come due. Since the chances of eventual arrest are so high and the takings so low, those who live off crime are on the whole probably no better off than their neighbors who take jobs washing dishes or sweeping floors. In fact, their prospects may be worse. Considering the employment market and the scarcity of housing, criminals released from prison stand less chance of remaking their lives than they formerly did. This is one reason why black men are so numerous among the homeless. Many go direct from prison cells to the streets. For them, a criminal life is less a livelihood than part of a self-destructive spiral.

So long as we use imprisonment as a punishment, there will be debates over who deserves to be locked away. One reason we put men and women behind bars is to protect society: if not incarcerated, they might continue preying on the rest of us. Also, we may feel that their offenses were so serious that only some years in a cell will impress upon them the gravity of their acts. Nor are these the only reasons. We also imprison people as expressions of outrage and revenge. Or in hopes that correctional programs will prove rehabilitating. Along with the belief that knowing you can be sent to prison will scare most citizens into behaving lawfully.

There is also controversy over what constitutes a "serious" crime. One criterion, certainly, is economic: how much did the person steal? The sums can be quite high. Not so long ago, *Fortune* magazine devoted an article to "corporate crooks." It told of one manager who embezzled $1 million by passing fake invoices through his company's billing system. Another involved a banker who secretly withdrew $4 million from various accounts. The latter felon received a sentence of two years. The former's was somewhat sterner: two to six years, depending on his conduct and prospect for parole.

Both of these culprits were white men in white-collar occupations. If their sentences are any gauge, their million-dollar thefts were not deemed as serious as offenses described as "violent" crimes, for which prison terms can run to ten or more years, even though they involved considerably less money.

The justification generally given is that people who engage in robbery are in fact more dangerous than individuals who embezzle large sums. According to this reasoning, if we wish to maintain a civilized society, we should be able to expect a reasonable degree of safety. Violent crimes threaten our lives and health; those who commit them are predators. Moreover, robbery and rape involve more than weapons, and actual or threatened force. They are acts of terror, intimidating not only the victims, but everyone else who may become prey.

So long as blacks commit more than their share of violent crimes, they will account for more than their share of prison cells. Moreover, American society has shown itself increasingly impatient with alternatives like community service, or release on one's own recognizance, not to mention furloughs. And here, too, race intrudes. The feeling persists that a black man who rapes or robs a white person has inflicted more harm than black or white criminals who prey on victims of their own race. It is as if an assault by a black is an act of desecration that threatens the entire white race. And that is why Willie Horton—the black man who raped a white woman—played so signal a role in electing a president.

CHAPTER TWELVE

A POLITICS BASED ON RACE

THAT A BOOK about race concludes with a chapter on politics should not occasion surprise. Problems associated with race continue to beset this nation, as they have since its earliest origins. Americans of all persuasions look to the political process, if not always for solutions, then for gradual progress and piecemeal remedies. In this view, politics is seen as a means for achieving compromise and coping with social change. So conceived, the process can work to redistribute resources, redress injustices, and improve the atmosphere in which people live and work. This, at least, has been the hope.

To the minds of many people, the civil rights movement of the 1960s provided a memorable model. By combining protest and pressure, plus appeals to majority opinion, many discriminatory practices were officially ended. Further moves toward racial equity helped to enlarge the black middle class. Since much remains to be done in the realm of race, it should be asked what can still be expected from the political process.

Of course, politics is a mélange of activities, taking place in the streets as well as within conference rooms. It ranges from judicial decisions and administrative rulings to legislative trade-offs and moral leadership. And where race is concerned, the process can lead to a confrontation between minority and majority.

Of course, well-organized minorities can make their weight felt. Gun owners have proved that, as have opponents of abortion. Pursuing this theory, it could be argued that since black Americans have an intense interest in racial redress, they should be able to mobilize their numbers with similar effectiveness. On occasion that appeared to happen, especially during the 1960s and 1970s, when the Congress passed some serious civil rights laws. Recourse to the courts also succeeded, not least because judges saw individual plaintiffs as having broad backing in the black community.

Yet the political power of black Americans faces limitations. For one thing, many black Americans are preoccupied with personal problems and are not easily organized. Money plays a vital role in politics, if only to make one's case heard, and blacks have less available cash than many other groups. Moreover, black voters tend to be concentrated in segregated areas, which means they have little sway over politicians in other districts. Indeed, the majority of lawmakers in the United States have few if any black residents in their constituencies. While governors and senators have more varied electorates, in twenty-one of the states, black comprise less than 5 percent of the population.

Political measures intended to redress relations between the races require either support from white voters, or neutrality, or indifference. For a period of about thirty years—roughly from 1945 until 1975—white Americans found themselves embarrassed by blatant cases of discrimination. It was during these decades that Harry Truman and Lyndon Johnson occupied the White House. Throughout most of this period, also, the Supreme Court led by Earl Warren called for enforcement of desegregation decisions. At least equally important were social and economic changes, largely induced by World War II, that spread education and sophistication to a growing middle class. And as has been noted in earlier chapters, throughout most of these years, black citizens remained remarkably civil, and refrained from unsettling white sensibilities.

Starting about 1975, changes began to be seen in the attitudes of white voters who had been willing to support measures aimed at assisting blacks. This shift was ratified in the 1980 election of Ronald

Reagan, which moved race closer to the center of the political stage. Reagan's reelection in 1984, and the succession four years later of George Bush, helped to consolidate this drive.

At the most visible level, growing numbers of white people are expressing misgivings over how black people are conducting themselves. Along with complaining about welfare dependency and violent crime, more and more whites have come out against preferential programs, and increasingly condemn blacks for casting their race as victims who have no control over their condition. In the same vein, white Americans are franker to admit their support for racial barriers, all the while denying that they have gained any advantages because they are white. More typically, they describe themselves as bystanders, who must watch while their country is held hostage by a demanding minority. In their view, the behavior of blacks is a major explanation for what ails America.

One of the two major parties—the Republicans—has all but explicitly stated that it is willing to have itself regarded as a white party, prepared to represent white Americans and defend their interests. Of course, Republican administrations make sure that they appoint a few black officials, either vocal conservatives or taciturn moderates willing to remain in the background. (And they were especially adroit in finding apt candidates for the Supreme Court and Chairman of the Joint Chiefs of Staff.) An unwritten plank in the party's strategy is that it can win the offices it wants without black votes. More than that, by sending a message that it neither wants nor needs ballots cast by blacks, it feels it can attract even more votes from a much larger pool of white Americans who want a party willing to represent their racial identity.

By the close of 1992, twenty of the preceding twenty-four years will have been an era of Republican hegemony. Even Jimmy Carter's single term served as an interlude for enlarging the Republicans' constituency. And while the Congress theoretically remains in Democratic hands, on racial matters it cannot muster enough power to challenge Republican presidencies. At best, it must content itself with rearguard actions, like clarifying the grounds for redress in discrimination suits.

A politics purposively permeated by race has consolidated enough white Americans as a self-conscious racial majority. This is not to say that they are bigots or reactionaries. It is rather that they feel threatened, not always in ways they understand. But what, precisely, is the threat? After all, the United States is not South Africa, where whites are heavily outnumbered by indigenous blacks, who might mobilize their strength to dominate the society.

Of course, there is fear of crime. It crops up in every poll, and has become a conversational staple. Still, most white Americans do not live in or near areas where violence stalks the streets. Nor are many whites in situations where they may fail to obtain positions or promotions due to preferential policies favoring black applicants. Nor does a significant share of the taxes paid by white householders support black families on welfare or out-of-wedlock children.

How, then, can a minority so unsettle a national majority? One source of anxiety, is what is seen as an increasingly obtrusive presence of black people in places where they do not belong. Whether as teenagers on the streets or militants on college campuses, blacks are regarded as unduly arrogant and outwearing their welcome. Taken together, whites see their country as being despoiled by persons who lack either the quality or qualifications for the positions they claim.

Apart from some blatant Willie Horton episodes, racial references tend to be conveyed in nuances and codes, including allusions to crime and comments on quotas. In his 1990 campaign for another Senate term, Jesse Helms of North Carolina confined his overtures to white voters. "You needed that job, and you were the best qualified," one of his commercials ran. "But it had to go to a minority because of a racial quota." White voters from all regions and classes have little trouble intuiting where candidates like Helms stand. What makes these efforts easier is that each year the electorate grows more middle class, more middle-aged, and increasingly suburban. If and when its rolls need expanding, the white majority is ready to absorb upwardly mobile Hispanics and Asians, who are already being encouraged to separate and differentiate themselves from black Americans.

But, it may be protested, any talk of a unified "white" outlook makes very little sense. Some 200 million Americans answer to that description, and they represent a wide range of origins and hold diverse views on race. Indeed, as an earlier chapter pointed out, since "white" people comprise so large and varied a group, they display little of the political and cultural coherence associated with the "black" community.

When Alexis de Tocqueville visited the United States in the 1830s, he referred to his hosts as "Anglo-Americans," since the great majority then claimed British origins. However, soon thereafter that designation became inapplicable, since with the advent of other immigrants, America became a miscellany of ethnic groups. Yet as a matter of fact, and as earlier chapters made clear, each year finds less ethnic emphasis and diversity among and within white Americans. Whole stretches of the country, most especially the suburbs, are now close to being generically white. In many major particulars, white Americans have reverted to Tocqueville's "Anglo-American" model.

This is not to assert that white Americans spend much of their time musing about their "whiteness" in an open way. Still, the emphasis placed on race by Republican candidates and administrations embodies just that aim. It wants to remind white people how much they have invested in maintaining the status of their race. Thus the attacks on affirmative action suggest that these policies will diminish the benefits of being white for those who have always believed that they could take that advantage for granted.*

The way people cast their ballots often provides an index of how they think and feel about race. These sentiments usually surface in contests that find black and white candidates opposing one another. As it happens, in most such elections, most black voters support the black contender and most whites line up behind the white. Of course, the colors of the candidates are not the only variables at work. Ideology always plays a role, as do party labels and impressions of personality and character. So if a white person does not vote for a black candidate, it should not automatically be concluded that race was the reason.

At the same time, we know that many citizens feel contented and comfortable when they see persons of their origin holding public office. This has long been the role of "ethnic politics": recent citizens feel they have come closer to acceptance when members of their

* Of course, race is not the only exacerbating issue. Republican support for the "right to life" coalition has much in common with contriving an omnibus "whiteness." In a similar way, anti-abortion rallies bring together Roman Catholics, Fundamentalist Protestants, Mormons, and Orthodox Jews. What binds these activists is a belief in their moral superiority. Nor is it surprising that those most actively opposing abortion are almost entirely white.

group get honors and recognition. So it is hardly unusual that black Americans want to have fellow blacks in governmental positions. (Whether the same reasoning can be applied to whites voting for whites will be examined shortly.)

In politics, as in other areas, black behavior has been put on display. Blacks who get elected to office receive extra scrutiny, if only to see how they will conduct themselves once power is in their hands. Hence, too, the murmurings among whites that black voters sometimes seem to settle for representatives with less-than-shining credentials. Whites have also been heard to complain that blacks appear unwilling to condemn dubious behavior on the part of "their" politicians, or at least will not do so in racially mixed circles. These and similar remarks suggest that blacks need white counseling, as if they were somehow unaware of their own interests. In fact, it makes sense for members of a racial minority to pull together. Blacks have had a long history of being divided and conquered, especially in the white media, and this practice persists. Indeed, as many black Americans see it, whites take a special delight in dissecting and exploiting differences among blacks.

If black citizens have a chance to vote for some of their race, they often do so with enthusiasm. When David Dinkins ran for mayor of New York City in 1989, polls found that 91 percent of the black voters gave him their support. Surveys showed that when Douglas Wilder sought the governorship of Virginia that year, he received 95 percent of the black votes. And in the thirty states where Jesse Jackson competed for the Democratic nomination in 1988, he attracted 92 percent of the ballots cast by blacks. Figures like these make it clear that even if some black voters had mixed feelings about Dinkins or Wilder or Jackson, they very much wanted those men to win. At the same time, Dinkins and Wilder were both Democrats running against Republicans. And for more than half a century, the overwhelming majority of black voters have been loyal Democrats. Indeed, black voters have also turned out for white Democrats at much the same rate as they do for candidates of their own race. So it is appropriate to ask how far, if at all, voting by blacks can be said to be race-based.

A good test can be found in Michigan's 1986 contest for governor. That year the Republican party nominated a black man, the sheriff of

Wayne County, to run against James Blanchard, the white Democrat who was seeking reelection. For as long as most people can remember, Michigan's black residents have usually voted Democratic by overwhelming margins. So the nomination of William Lucas by the Republicans would reveal whether or how far race might outweigh party loyalty.

As it turned out, the Democrat won handily with 68 percent of the overall vote. (Four years later, his margin had been a thin 51 percent.) A *Detroit News* survey showed how voters of the two races divided their ballots. It found that 20 percent of the black voters had supported Lucas, whereas in previous elections, Republicans were lucky to get ten percent of Michigan's black votes. But at least equally striking was the survey's finding that over three-quarters of the black voters gave their ballots to a white candidate for governor. Indeed, black Americans have always cast most of their votes for white candidates, since in most elections only whites are running. Yet there has been little reciprocity from whites when black aspirants seek office.

Indeed, many of Michigan's white Republicans openly abandoned Lucas, and crossed over to Blanchard for this election; they seemed to be saying that despite their usual partisan allegiance, they would rather vote for a white Democrat than a black Republican. Thus, more whites than blacks ended up voting on the basis of race.

Three years later, similar sentiments were displayed in New York City, when David Dinkins ran for Mayor. Historically, New York has been a Democratic stronghold, mustering majorities even for lackluster candidates like Walter Mondale and Michael Dukakis. However in 1989, over 70 percent of the white voters—most of them regular Democrats—supported Dinkins' Republican opponent, producing an unprecedented percentage for that party. It was not surprising that many voters of Italian origin chose to back a candidate named Rudolph Giuliani. But so did 63 percent of the Jewish voters, as well as 62 percent of New Yorkers with postgraduate degrees. No segment of white voters gave more than 36 percent of its votes to David Dinkins. He won only because blacks and Hispanics turned out in greater than customary numbers.

As was noted earlier, it can be understood if blacks—or Jews or Mormons or Italian-Americans—want to see people of their origins holding office. However, it is less easy to contend that white Americans taken together constitute a "group" whose members share common characteristics and origins. So when whites vote for fellow whites, their reasons are not strictly analogous to those that impel blacks to vote for blacks.

Of course, when white voters support the white candidate in an interracial contest, it is perfectly possible to argue that they can do so for other than racial reasons. In 1983, many Chicago voters said they would not support Harold Washington because of problems related to his personal finances. In New York's 1989 mayoral election, similar comments were heard concerning David Dinkins. In politics, as elsewhere, few of us want to reveal our real motives, whether to interviewers or even to ourselves. So we should not expect many white Americans to openly attest that they are supporting a white candidate simply because they do not want the black contender to win. But a more critical concern is that they fear what may happen if or when blacks gain political power.

When black citizens have an opportunity to vote for someone of their race, they do so in the expectation that if that candidate wins, he or she will form a "black" administration, or at least one that will be more visibly multiracial. It would certainly mean more blacks holding high positions, who would formulate policies more attuned to the needs of black citizens.

For many whites, such prospects can generate alarm. These fears rise to the surface when, in the course of a campaign, white voters hear—or think they hear—blacks saying, "It's our turn." These words are interpreted as meaning that whites have heretofore run the city; now blacks want that power.

Behind these imaginings, of course, is the dread that blacks will treat whites as whites have treated blacks. Louis Farrakhan once said as much: "You fear we'll do to you what you did to us." Here the fears of white Americans and white South Africans share some common ground. To both, "our turn" means turning the tables. Indeed, this reaction suggests that whites are far from unaware of the inequities blacks have suffered at white hands.

Is this to say that even middle-aged gentlemen like David Dinkins and Douglas Wilder rouse such anxieties? The answer is they can, at least among voters who choose to look less at the candidates themselves than at a racial power they appear to represent. These fears have already helped to redefine the Democratic party. The increased visibility of black men and women in its councils has some bearing on the fact that none of its presidential candidates has won a majority of the white electorate since Lyndon Johnson's victory in 1964.

Whether the Democrats are becoming a "black" party will be less settled by statistics than in white perceptions. At its 1988 convention, 20 percent of the delegates were black, a fact that became quite apparent as television cameras swept across the hall. The presence of Jesse Jackson augmented that impression, as did the choice of Ronald Brown as national chairman. To many white voters, the Democrats now look sufficiently "black" to make them think twice about supporting its candidates. As has been noted, the Republicans have been happy to build on these beliefs.

There are several cities and—thus far—one state that have predominantly white populations, where blacks have not only run for office but have defeated white opponents. Indeed, this has sometimes come about because a majority of the white voters supported the black candidate. The first such election took place in Los Angeles in 1973, when Tom Bradley was elected mayor mainly with white votes, at a time when the city's population was less than 20 percent black. (Carl Stokes became mayor of Cleveland six years earlier, but in that election most of the city's whites backed his opponent.) More recently, in 1989, in Seattle and New Haven, black mayoral candidates defeated white opponents with 58 percent and 68 percent of the votes, in both cases winning majority support from whites. In 1991, in Kansas City, Missouri, where only about a quarter of the electorate is black, a black clergyman won over a white businessman in the contest for mayor. Kansas City also has a black member in the House of Representatives, from a largely white district. And, in 1990, an almost entirely white district in Connecticut elected a black man to Congress on the Republican ticket. The table on the next page shows that Southern and Northern cities, like Roanoke in Virginia and Rockford in Illinois, have chosen black mayors even though their populations are dominantly white.

Perhaps white voters in these areas are more liberal or open-minded than whites elsewhere. In fact, the major determinant of white support is how black politicians are perceived by the white electorate. In part, this depends on the candidate's actual views and

BLACK POPULATIONS OF CITIES THAT HAVE ELECTED BLACK MAYORS

City	%
Detroit	75.7%
Atlanta	66.6%
Washington, D.C.	65.8%
Birmingham	63.3%
New Orleans	61.9%
Baltimore	59.2%
Newark	58.5%
Memphis	54.8%
Camden	56.4%
Cleveland	46.6%
Oakland	43.9%
Dayton	40.4%
Philadelphia	39.8%
Chicago	39.1%
Hartford	38.9%
New Haven	36.1%
Newport News	33.6%
Charlotte	31.8%
Kansas City	29.6%
Tallahassee	29.1%
New York	28.7%
Roanoke	24.3%
Rockford	15.0%
Los Angeles	14.0%
Denver	12.8%
Seattle	10.1%

attributes. However, the more crucial characteristics are those whites decide to impute to blacks who are running for office. In Kansas City and Seattle, cities with comparatively few black residents, the black candidates tended to be seen as persons in their own right, rather than as representing a racial constituency. This was certainly so with Edward Brooke, Massachusetts' Republican senator from 1967 until 1979, when blacks numbered only about 3 percent of the state's population.

Thus far, black candidates who gain white support have come from middle-class backgrounds and display a middle-class demeanor. Julian Bond and Andrew Young in Georgia fit this description, as does Kurt Schmoke, a former Rhodes Scholar who became Baltimore's mayor. Michael White, who won the mayoralty of Cleveland in 1989, had been elected president of the largely white student body at Ohio State University. Others are also respectably middle-aged, having devoted many years to building careers in public life. This certainly describes Douglas Wilder of Virginia and David Dinkins in New York. While they are undeniably "black," to many whites they seem more "colored," as evidenced by the ease with which they move within the white world. And even when they allude to injustices their people have suffered, they do so without a bitterness and rancor that tends to unsettle whites. In some cases, they will make an explicit point of dissociating themselves from figures who speak in a sharper voice. Thus David Dinkins explicitly repudiated Louis Farrakhan, while Douglas Wilder let Jesse Jackson know that he did not want him sojourning in Virginia during his campaign.

These individuals have been called "crossover" politicians, since they make a frank appeal for white votes. Quite obviously, they must tread a fine line. While they cannot ignore their home base, they have to hope it will remain loyal, since they must spend most of their time courting white votes. Indeed, the thrust of their campaigns has to center on allaying white anxieties. They must come close to presenting themselves as if they had no black connections, and certainly not as aspiring to represent "black power." There are even risks in taking time off to address an all-black meeting. With television turning everywhere, the sight of cheering black supporters could induce tremors in white viewers.

For at least a generation, all three branches of government have sought to raise the representation of black Americans in elected positions. As it happens, Republicans have joined with Democrats in this effort, although for quite different reasons. The Federal Voting Rights Act, enacted in 1965, was intended to oversee Southern states and localities, due to that region's history of preventing its black citizens from voting. The Civil Rights Division of the Justice Department was empowered to intervene when and where it believed the number of black voters to be suspiciously low. While tests and threats are no longer employed, a new set of concerns has amplified the voting rights issue. Now the question is not whether black citizens can register and vote, but what results they secure when they do cast their ballots.

A 1982 amendment to the Voting Rights Act provides that the

Justice Department may also take action if it suspects that members of any racial group

> have less opportunity than other members of the electorate to participate in the political process and to elect representatives of their choice.

This proviso deserves close examination. If black citizens no longer face barriers to voting, how might they still have "less opportunity" than, say, whites when it comes to their capacity "to participate in the political process"? And what might be thwarting them from being able "to elect representatives of their choice"?

So long as all electoral districts have approximately the same populations, as they now tend to do, all voters and their votes would seem to have the same weight and worth. Of course, it is possible to draw district lines so that the votes cast for one party end up electing more of its candidates to office. By the same token, many of the other party's votes will be "wasted," by bunching that party's supporters in certain districts, giving their winning candidates unnecessarily large majorities. This is the venerable art of gerrymandering, which has been given new life as computers fine-tune district lines. But if gerrymandering aims at giving one political party an edge, the Voting Act's reference to "representatives of their choice" has an additional meaning where race is involved.

A complaint of many black voters is that even now, they are overwhelmingly governed by white people. Not only has every President of the United States been white, but so is every current senator and all but one of the governors; in addition, almost three quarters of all black citizens live in districts that have white representatives in the Congress.

It is the view of many black citizens that they lack "representatives of their choice," since it is not their choice to have laws made in their name by white officeholders. Even if they voted for the whites who won, in many cases they would rather be represented by a person of their own race. Many whites feel the same way; but it is not a bothersome issue, since almost all of them have white representatives. So in terms of equity, it could be concluded that because of the way the system works, black voters have fewer opportunities than whites to cast ballots that will give them "representatives of their choice." On this reasoning, having the right to vote is not enough. It should also be a vote that achieves a desired result. Hence the feeling that electoral systems should be rearranged so that black Americans will be able to put more people of their race in office.

On this matter, if not others, Justice Department officials in the Reagan and Bush administrations have been willing to aid black Americans. Federal lawyers have filed a succession of suits ordering states and localities to create new constituencies with predominantly black populations, with the aim of winning more seats for black candidates. Nor is this strategy pursued only in the courts. In several state legislatures, Republican members have offered to use their influence to increase the number of solidly black seats. Some have even made computer programs available to assist in this effort.

Insofar as black voters want their representation increased by districts drawn primarily by race, it could be seen as another step toward racial isolation. Why, some white commentators have asked, must the effectiveness of legislators be judged by the colors of their skins? The response to this question is that under the ideal of integration, blacks end up as a powerless minority in white-dominated settings. So since residential segregation already exists, why not use it to strengthen the role of blacks in politics?

Of course, there should be no mystery as to why Republicans have favored the drawing of dominantly black districts. Since black Americans tend to support the Democratic party, heavy majorities in more of these constituencies would dissipate Democratic strength. Gerrymandering based on race would also serve to scatter white Democratic voters among districts with Republican majorities. In exchange for helping to elect a few more black representatives, the Republicans hope to decrease the delegations of white Democrats.

Efforts to ensure race-based results have taken other forms as well. One involves challenging at-large elections and those involving multimember constituencies. For example, some cities and school districts have at-large elections for their lawmaking bodies or boards of education. When, say, eight seats are to be filled, each voter may check that many names from a larger list of candidates, and the eight persons with the most votes win. Some states have also had systems for electing several judges or a group of legislators from a single large district. Here, too, those getting the most votes are declared elected.

These arrangements have been contested on the grounds that they produce racially discriminatory results. Put very simply, black candidates on the list of candidates are less likely to win in at-large elections and multimember districts. The reasons have to do with demography and discrimination. In most cities and counties and larger districts within states, blacks make up only a minority of the residents. So if black candidates enter, they need to attract considerable numbers of white votes if they hope to end up among the winners. Unfortunately, in most areas using at-large and multimember systems, not enough whites have been willing to give their votes to black contenders. As a result, all-white slates usually get elected. The Justice Department has therefore filed suits demanding that these systems be replaced with single-member districts, with the added warning that one or more should have enough black residents to ensure that "representatives of their choice" will end up in office.

One further reform warrants mention. In Southern and border states, as well as some Northern cities, obtaining the Democratic nomination often ensures victory at the general election. Because it is an important balloting, most Democratic primaries have several candidates seeking their party's nomination for mayor or governor, or other state or city offices. Fairly frequently, there will be a single black candidate on the ballot, while all the others are white. In more than a few of these cases, after the ballots have been counted, it emerges that the black candidate heads the list with something like 42 percent of the votes, while the three whites have divided up the other 58 percent.

At this point, two options are available. The first, which is more generally used, is to call the voters back for a runoff primary. Since this second balloting eliminates all but the two front-runners, it will pit the black candidate against the top white contender. However, growing numbers of black voters have found themselves frustrated by the runoff system. And with good reason. Their experience has been that if a black candidate gets 42 percent of the votes in the initial primary, he will be unlikely to pick up many new votes in the second go-round. The reason is that at the runoff stage, supporters of the eliminated white candidates will rally around the remaining white contender, supplying him with the necessary majority. Because black candidates seldom win in runoffs, it has been contended that a two-stage system also denies black voters a fair chance "to elect representatives of their choice."

Many Republicans, including Justice Department officials, favor the idea of compelling the Democrats to abandon runoff primaries. Nor should this be surprising. If black front-runners can secure Democratic nominations with only 40 percent of the ballots, come the November election, Republican candidates will be able to attract many of the white Democrats who had supported the white contenders in the earlier primary.

Many whites aligned with the Democratic party believe that the overall liberal cause will suffer if more predominantly black districts are created. The point is not, they emphasize, that the blacks who are elected to office will not do as good a job as the whites they replace. Rather, they argue, concentrating black votes will put at risk seats that might have gone to white liberals. The consequence will be to strengthen the representation of Republicans and conservatives. And if blacks insist on obtaining Democratic nominations with 40 percent of the ballots, the result will also be more Republican victories. In reply, black voters may ask why they should be the ones to sacrifice in order to hold conservatives at bay.

Black Americans prefer to define their own interests in their own ways, and having more of their own people in office now has high priority. Increasing the number of black lawmakers, even if they come mainly from predominantly black districts, should strengthen black political power at all governmental levels. Black caucuses can expand their influence if their members act in concert and are prepared to strike deals with other interests. But to become a pivotal force, such groups must be prepared to act as a balance of power, which also means being ready to play on white divisions. These tactics call for a combination of sophistication and discipline, and are certainly worth a try. What dividends they will yield remains to be seen. As was noted in the opening of this chapter, on matters of major concern to blacks, white America is no longer in a mood to give very much away.

As hardly needs detailing, black political power is most visible in cities that have large poor populations and a declining economic base. Black mayors, black police chiefs, and black agency heads find themselves confronted with problems seldom faced by their white predecessors. Despite promises of becoming showcases of self-help, all too many cities have drifted into decay and dependency. While Detroit and Atlanta and Baltimore have plenty of decent and hard-working citizens, what they can contribute is overwhelmed by those around them who seem unable to make it on their own.

With economic investment going to the suburbs—or distant states or overseas—fewer and fewer central cities can cover their costs through local taxes. Federal administrations have taken the view that they reap little benefit by propping up declining cities. State legislators, who come largely from small towns and suburbs, cannot be counted on to sympathize with a terrain they seldom visit and do not care to know. Admittedly, many white communities are poor, due to loss of industries or population or because they were never very productive. But since their misfortunes are not placed in a racial context, they often end up with proportionately more aid than urban dwellers.

Politics worked well in the early struggles for civil rights: the right to vote, fair treatment in the courts, and entry to hotels and restaurants and other public accommodations. But after those victories, those concerned with racial redress began to talk of more radical measures. Debates over affirmative action, of qualifications versus quotas, deflect attention from more chronic disparities; in fact, that may be their purpose. At issue is whether government can or will commit itself to so raise black Americans that they will stand on a social and economic parity with members of other races.

In a not-so-distant past, a great deal was said about the need for "massive" infusions of cash to remedy the ills resulting from poverty and racial inequity. To Lyndon Johnson's "War on Poverty" were added calls for a domestic "Marshall Plan," which would devote billions in public dollars to inner cities and other impoverished areas. But today such proposals are seldom heard. The chief reason is that few white Americans feel an obligation to make further sacrifices on behalf of the nation's black minority. They see themselves as already overtaxed; feel the fault is not theirs; and that money cannot achieve a cure. About the only funding the public approves is for more police and prisons.

Nor is it a lack of leadership or a failure of will that has made common action so remote. The reasons rest with a past that has shaped our present; and a present that makes use of that past. Race has made America its prisoner since the first chattels were landed on these shores. So the causes of disharmony run deeper than the condition of the parties, or the capacities of government. A nation that has done so much to stress racial divisions should not be surprised if the result is not compassion and fellow feeling, but withdrawal and recriminations.

As was noted in the Preface of the book, Gunnar Myrdal saw America beset by a social and moral paradox. Of all the world's nations, the United States speaks eloquently of universal justice and equal opportunity. Yet its treatment of its principal minority belies those basic commitments. But it may have been that Myrdal misread America's ideals. Alexis de Tocqueville, an earlier visitor, heard the same professions about equity and equality. However, he soon concluded that they were never intended to apply to members of the black race. White Americans, he observed, "scarcely acknowledge the common features of humanity in this stranger whom slavery has brought among them." Nor, Tocqueville added, would this racism disappear once slavery ended. In fact, he predicted, "the abolition of slavery will, in the common course of things, increase, the repugnance of the white population for the blacks." The analysis in *Democracy in America,* reproduced below, found racial enmities so ingrained they would plague the future as they had haunted the past. His observations, set down a century and a half ago, might have been written today.

White Americans, Tocqueville noted, could countenance slavery only by persuading themselves that human beings of African origin were inherently "inferior to the other races of mankind" and hence suited for bondage. This view, so firmly entrenched, would persist after emancipation. "You may set the Negro free," he told his American readers, "but you cannot make him otherwise than an alien to those of European origin." So citizenship for black Americans would always be shadowed by their past; they would ever remain aliens among the nation's native-born inhabitants.

Sooner or later, Tocqueville said black Americans would "revolt at being deprived of almost all their civil rights." And by this he meant not just legal entitlements, but social and economic parity. Hence the visitor's final forecast, which haunts all phases of current life, from party politics to violent crime: "The danger of a conflict be-

ALEXIS DE TOCQUEVILLE ON THE RACES IN AMERICA

- The most formidable of all the ills that threaten the future of the Union arises from the presence of a black population upon its territory.

  The whites and the blacks are placed in the situation of two foreign communities. These two races are fastened to each other without intermingling; and they are unable to separate entirely or to combine.

- The Europeans chose their slaves from a race differing from their own, which many of them considered as inferior to the other races of mankind. Nor is this all: they scarcely acknowledge the common features of humanity in this stranger whom slavery has brought among them.

  Although the law may abolish slavery, God alone can obliterate the traces of its existence. You may set the Negro free, but you cannot make him otherwise than an alien to those of European origin.

- White Americans first violated every right of humanity by their treatment of the Negro. But with his liberty, he will acquire a degree of instruction that will enable him to appreciate his misfortunes and to discern a remedy for them.

  If the Negroes are to be raised to the level of freemen, they will soon revolt at being deprived of almost all their civil rights. And as they cannot become the equals of the whites, they will speedily show themselves as enemies.

- If I were called upon to predict the future, I should say that the abolition of slavery will, in the common course of things, increase the repugnance of the white population for the blacks.

  The danger of a conflict between the white and the black inhabitants perpetually haunts the imagination of the Americans, like a painful dream.

tween the white and the black inhabitants perpetually haunts the imagination of the Americans, like a painful dream."

Alexis de Tocqueville knew that relations between the races—or their lack—are not formed in isolation. If race figures so centrally in the life of the United States, it has much to do with the kind of country America is and has been from its start. A combination of forces has served to heighten racial awareness and exacerbate tensions.

America is hardly the only nation to perpetuate racial prejudice and ethnic bigotry. Nor is it the worst by most objective measures. Even today, in Ireland and Lebanon, Ethiopia or Sri Lanka, people are marked for slaughter because of tribal animosities and religious rivalries. Throughout Europe, the arrival of immigrants of African descent has generated new tensions, many of them strikingly similar to those long known in the United States.

Still, the United States considers itself more socially advanced than Lebanon and Sri Lanka, which means it sets a higher standard for human life and racial harmony. Most Americans are not especially surprised when they hear of groups murdering one another in Third World countries. Even compared with Europe, the United States has always prided itself on emphasizing equal treatment and social mobility. Given these aims and ideals, the United States carries a greater obligation to achieve amity and equity in relations between the races. The fact that it remains so far from its own goals, justifies its subjection to scrutiny and vulnerability to censure.

If America is short on excuses, it has no lack of explanations, most of them centering on its special history and circumstances. As was noted, to expect tolerance and fellow feeling from white Americans is to ask a great deal, considering the competitive pressures pervading their lives.

Hence the weight Americans have chosen to give to race, in particular to the artifact of "whiteness," which sets a floor on how far people of that complexion can fall. No matter how degraded their lives, white people are still allowed to believe that they possess the blood, the genes, the patrimony of superiority. No matter what happens, they can never become "black." White Americans of all classes have found it comforting to preserve blacks as a subordinate caste: a presence, which despite all its pain and problems, still provides whites with some solace in a stressful world.

In the end, there remains the question of responsibility. The American tradition has said that all individuals are expected to make it on their own. Both the earliest settlers and current immigrants have known they had to enter the competition and create lives for themselves. Demands for special dispensations have never stirred much sympathy or support. (Even the Freedman's Bureau, set up after the Civil War, had a brief and controversial history.) So most white Americans feel it is time for blacks to put their lives together and make what they can of themselves. They should muster the will to stay in school and gain the skills needed in today's economy. They can avoid having children they cannot support, just as they can steer clear of pursuits that end in self-destructive spirals.

Just to cite a single example: black youths have taken to carrying guns and firing them at one another, making homicide the most frequent cause of death among young men of their race. In part, these deaths are ways of settling scores within the drug industry, much as bootleggers dealt with competitors during Prohibition. More frightening are killings that result from random arguments or perceived disrespect. Not to mention scattered shots from rooftops or cars, which end up hitting children on the street. These would certainly seem to be acts for which the perpetrators should be held strictly responsible. How can the blame for such mayhem be laid at the door of white racism?

Yet it may also be asked *why* so many young men are engaging in what amounts to a self-inflicted genocide. While in one sense these are "free" acts, performed of personal volition, when they become so widespread, they must also be seen as expressing a despair that suffuses much of their race. These are young men who do not know whether they will live another year, and many have given up caring. If they are prepared to waste the lives of others, they will hardly be surprised if their turn comes next. No other American race is wounding itself so fatally. Nor can it be said that black Americans chose this path for themselves.

So in allocating responsibility, the response should be clear. It is white America that has made being black so disconsolate an estate. Legal slavery may be in the past, but segregation and subordination have been allowed to persist. Even today, America imposes a stigma on every black child at birth.

Of course, life can be unfair. We cannot vouchsafe that every infant will be born with sight or hearing or the full use of his or her limbs. However, not all disabilities derive from nature; many are contrived by society. Some have argued that black Americans deserve reparations for their centuries of bondage and subjection. That is what the argument about affirmative action is essentially about. Others claim that ratifying their status as victims will only perpetuate condescension and subordination. Moreover, it insults the many black Americans who have surmounted the most daunting of obstacles, and made decent lives for themselves.

A huge racial chasm remains, and there are few signs that the coming century will see it closed. A century and a quarter after slavery, white America continues to ask of its black citizens an extra patience and perseverance that whites have never required of themselves. So the question for white Americans is essentially moral: is it right to impose on members of an entire race a lesser start in life, and then to expect from them a degree of resolution that has never been demanded from your own race?

PART THREE

STATISTICAL SOURCES

Most of the statistical materials in *Two Nations* come from official sources. Where possible, preliminary figures from the 1990 census have been used. But because most census reports will not be available until late 1992 or even 1993, an alternative source has been the Current Population Survey, which is based on monthly interviews with some 65,000 households. These include studies of household income, family arrangements, child support payments, criminal victimization, educational attainment, and fertility expectations. In every instance, figures used in this book have been the most recent available. And in one or two cases, where figures still seem applicable, data from the 1980 census has been drawn on.

Other tables have been derived from reports issued by the Bureau of Labor Statistics, the Bureau of Justice Statistics, the National Center for Education Statistics, and the National Center for Health Statistics, as well as documents from the Department of Health and Human Services.

Some government publications place persons of Hispanic origin within the black and white racial groupings. Others put them in a separate category, to differentiate them from blacks and whites. Wherever the sources permit, *Two Nations* has separated out Hispanics, to keep the book's emphasis on race as coherent as possible. Where this has not been possible, readers should bear in mind that the figures for whites may be inflated by the inclusion of considerable numbers of Hispanics.

The 1990 census, like all of its predecessors, failed to find many of the people residing in this country. Most demographers agree that something like 5.25 million persons should be added to the reported total of 248,709,873. So while the official count puts blacks at 12.1 percent of the population, in reality they come closer to 12.4 percent. For editorial reasons, *Two Nations* has used the 12.1 percent figure. Where this is done, readers may want to make their own mental adjustments.

The following section contains additional tables that would have burdened the textual chapters of this book. They are provided for readers who want further statistical insights and more detailed information.

RACIAL AND HISPANIC POPULATIONS IN EACH STATE: 1970 AND 1990

	1970	1990	1970	1990	1970	1990
	Alabama		Alaska		Arizona	
White	72.8%	73.3%	77.5%	73.9%	76.1%	71.7%
Black	25.9%	25.2%	2.9%	4.0%	2.9%	2.8%
Hispanic	1.1%	0.6%	1.5%	3.2%	14.9%	18.8%
Other	0.2%	0.9%	18.1%	18.9%	6.1%	6.7%
	Arkansas		California		Colorado	
White	80.4%	82.2%	77.5%	57.3%	85.7%	80.7%
Black	18.1%	15.9%	6.9%	7.0%	2.9%	3.9%
Hispanic	1.3%	0.8%	11.9%	25.8%	10.2%	12.9%
Other	0.2%	1.1%	3.7%	9.9%	1.2%	2.5%
	Connecticut		Delaware		Florida	
White	91.4%	83.9%	83.8%	79.2%	78.6%	73.3%
Black	5.9%	7.9%	14.1%	16.7%	15.0%	13.1%
Hispanic	2.2%	6.4%	1.5%	2.4%	6.0%	12.2%
Other	0.5%	1.8%	0.6%	1.7%	0.4%	1.4%
	Georgia		Hawaii		Idaho	
White	73.2%	70.1%	36.7%	31.4%	95.8%	92.2%
Black	25.6%	26.8%	0.9%	2.3%	0.3%	0.3%
Hispanic	1.0%	1.7%	3.2%	7.3%	2.3%	5.3%
Other	0.2%	1.4%	59.2%	59.0%	1.6%	2.2%
	Illinois		Indiana		Iowa	
White	83.2%	74.9%	90.8%	89.6%	97.9%	95.9%
Black	12.6%	14.6%	6.7%	7.7%	1.1%	1.7%
Hispanic	3.5%	7.9%	2.2%	1.8%	0.7%	1.2%
Other	0.7%%	2.6%	0.3%	0.9%	0.3%	1.2%
	Kansas		Kentucky		Louisiana	
White	92.2%	88.4%	91.3%	91.7%	68.3%	65.8%
Black	4.7%	5.7%	7.1%	7.1%	29.5%	30.6%
Hispanic	2.4%	3.8%	1.4%	0.6%	1.9%	2.2%
Other	0.7%	2.1%	0.2%	0.6%	0.3%	1.4%
	Maine		Maryland		Massachusetts	
White	99.1%	98.0%	80.4%	69.6%	95.2%	87.7%
Black	0.3%	0.4%	17.7%	24.6%	3.0%	4.6%
Hispanic	0.2%	0.6%	1.2%	2.6%	1.2%	4.8%
Other	0.4%	1.0%	0.7%	3.2%	0.6%	2.9%
	Michigan		Minnesota		Mississippi	
White	86.8%	82.2%	97.2%	93.8%	62.4%	63.2%
Black	11.0%	13.9%	0.9%	2.1%	36.5%	35.4%
Hispanic	1.7%	2.2%	1.0%	1.2%	0.7%	0.6%
Other	0.5%	1.7%	0.9%	2.9%	0.4%	0.8%
	Missouri		Montana		Nebraska	
White	88.2%	86.9%	94.6%	91.8%	95.2%	92.5%
Black	10.1%	10.7%	0.3%	0.3%	2.7%	3.6%
Hispanic	1.3%	1.2%	1.0%	1.5%	1.4%	2.3%
Other	0.4%	1.2%	4.1%	6.4%	0.7%	1.6%

RACIAL AND HISPANIC POPULATIONS IN EACH STATE: 1970 AND 1990

	1970	1990	1970	1990	1970	1990
	Nevada		**New Hampshire**		**New Jersey**	
White	87.5%	78.7%	99.1%	97.3%	84.9%	74.0%
Black	5.7%	6.4%	0.3%	0.6%	10.5%	12.7%
Hispanic	4.2%	10.4%	0.3%	1.0%	4.0%	9.6%
Other	2.6%	4.5%	0.3%	1.1%	0.6%	3.7%
	New Mexico		**New York**		**North Carolina**	
White	60.1%	50.5%	80.5%	69.3%	76.1%	75.0%
Black	1.9%	1.8%	11.0%	14.3%	22.0%	21.9%
Hispanic	30.3%	38.2%	7.4%	12.3%	0.9%	1.1%
Other	7.7%	9.5%	1.1%	4.1%	1.0%	2.0%
	North Dakota		**Ohio**		**Oklahoma**	
White	96.7%	94.2%	89.5%	87.0%	87.3%	81.0%
Black	0.4%	0.5%	9.0%	10.6%	6.6%	7.4%
Hispanic	0.4%	0.7%	1.2%	1.3%	2.0%	2.7%
Other	2.5%	4.6%	0.3%	1.1%	4.1%	8.9%
	Oregon		**Pennsylvania**		**Rhode Island**	
White	96.0%	90.7%	90.3%	87.7%	95.9%	89.3%
Black	1.3%	1.6%	8.5%	9.0%	2.6%	3.4%
Hispanic	1.1%	4.0%	0.9%	2.0%	0.8%	4.6%
Other	1.6%	3.7%	0.3%	1.3%	0.7%	2.7%
	South Carolina		**South Dakota**		**Tennessee**	
White	68.9%	68.5%	94.4%	91.2%	83.0%	82.6%
Black	30.4%	29.7%	0.2%	0.4%	15.5%	15.9%
Hispanic	0.5%	0.9%	0.4%	0.8%	1.3%	0.7%
Other	0.2%	0.9%	5.0%	7.6%	0.2%	0.8%
	Texas		**Utah**		**Vermont**	
White	70.8%	60.7%	94.3%	91.2%	99.2%	98.1%
Black	12.2%	11.6%	0.6%	0.6%	0.2%	0.3%
Hispanic	16.4%	25.5%	3.2%	4.9%	0.4%	0.7%
Other	0.6%	2.2%	1.9%	3.3%	0.2%	0.9%
	Virginia		**Washington**		**West Virginia**	
White	80.2%	76.0%	93.7%	86.8%	95.4%	95.8%
Black	18.4%	18.6%	2.1%	3.0%	3.9%	3.1%
Hispanic	0.9%	2.6%	1.7%	4.4%	0.5%	0.5%
Other	0.5%	2.8%	2.5%	5.8%	0.2%	0.6%
	Wisconsin		**Wyoming**		**U.S.A.**	
White	95.1%	91.3%	93.0%	90.9%	83.3%	75.3%
Black	2.8%	4.9%	0.8%	0.8%	10.9%	11.9%
Hispanic	1.4%	1.9%	4.2%	5.7%	4.5%	9.0%
Other	0.7%	1.9%	2.0%	2.6%	1.3%	3.8%

POPULATION COMPOSITION: 1790–1990

	Whites	Enslaved Blacks	Free Blacks
1790	80.7%	17.8%	1.5%
1800	81.1%	16.9%	2.0%
1810	81.0%	16.4%	2.6%
1820	81.6%	16.0%	2.4%
1830	81.9%	15.6%	2.5%
1840	83.2%	14.5%	2.3%
1850	84.3%	13.8%	1.9%
1860	85.7%	12.6%	1.7%
	Whites	**Blacks**	**Others***
1870	87.1%	12.7%	0.2%
1880	86.5%	13.1%	0.4%
1890	87.5%	11.9%	0.6%
1900	87.7%	11.6%	0.7%
1910	88.7%	10.7%	0.6%
1920	89.5%	9.9%	0.6%
1930	89.6%	9.7%	0.7%
1940	89.7%	9.8%	0.5%
1950	89.3%	9.9%	0.8%
1960	88.6%	10.5%	0.9%
1970	87.5%	11.1%	1.4%
1980	83.2%	11.7%	5.1%
1990	80.3%	12.1%	7.6%

*Other races were not reported separately until 1860.

RACIAL CHOICES OF HISPANIC AMERICANS: 1990
(Totals = Across)

	White	Black	Other Races	No Race
Florida	80.9%	3.7%	0.7%	14.7%
New Mexico	65.9%	0.4%	1.4%	32.3%
Texas	57.2%	1.0%	0.7%	41.1%
Arizona	49.0%	0.8%	2.5%	47.7%
California	45.5%	1.5%	2.5%	50.5%
New York	41.8%	13.1%	1.8%	43.3%

STATES WITH THE MOST NATIVE AMERICANS AND ASIANS: 1990*

Native Americans		Asians	
Alaska	15.6%	Hawaii	61.8%
New Mexico	8.9%	California	9.6%
Oklahoma	8.0%	Washington	4.3%
South Dakota	7.3%	New York	3.9%
Montana	6.0%	Alaska	3.6%
Arizona	5.6%	New Jersey	3.5%
North Dakota	4.1%	Nevada	3.2%

* Asians includes Pacific Islanders.

STATES: RACIAL RANKINGS

Percentage White		Percentage Black	
Vermont	98.1%	Mississippi	35.4%
Maine	98.0%	Louisiana	30.8%
New Hampshire	97.3%	South Carolina	29.7%
Iowa	95.9%	District of Columbia	27.4%
West Virginia	95.8%	Georgia	26.8%
North Dakota	94.2%	Alabama	25.2%
Minnesota	93.8%	Maryland	24.6%
Nebraska	92.5%	North Carolina	21.9%
Idaho	92.2%	Virginia	18.6%
Montana	91.8%	Delaware	16.7%
Kentucky	91.7%	Arkansas	15.9%
Wisconsin	91.3%	Tennessee	15.9%
South Dakota	91.2%	Illinois	14.6%
Utah	91.2%	New York	14.3%
Wyoming	90.9%	Michigan	13.9%
Oregon	90.7%	Florida	13.1%
Indiana	89.6%	New Jersey	12.7%
Rhode Island	89.3%		
Kansas	88.4%	**U.S.A.**	**11.9%**
Massachusetts	87.7%		
Pennsylvania	87.7%	Texas	11.6%
Ohio	87.0%	Missouri	10.7%
Missouri	86.9%	Ohio	10.6%
Washington	86.8%	Pennsylvania	9.0%
Connecticut	83.9%	Connecticut	7.9%
Tennessee	82.6%	Indiana	7.7%
Michigan	82.2%	Oklahoma	7.4%
Arkansas	82.2%	Kentucky	7.1%
Oklahoma	81.0%	Calfornia	7.0%
Colorado	80.7%	Nevada	6.4%
Delaware	79.2%	Kansas	5.7%
Nevada	78.7%	Wisconsin	4.9%
Virginia	76.0%	Massachusetts	4.6%
		Alaska	4.0%
U.S.A.	**75.3%**	Colorado	3.9%
		Nebraska	3.6%
North Carolina	75.0%	Rhode Island	3.4%
Illinois	74.9%	West Virginia	3.1%
New Jersey	74.0%	Washington	3.0%
Alaska	73.9%	Arizona	2.8%
Alabama	73.3%	Hawaii	2.3%
Florida	73.3%	Minnesota	2.1%
Arizona	71.7%	New Mexico	1.8%
Georgia	70.1%	Iowa	1.7%
Maryland	69.6%	Oregon	1.6%
New York	69.3%	Wyoming	0.8%
South Carolina	68.5%	New Hampshire	0.6%
Louisiana	65.8%	Utah	0.6%
District of Columbia	65.1%	North Dakota	0.5%
Mississippi	63.2%	Maine	0.4%
Texas	60.7%	South Dakota	0.4%
California	57.3%	Idaho	0.3%
New Mexico	50.3%	Montana	0.3%
Hawaii	31.4%	Vermont	0.3%

BLACK POPULATIONS OF CITIES

	1990	1970	1950*
Detroit	75.7%	43.7%	16.4%
Altanta	66.6%	51.3%	36.6%
Washington, D.C.	65.8%	71.1%	35.4%
Birmingham	63.3%	42.0%	39.9%
New Orleans	61.9%	45.0%	32.0%
Baltimore	59.2%	46.4%	23.8%
Newark	58.5%	54.2%	17.2%
Jackson	55.7%	39.7%	27.0%
Richmond	55.2%	42.0%	31.7%
Wilmington	52.4%	43.6%	15.7%
Flint	47.9%	28.1%	8.6%
St. Louis	47.5%	40.9%	18.0%
Cleveland	46.6%	38.3%	16.3%
Philadelphia	39.8%	33.6%	18.3%
Chicago	39.1%	32.7%	14.1%
Norfolk	39.1%	28.3%	29.7%
Hartford	38.9%	27.9%	7.2%
Cincinnati	37.9%	27.6%	15.6%
New Haven	36.1%	26.3%	6.0%
Little Rock	34.0%	25.0%	23.0%
Charlotte	31.8%	30.3%	28.0%
Buffalo	30.7%	20.4%	6.5%
Milwaukee	30.4%	14.7%	3.6%
Louisville	29.7%	23.8%	15.7%
Kansas City, Mo.	29.6%	22.1%	12.3%
Dallas	29.5%	24.9%	13.2%
Kansas City, Kans.	29.3%	20.4%	20.6%
New York City	28.7%	21.1%	9.8%
Houston	28.1%	25.7%	21.1%
Miami	27.4%	22.7%	16.3%
Boston	25.6%	16.3%	5.3%
Tampa	25.0%	19.7%	22.0%
Jacksonville	24.4%	22.3%	35.5%
Indianapolis	22.6%	18.0%	15.0%
Columbus	22.6%	18.5%	12.5%
Oklahoma City	16.0%	13.7%	9.3%
Los Angeles	14.0%	17.9%	10.7%
Omaha	13.1%	9.9%	6.7%
Minneapolis	13.0%	4.4%	1.6%
Denver	12.8%	9.1%	4.4%
Wichita	11.3%	9.7%	5.0%
San Francisco	10.9%	13.4%	10.5%
Seattle	10.1%	7.1%	5.8%
San Diego	9.4%	7.6%	5.5%
Portland	7.7%	5.6%	3.5%
St. Paul	7.4%	3.5%	2.0%
Des Moines	7.1%	5.7%	4.6%
Phoenix	5.2%	4.8%	6.2%
San Jose	4.7%	2.5%	2.2%
Albuquerque	3.0%	2.2%	2.0%

* Percentages for 1950 include other "nonwhites."

BIRTHS TO UNMARRIED WOMEN
Black Percentages as Multiples of White Percentages

Mississippi	5.83
Alabama	5.73
Georgia	5.17
North Carolina	5.09
Michigan	5.00
Louisiana	4.93
Nebraska	4.88
Wisconsin	4.81
South Carolina	4.72
Tennessee	4.65
Illinois	4.62
Arkansas	4.59
Minnesota	4.56
Missouri	4.53
Utah	4.37
Virginia	4.34
Iowa	4.32
New Jersey	4.31
Delaware	4.27
Pennsylvania	4.27
Indiana	4.14
Kansas	4.14
Ohio	3.97
Connecticut	3.85
Kentucky	3.75
Maryland	3.75
Florida	3.73
Oklahoma	3.73
Nevada	3.72
Texas	3.59
U.S.A.	3.59
New York	3.09
Massachusetts	3.07
Rhode Island	3.03
West Virginia	2.96
Oregon	2.78
Montana	2.55
Colorado	2.52
Washington	2.40
Wyoming	2.30
Arizona	2.24
California	2.20
Vermont	2.06
Alaska	2.04
New Hampshire	1.96
New Mexico	1.70
Idaho	1.64
South Dakota	1.55
North Dakota	1.45
Hawaii	1.19
Maine	0.98

WOMEN WHO HAD ABORTIONS IN 1988

Abortions per 1,000 Births	White Women	Black Women
All Women	257	587
Unmarried	1,131	777
Married	68	261
Under 18 years	771	697
18 through 24	350	608
25 and older	179	546
Having Their:		
First Abortion	60.4%	47.1%
Second Abortion	25.5%	29.9%
Third or More	14.1%	23.0%
	100.0%	100.0%
Children:		
None	57.2%	36.6%
One	20.5%	31.2%
Two or More	22.3%	32.2%
	100.0%	100.0%

LOCATIONS OF FAMILIES HEADED BY WOMEN

	White	Black
Central Cities	28.1%	59.7%
Suburbs	46.7%	21.9%
Nonmetropolitan	25.2%	18.4%
	100.0%	100.0%

MARITAL STATUS OF WOMEN BETWEEN 35 AND 40*

	White	Black
Married	74.3%	42.5%
Formerly Married	17.5%	33.0%
Never Married	8.2%	24.5%
	100.0%	100.0%

* Hispanic women omitted.

CHILDREN LIVING ONLY WITH THEIR MOTHERS

	White	Black	Black Multiple
1960	6.1%	19.9%	3.2
1970	7.8%	29.5%	3.78
1980*	12.8%	43.9%	3.43
1990*	14.2%	51.2%	3.60

* Hispanic children omitted.

FAMILIES HEADED BY WOMEN

Black	56.2%
Puerto Rican	44.0%
Native American	24.3%
Native Hawaiian	21.5%
Mexican	18.5%
White	17.3%
Cuban	16.1%
Japanese	12.0%
Filipino	10.0%
Chinese	6.5%

RACIAL RATIOS OF DEATH CAUSES
Black Rates as Multiples of White Rates

Tuberculosis	7.00
Homicides	6.43
H.I.V.-A.I.D.S.	3.38
Meningitis	3.33
Anemias	3.14
Kidney Diseases	2.83
Alcohol-Induced Causes	2.75
Infant Deaths	2.69
Infections	2.60
Nutritional Deficiencies	2.50
Diabetes	2.36
Drug-Induced Causes	2.16
Cerebrovascular Diseases	1.87
All Other Accidents	1.77
Liver Diseases	1.73
Pneumonia and Influenza	1.44
Heart Diseases	1.40
Cancers	1.32
Duodenal & Stomach Ulcers	1.21
Congenital Anomalities	1.14
Atherosclerosis	1.12
Motor Vehicle Accidents	0.94
Pulmonary Diseases	0.84
Suicides	0.56

CHILDREN WHOSE MOTHERS HAVE NEVER BEEN MARRIED

	White	Black	Black Multiple
1960	0.11%	2.1%	19.1
1970	0.22%	4.6%	20.9
1980*	0.73%	13.2%	18.0
1990*	2.69%	35.3%	13.1

* Hispanic children omitted.

DOES COMMUNITY SIZE MAKE A DIFFERENCE?
Black Families in Illinois: 1980

	Number of Black Families	With Women as Heads
Chicago	167,921	50.8%
East St. Louis	8,017	57.5%
Peoria	3,403	50.0%
Kankakee	1,481	54.0%
Mount Vernon	223	55.2%
Quincy	154	53.2%

LIFE EXPECTANCIES AT BIRTH

	White	Black	Ratio
1990	76.0	70.3	.93
1980	74.4	68.1	.92
1970	71.7	64.1	.89
1960	70.6	63.6	.90
1950	69.1	60.8	.88
1940	64.2	53.1	.83

INFANT MORTALITY RATES
(Deaths per 1,000 Births)

	White	Black	Multiple
1990	8.1	16.5	2.04
1988	8.5	17.6	2.07
1980	11.0	21.4	1.95
1970	17.8	32.6	1.83
1960	22.9	43.9	1.92
1950	26.8	43.9	1.64
1940	43.2	72.9	1.69

BLACK REPRESENTATION WITHIN INDUSTRIES*
Black Workers = 10.1% of Total Workforce

Industry	Percent
Rug and Carpet Manufacturing	31.3%
Tobacco Processing	29.0%
Meat Processing	25.1%
Private Protection Services	22.1%
Knitting Mills	20.2%
U.S. Postal Service	19.9%
Rubber Tires	18.6%
Garbage Disposal	17.9%
Laundries & Cleaners	16.8%
Hospitals	16.1%
Hotels & Motels	15.4%
Government Agencies	15.1%
Child-Care Services	13.6%
Shoe Stores	12.1%
Department Stores	12.0%
Libraries	9.7%
Durable Goods Manufacturing	8.6%
Construction	6.5%
Printing & Publishing	5.8%
Motor Vehicle Dealers	5.4%
Advertising Agencies	5.2%
Book & Stationery Stores	4.8%
Agriculture	4.4%
Jewelry Stores	4.4%
Coal Mining	4.2%
Law Offices	4.2%
Toys and Sporting Goods	3.9%
Retail Hardware Stores	3.2%
Scientific Instruments	3.1%
Accountants' Offices	3.1%
Retail Florists	2.8%
Chiropractors' Offices	2.5%
Optometrists' Offices	1.7%

* Includes workers at all levels in an industry.

BLACK PROPORTIONS IN THE ARMED SERVICES

	Enlisted		Officers	
	Men	Women	Men	Women
Army	28.0%	43.3%	9.4%	17.9%
Navy	13.4%	21.8%	2.9%	6.2%
Marines	20.2%	26.4%	4.4%	6.7%
Air Force	16.4%	22.4%	5.6%	10.3%
Total	20.1%	30.5%	5.7%	12.3%

LABOR UNIONS

Workers Who Belong	White	Black
Men	18.8%	24.4%
Women	11.7%	18.0%

Weekly Wages	White	Black
Members	$521	$440
Non-members	$402	$302

OCCUPATIONS AND EMPLOYMENT: 1960–1990

Men	White 1960	White 1990	Black 1960	Black 1990
Total	41,314,000	56,432,000	4,372,000	5,915,000
White Collar	36.0%	47.2%	12.1%	30.4%
Service	9.8%	13.4%	25.1%	21.3%
Blue Collar	54.2%	39.4%	62.8%	48.3%
	100.0%	100.0%	100.0%	100.0%
Adults Employed	95.6%	89.2%	87.3%	73.8%

Women	White 1960	White 1990	Black 1960	Black 1990
Total	19.456,000	45,654,000	2,848,000	6,051,000
White Collar	58.1%	72.5%	18.2%	57.7%
Service	23.5%	17.6%	66.6%	27.8%
Blue Collar	18.4%	9.9%	15.2%	14.5%
	100.0%	100.0%	100.0%	100.0%
Adults Employed	43.4%	70.0%	51.8%	62.3%

UNEMPLOYMENT AND EDUCATIONAL ATTAINMENT
Persons Aged 25 to 34

	White	Black	Multiple
Completed College	2.2%	4.5%	2.05
Completed High School	5.3%	12.9%	2.43
Dropped Out High School	11.4%	25.3%	2.22

UNEMPLOYMENT AND MARITAL STATUS
Men Aged 25 and Older

	White	Black	Multiple
Currently Married	3.0%	5.8%	1.93
Formerly Married	6.1%	10.4%	1.70
Never Married	6.2%	14.7%	2.37

FAMILIES BELOW THE POVERTY LINE*

	White	Black	Multiple
Northeast	4.8%	21.4%	4.46
Midwest	4.6%	33.7%	5.11
South	7.3%	28.4%	3.89
West	5.7%	22.9%	4.02

* Hispanic families not included.

BLACK SHARE OF AGGREGATE FAMILY INCOME

1947	4.7%
1959	5.4%
1969	6.1%
1974	6.5%
1979	6.8%
1984	6.9%
1989	7.2%

BLACK STUDENTS ATTENDING PREDOMINANTLY WHITE SCHOOLS

City	%
Colorado Springs	88.6%
San Jose	67.6%
Tucson	63.0%
Albuquerque	51.8%
Toledo	34.2%
Oklahoma City	27.9%
San Diego	26.5%
Seattle	25.8%
Fort Worth	22.1%
Austin	21.8%
Denver	19.0%
Milwaukee	11.8%
Philadelphia	10.6%
El Paso	9.8%
Dade (Miami)	8.2%
New York	6.8%
Los Angeles	4.9%
Dallas	4.6%
Houston	3.4%
Chicago	2.4%
Oakland	1.5%
Newark	1.0%
Jersey City	0.3%
San Francisco	0.0%

EDUCATIONAL ATTAINMENT
Persons aged 25 to 35

Completed High School			
	Black	White	Multiple
1940	12.3%	41.2%	3.35
1950	23.6%	56.3%	2.39
1960	38.6%	63.7%	1.65
1970	58.4%	77.8%	1.33
1980*	82.2%	89.8%	1.10
1989*	82.2%	89.3%	1.09

Four or More Years of College			
	Black	White	Multiple
1940	1.6%	6.4%	4.00
1950	2.8%	8.2%	2.93
1960	4.8%	11.8%	2.45
1970	7.3%	17.3%	2.36
1980*	11.5%	25.3%	2.20
1988*	12.7%	24.4%	1.92

* Hispanics not included.

PRINCIPAL UNDERGRADUATE MAJORS

Black	Hispanic		White	Asian
26.0%	23.7%	Business	24.4%	18.4%
7.5%	8.2%	Education	9.3%	3.3%
17.8%	16.7%	Science & Engineering	16.1%	34.0%
18.2%	13.3%	Social Sciences & Psychology	15.4%	13.2%
3.8%	6.2%	Languages & Literature	5.6%	3.9%
6.9%	4.9%	Health & Nursing	6.6%	4.8%
0.4%	0.5%	Area & Ethnic Studies	0.3%	0.7%
19.4%	26.5%	All Other Fields	22.3%	21.7%
100.0%	100.0%		100.0%	100.0%

DEGREES CONFERRED (Totals = Across)

Black	Hispanic		White	Asian
6.5%	2.1%	Bachelor's (1977)	89.5%	1.5%
5.7%	2.9%	Bachelor's (1989)	84.5%	3.8%
4.3%	1.8%	Doctorates (1977)	91.4%	2.2%
3.5%	2.4%	Doctorates (1989)	89.3%	2.7%
5.1%	3.2%	Medicine (1989)	86.0%	5.3%
4.9%	2.9%	Law (1989)	89.9%	1.9%

PUBLIC SCHOOL ENROLLMENTS: SELECTED CITIES AND STATES

	White	Black	Hispanic	Asian
Washington, D.C.	4.0%	91.4%	3.5%	1.1%
San Antonio	6.9%	12.1%	80.6%	0.4%
Newark	9.7%	63.9%	25.6%	0.6%
Phoenix	12.0%	13.0%	69.0%	0.6%
Chicago	12.4%	59.7%	24.9%	2.9%
Birmingham	13.0%	86.0%	0.4%	0.5%
San Francisco	14.0%	20.0%	20.0%	45.0%
Baltimore	18.6%	80.2%	0.3%	0.6%
Jackson	21.0%	77.0%	1.0%	1.0%
New York City	21.0%	38.0%	34.0%	7.0%
Miami	21.1%	33.3%	44.4%	1.1%
Boston	23.0%	48.0%	19.0%	9.0%
Kansas City, Mo.	26.0%	68.0%	4.0%	1.0%
Milwaukee	32.0%	55.0%	8.0%	3.0%
Denver	35.0%	22.0%	38.0%	4.0%
Cincinnati	38.2%	60.7%	0.2%	0.8%
Bakersfield	39.0%	15.0%	43.0%	0.1%
San Diego	41.4%	16.4%	23.2%	18.6%
Oklahoma City	47.0%	39.6%	6.7%	2.7%
Seattle	47.0%	24.0%	5.0%	21.0%
Columbus	51.0%	46.3%	0.4%	2.3%
Houston	53.7%	9.5%	28.0%	8.6%
Akron	59.6%	38.7%	0.3%	1.3%
Jacksonville	60.1%	36.3%	1.2%	2.2%
Des Moines	82.0%	11.5%	2.0%	4.2%
New Mexico	43.1%	2.2%	45.1%	0.8%
Texas	51.0%	14.4%	32.5%	2.0%
California	53.7%	9.0%	27.5%	9.1%
Florida	65.4%	23.7%	9.5%	1.2%
New York	68.4%	16.5%	12.3%	2.7%
U.S.A.	70.4%	16.1%	9.9%	2.8%

HIGH SCHOOL AND COLLEGE
(Totals = Across)

Black	Hispanic		White	Asian
16.1%	9.9%	Public School Students	70.4%	2.8%
8.1%	2.9%	Public School Teachers	85.8%	0.3%
8.3%	5.5%	High School Students Taking NCEE Program*	12.7%	24.3%
9.9%	6.8%	High School Graduates Completing College	20.2%	27.3%

* Courses recommended by the National Council on Excellence in Education for all college-bound high school students.

PRISON POPULATIONS: SELECTED STATES

	Imprisonment Rates		Ratio of Blacks to Whit Rate	Racial Income Ratio	Violent Crime Rate
	White	Black			
Nebraska	38	584	15.4	$662	26.3
Pennsylvania	32	429	13.4	625	35.9
Michigan	41	391	9.5	725	80.4
Maryland	61	528	8.7	704	83.3
Delaware	101	770	7.6	571	42.7
Okalahoma	104	569	5.5	641	43.6
Mississippi	59	292	4.9	495	27.4
North Carolina	82	366	4.5	633	47.6

Imprisonment rates are the number of inmates per 10,000 men of each race aged 18 to 30 within each state.
Income ratios give black earnings for each $1,000 received by whites within the state.
Violent crime rates are based on number of reported robberies, rapes, murders, and aggravated assaults per 10,000 population.

BLACK OFFICERS' REPRESENTATION ON CITY POLICY FORCES COMPARED WITH BLACK PROPORTION OF THE CITIES' POPULATIONS

	Blacks on Force	Ratio to Population
Washington, D.C.	54.8%	.78
Atlanta	51.7%	.78
Pittsburgh	18.8%	.78
Detroit	48.0%	.76
Boston	15.9%	.71
Los Angeles	11.3%	.67
San Francisco	8.5%	.67
Chicago	22.4%	.56
Philadelphia	19.2%	.51
Cleveland	21.7%	.50
Houston	13.5%	.49
Kansas City, Mo.	12.9%	.47
Denver	5.5%	.46
Newark	25.4%	.44
New York	11.0%	.44
Baltimore	21.8%	.40
Dallas	11.5%	.39

REFERENCES

ix " 'Two nations' ": Benjamin Disraeli, *Sybil; or, The Two Nations* (1845).

ix " 'Our nation is moving . . .' ": *Report of the National Advisory Commission on Civil Disorders* (Bantam Books, 1968).

ix " 'The most formidable . . .' ": *Democracy in America,* translated by Henry Reeve and edited by Phillips Bradley (Vintage Books, 1956).

x "black and white breakdowns . . .": According to the most recent government studies, 57.2 percent of white mothers and 24.5 percent of black mothers breast-feed their babies. Black Americans account for 30.8 percent of all arrests, and 33.4 percent of those for embezzlement. Black women comprise 13.3 percent of all working women, and 2.5 percent of those employed as dental hygienists. Altogether, 418,717 white persons (0.5 percent of those who are employed) bicycle to work, and 26,916 black persons (0.3 percent) use this mode of transportation.

xi "among these authors . . .": J. Anthony Lukas, *Common Ground* (Knopf, 1985); Elijah Anderson, *Streetwise: Race, Class, and Change in an Urban Community* (University of Chicago Press,1990); Nicholas Lemann, *The Promised Land* (Knopf, 1991): Alex Kotlowitz, *There Are No Children Here* (Doubleday, 1991).

xii Gunnar Myrdal, *An American Dilemma: The Negro Problem and Modern Democracy* (Harper and Brothers, 1944).

xii Murray's best-known work is *Losing Ground: American Social Policy, 1950–1980* (Basic Books, 1984); and Wilson's is *The Truly Disadvantaged: The Inner City, the Underclass, and Public Policy* (University of Chicago Press, 1987). An interchange between Ravitch and Asante can be found in *The American Scholar* (Spring 1991).

25 " 'Nobody wishes more than I . . .' ": Letter to Benjamin Banneker, August 30, 1791, in *Thomas Jefferson: Writings,* edited by Merrill D. Peterson (The Library of America, 1984).

26 William Shockley's views were confined to speeches before lay audiences. For Arthur Jensen, see "How Much Can We Boost IQ and Scholastic Achievement?" *Harvard Educational Review* (February 1969).

28 "ideological positions . . .": See Nicholas Pastore, *The Nature-Nurture Controversy* (Kings Crown Press, 1949).

28 " 'ice people' . . . 'sun people' ": These phrases were devised by Leonard Jeffries, a professor of political science at the City University of New York. They are quoted in Arthur M. Schlesinger, Jr., *The Disuniting of America: Reflections on a Multicultural Society* (Whittle, 1991).

29 "cannot be called racists . . .": Mayor Coleman Young, quoted in Ze'ev Chafets, *Devil's Night and Other Tales of Detroit* (Random House, 1990).

30 James Baldwin, *The Fire Next Time* (Dial Press, 1963).

33 " 'two thoughts . . .' ": W. E. B. Du Bois, *The Souls of Black Folk* (1903) in *W. E. B. Du Bois: Writings,* edited by Nathan Huggins (The Library of America, 1986).

34 " 'a different people . . .' ": August Wilson, quoted in *New York Times* (April 15, 1990).
34 " 'At no moment . . .' ": Toni Morrison, quoted in *New York Times* (January 15, 1986).
35 "some 85 percent . . .": See, for example, the survey reported in *New York Times* (April 1, 1987).
36 "Starrett City . . . Atrium Village": *New York Times* (July 24, 1987).
37 "10 to 20 percent . . .": Gerald Jaynes and Robin Williams, eds., *A Common Destiny: Blacks and American Society* (National Academy Press, 1989).
39 Ralph Ellison, *Invisible Man* (Random House, 1952).
41 " 'What is Africa . . .' ": Quoted in *W. E. B. Du Bois: Writings,* edited by Nathan Huggins (The Library of America, 1986).
43 " 'African-American . . .' ": *Political Trendletter* (Joint Center for Political and Economic Studies, March 1991).
43 "African names . . .": Communication from Professor Richard Allen, University of Michigan, September 2, 1989. Also see his article in the *American Political Science Review* (June 1989).
44 "from the Caribbean . . .": See Thomas Sowell, "The Fallacy of Racial Politics, *Harpers* (June, 1984).
46 "Bangladesh . . .": Colin McCord and Harold Freeman, "Excess Mortality in Harlem, *New England Journal of Medicine* (January 18, 1990).
47 "victims of violent crimes . . .": Catherine Whitaker, *Black Victims* (Bureau of Justice Statistics, 1990).
49 "deliberately encouraging drug use . . .": *New York Times,* October 29, 1990).
52 "support racial integration . . .": Howard Schuman, Charlotte Steeh, and Lawrence Bobo, *Racial Attitudes in America* (Harvard University Press, 1985).
61 " 'the nigger. . .' ": James Baldwin, *The Fire Next Time* (Dial Press, 1963).
61 " 'sex and race . . .' ": Gunnar Myrdal, *An American Dilemma: The Negro Problem and Modern Democracy* (Harper and Brothers, 1944).
68 Table on Families Headed by Women: For 1950 through 1980, the Decennial Censuses; for 1990, *Household and Family Characteristics,* Series P-20, No. 447 (Bureau of the Census, 1990).
69 "remained remarkably stable . . .": Herbert Gutman, *The Black Family in Slavery and Freedom: 1750–1925* (Random House, 1977).
69 " 'men's liberation . . .' ": Stanley Lebergott, *The American Economy: Income, Wealth, and Want* (Princeton University Press, 1976).
70 "no child support . . .": *Child Support and Alimony,* Series P-60, No. 173 (Bureau of the Census, 1991).
71 Table on Fertility Rates: *Advance Report of Final Natality Statistics,* Vol. 39, No. 4 (National Center for Health Statistics, 1990).
72 "aunts and grandparents . . .": *Household and Family Characteristics,* Series P-20, No. 447 (Bureau of the Census, 1990).
73 " 'absence of a father . . .' ": Andrew Cherlin, *Marriage, Divorce, Remarriage* (Harvard University Press, 1981).
73 " 'lack of a male income . . .' ": Also Cherlin, as above.
73 "less than $14,000 . . .": *Money Income and Poverty Status in the United States,* Series P-60, No. 174 (Bureau of the Census, 1991).
74 Table on Marital Status: For 1960, the Decennial Census. For 1990, *Household and Family Characteristics,* Series P-20, No. 447 (Bureau of the Census, 1990).
74 "years of college . . .": *Educational Attainment in the United States,* Series P-20, No. 428 (Bureau of the Census, 1988).
75 "mortality rate for black men . . .": *Births, Marriages, Divorces, and Deaths,* Vol. 40, No. 1 (National Center for Health Statistics, 1991).
75 "separated or divorced . . .": *Educational Attainment in the United States,* Series P-20, No. 428 (Bureau of the Census, 1988).

76 Table on Pregnancies and Births: Figures from Cheryl Hayes, ed., *Risking the Future: Adolescent Sexuality, Pregnancy, and Childbearing* (National Academy Press, 1987); plus "Teenage Abortion, Birth, and Pregnancy," *Family Planning Perspectives* (March–April 1989).

77 Table on Pregnancy Rates: E. F. Jones et al., "Teenage Pregnancy in Developed Countries, *Family Planning Perspectives* (March–April 1985).

77 "in hopes of becoming pregnant . . .": *Wanted and Unwanted Childbearing in the United States.* Advance Data 189 (National Center for Health Statistics, 1990).

78 "Equilla and Zanquisha . . .": Cathy Jackson, "Names Can Hurt," *Essence* (April 1989).

78 "Women of Mexican ancestry . . .": *Advance Report of Final Natality Statistics,* Vol. 39, No. 4 (National Center for Health Statistics, 1990).

80 "outside of marriage . . .": *Advance Report of Final Natality Statistics,* Vol. 39, No. 4 (National Center for Health Statistics, 1990).

80 Table on Out-of-Wedlock Births: Figures from 1950 through 1980 from editions of *The Statistical Abstract of the United States* (U.S. Government Printing Office). For 1988, *Advance Report of Final Natality Statistics,* Vol. 39, No. 4 (National Center for Health Statistics, 1990).

80 "availing themselves of abortion . . .": *Induced Terminations of Pregnancy,* Vol. 39, No. 12 (National Center for Health Statistics, 1991).

81 "users of birth control . . .": *Contraceptive Use in the United States,* Advance Data No. 182 (National Center for Health Statistics, 1990).

83 Table on Births to Unmarried Women: *Natality: 1988* (National Center for Health Statistics, 1991).

84 Table on Out-of-Wedlock Birthrates: For black and white women: *Advance Report of Final Natality Statistics,* Vol. 39, No. 4 (National Center for Health Statistics, 1990). For Mexican, Puerto Rican, and Cuban women: *Births of Hispanic Parentage,* Vol. 36, No. 11 (National Center for Health Statistics, 1988). For Hawaiian, Filipino, Chinese, and Japanese women: *Characteristics of Asian Births,* Vol. 32, No. 10 (National Center for Health Statistics, 1984). For Native American and Native Alaskan women: *Characteristics of American Indian and Alaska Native Births,* Vol. 36, No. 3 (National Center for Health Statistics, 1987).

84 "overrun by conquerors or colonizers . . .": For an analysis of groups whose homes were subjected to conquest or colonization, see John Ogbu, "Minority Status and Literacy in Comparative Perspective," *Daedulus* (Spring 1990).

85 "leave voluntarily . . .": See Greg Duncan, Martha Hill, and Saul Hoffman, "Welfare Dependence Within and Across Generations, *Science* (January 29, 1988).

86 "annual cash allowances . . ." *Quarterly Public Assistance Statistics* (Department of Health and Human Services, 1991).

87 Table on Families Receiving AFDC: *Characteristics and Financial Circumstances of AFDC Recipients* (Department of Health and Human Services, 1988).

88 "averages $2,995 . . .": *Child Support and Alimony,* Series P-60, No. 173 (Bureau of the Census, 1991).

88 "A California study . . .": Lenore Weitzman, *The Divorce Revolution* (Free Press, 1985).

88 "can expect to remarry . . .": *Cohabitation, Marriage, Marital Dissolution, and Remarriage.* Advance Data No. 194 (National Center for Health Statistics, 1991).

88 "New federal legislation . . .": For the law's provisions, see the report of the Senate Finance Committee on The Family Security Act of 1988 (U.S. Government Printing Office, 1988).

89 "preschool-age children . . .": *Child Care Arrangements.* Advance Data No. 187 (National Center for Health Statistics, 1990).

90 " 'take from the common good . . .' ": Michael Novak, ed., *The New Consensus on Family and Welfare* (American Enterprise Institute, 1988).

91 Table on Single Mothers Receiving AFDC: Percentage of single mothers extrapolated from the 1980 census, and number receiving AFDC from *Characteristics and Finan-*

cial Circumstances of AFDC Recipients (Department of Health and Human Services, 1988).

94 Table on Incomes and Earnings: *Money Income of Households, Families, and Persons in the United States,* Series P-60, No. 174 (Bureau of the Census, 1991). Unless otherwise noted, all the figures cited in Chapter 6 have been derived from this census study.

95 Table on Education and Earnings: *Money Income of Households, Families, and Persons in the United States.* Series P-60, No. 174 (Bureau of the Census, 1991).

96 "earnings of male attorneys . . .": *Earnings by Occupation and Education.* Subject Report PC80-2-8B (Bureau of the Census, 1984).

100 Table on Poverty. *Poverty in the United States: 1990*, Series P-60, No. 175 (Bureau of the Census, 1991).

100 "a white underclass . . .": See, for example, James Howard Kunstler, "Schuylerville Stands Still," *New York Times Magazine* (April 25, 1990). For some urban counterparts, see Jay MacLeod, *Ain't No Making It* (Westview Press, 1987).

101 Table on Earnings Ratios: For 1939 through 1969, *Historical Statistics of the United States.* For 1979 and 1989, *Current Population Reports,* Series P-60 (Bureau of the Census).

103 Table on Unemployment: For 1960 through 1988, *Statistical Abstract of the United States.* For 1989 and 1990, *Employment and Earnings* (Bureau of Labor Statistics, 1991).

105 " 'discouraged workers . . .' ": *Employment and Earnings* (Bureau of Labor Statistics, 1991). Unless otherwise noted, figures in this part of Chapter 6 and throughout much of Chapter 7 are derived from this report.

108 "Only one black person . . .": "The Richest People in America," *Forbes* (October 21, 1991).

108 "only one black chairman . . .": "The Corporate Elite," *Business Week* (November 25, 1991).

108 "black businesses . . .": See the analysis by the Joint Center for Political and Economic Studies published in *Focus* (October 1990).

109 Table on Self-Employment: *General Social and Economic Characteristics.* U.S. Summary: PC80-1-C1 (Bureau of the Census, 1983). These figures and those in the next note will have to suffice until detailed occupational data for 1990 are available.

110 "254 black optometrists . . .": *Detailed Occupations for the Civilian Labor Force.* Supplementary Report: PC80-S1-8 (Bureau of the Census, 1983).

113 Table on 1960 vs. 1990: 1960 figures from that year's census; 1990, from *Employment and Earnings* (Bureau of Labor Statistics, 1991).

115 Table on Women: Percentages for military personnel from Edwin Dorn, ed., *Who Defends America: Race, Sex, and Class in the Armed Foreces* (Joint Center for Political Studies Press, 1989).

116 "black college men . . .": *Fortune* (April 22, 1991).

119 "by no means new . . .": Much of the background material cited here, including the quotations from Lyndon Johnson and court decisions, relies on Melvin Urofsky's *A Conflict of Rights: The Supreme Court and Affirmative Action* (Scribner's, 1991).

120 "carefully controlled survey. . .": Jonathan Leonard, "The Impact of Affirmative Action on Employment," *Journal of Labor Economics* (October 1984).

122 " 'find his proper element . . .' ": "Report on Manufactures," *The Reports of Alexander Hamilton* (Harper & Row, 1964).

125 "25,831 doctoral degrees . . .": *Chronicle of Higher Education* (October 16, 1991).

125 "being productive scholars . . .": Ernest Boyer, *College: The Undergraduate Experience in America* (Harper & Row, 1986).

125 " 'archaic rules . . .' ": Jesse Jackson, quoted in *New York Times* (May 10, 1990).

126 "black medical students . . .": *Chronicle of Higher Education* (June 15, 1988).

127 "not an easy test . . .": See Lawrence Fuchs, *The American Kaleidoscope* (Wesleyan University Press, 1990).

134 "University of Virginia . . .": *Washington Post* (December 12, 1988).
134 "seniors with Asian backgrounds . . .": *Freshman Admissions at Berkeley: A Policy for the 1990s and Beyond* (University of California, Academic Senate, 1989). Unless otherwise noted, the quotations and figures concerning Berkeley are from this report.
135 "3.2 percent of the students . . .": The precentages for ethnic groups at individual colleges cited in this and the next chapter come from tabulations in the *Chronicle of Higher Eduction* (April 11, 1990).
136 "Massachusetts Institute of Technology . . .": Elaine Louie, "Unequal Contest," *New York Times* (August 6, 1989).
136 "Harvard . . . alumni children . . .": Jerome Karabel and David Karen, "Go to Harvard: Give Your Kid a Break," *New York Times* (December 12, 1990).
136 "Harvard officials . . .": *Chronicle of Higher Education* (May 27, 1991).
137 Table on Ethnicity and Admissions: Graduation rates from *Retention Update* (Office of Student Research, 1989).
138 "the minimal standard . . .": A similar policy has been pursued at UCLA. Applicants for the 1989 entering class had the following acceptance rates: 84.5 percent for Hispanic applicants and 72.7 percent for blacks, compared with 40.6 percent for Asians and 39.0 percent for whites. *UCLA Daily Bruin* (April 12, 1989).
140 "freshman calculus courses . . .": Communication from Professor Charles Akemann, December 10, 1989.
140 "Pennsylvania State University . . .": Abigail Thernstrom, "Permaffirm Action," *New Republic* (July 31, 1989).
140 "right for Harvard . . .": David Karen, "Who Gets into Harvard," Ph.D Thesis, Department of Sociology, Harvard University, 1985.
142 Table with SAT Scores: These and other aggregate SAT scores cited in this chapter, along with biographical information on the students taking the tests, come from unpublished reports provided by the College Board.
144 " 'no significant relation . . .' ": Educational Testing Service, *Annual Report, 1966–1967.* Also see David McClelland, "Testing for Competence rather than for 'Intelligence,' " *American Psychologist* (January 1973).
144 "in the business world . . .": See Daniel Goleman, "Successful Executives Rely on Their Own Kind of Intelligence," *New York Times* (July 31, 1984).
145 "full academic program . . .": *Digest of Education Statistics* (National Center for Education Statistics, 1991).
145 "a wider 'modern' consciousness . . .": The term "modern" is used by Jim Sleeper in his *The Closest of Strangers* (Norton, 1990).
145 "children of immigrants . . .": *Philadelphia Inquirer* (May 10, 1988).
145 " 'telephone test . . .' ": See "The Next Wave," *New York* (May 12, 1986).
146 " 'abandoned by the institution . . .' ": Jacqueline Fleming, *Blacks in College* (Jossey-Bass, 1984).
148 "ethnic or sexual bigotry . . .": Howard J. Ehrlich, ed., *Campus Ethnoviolence and the Policy Options* (National Institute Against Prejudice and Violence, 1990).
148 "biggest sports budgets . . .": *The Experiences of Black Intercollegiate Athletes at NCAA Division I Institutions* (American Institutes for Research, 1989).
153 "failed to graduate . . .": NCAA report on *Academic Performance of College Athletes,* summarized in *Chronicle of Higher Education* (July 10, 1991).
153 "students barred from playing . . .": *Chronicle of Higher Education* (February 28, 1990).
156–157 Tables on Black Enrollments and North Carolina system: Percentage figures are from the *Chronicle of Higher Education* (April 11, 1990).
158 "black students and faculty members . . .": See Adam Nossiter, "Separatism Down South," *Nation* (June 18, 1990).
163 Table on Black School Share and Segregation: *Status of School Desegregation* (National School Boards Association, 1989).

164 "retarded, disabled . . .": See Lori Granger and Bill Granger, *The Magic Feather* (Dutton, 1986).
165 " 'segregated once they are inside . . .' ": *New York Times* (February 18, 1990).
166 " 'attended desegregated schools . . .' ": Gerald Janyes and Robin Williams, eds., *A Common Destiny: Blacks and American Society* (National Academy Press, 1989).
166 " 'Thrusting the black child . . .' ": Harold B. Gerard, in Phyllis Katz and Dalmas Taylor, eds., *Eliminating Racism* (Plenum, 1988).
166 "optimal achievement . . .": Rita Mahard and Robert Crain, in Christine Rossell and Willis Hawley, eds., *The Consequences of School Desegration* (Temple University Press, 1983).
166 "high-school drop-out rates . . .": *New York Times* (May 1, 1990).
167 " 'intellectual and educational oppression . . .' ": *A Curriculum of Inclusion* (New York State Department of Education, 1989).
170 "see themselves in the curriculum . . .": Janice Hale-Benson, in Kofi Lomotey, ed., *Going to School: The African-American Experience* (State University of New York Press, 1990).
171 " 'Shakespeare or Emily Dickinson . . .' ": *Visions of a Better Way* (Joint Center for Political Studies, 1989).
172 " 'apparently irrelevant topics . . .' ": *New York Times* (June 24, 1988).
172 " 'telling . . . Eddie Murphy to shut up . . .' ": Janice Hale-Benson, quoted in *New York Times* (November 4, 1990).
172 "fewer than 5 percent . . .": *New York Times* (August 27, 1990).
173 Table on Teacher Examinations: *Minorities in Higher Education,* Sixth Annual Status Report (American Council on Education, 1987).
173 "Pre-Columbian sculptures . . . Lewis Howard Latimer . . .": Pat Brown of Indianapolis school system, quoted in *New York Times* (October 10, 1990).
174 "Caesarean section . . .": Larry Obadele Wiliams of the Atlanta school system, in *Southern Education Foundation News* (December 1990).
174 "Vaccination . . . carbon steel . . .": *African-American Baseline Essays* (Portland, Oregon, Public Schools, 1987).
174 " 'mental genocide . . .' ": Leonard Jeffries of the City University of New York, quoted in Andrew Sullivan, "Racism 101," *New Republic* (November 26, 1990).
175 "in private rather than public . . .": Richard Alba, *Ethnic Identity: The Transformation of White America* (Yale University Press, 1990).
177 " 'men are disproportionately at risk . . .' ": *Minorities in Higher Education,* Seventh Annual Status Report (American Council on Education, 1988).
178 Table on Degrees to Women: *Minorities in Higher Education,* Ninth Annual Status Report (American Council on Education, 1991).
180 "black men and women account for . . .": *Jail Inmates, 1990* (Bureau of Justice Statistics, 1991); *Prisoners in 1990* (Bureau of Justice Statistics, 1991); *Capital Punishment* (Bureau of Justice Statistics, 1990).
181 Table on Racial Arrest Rates: *Uniform Crime Reports for 1990* (Federal Bureau of Investigation, 1991). Disproportionate arrest rates are based on blacks' comprising 12.1 percent of the population.
183 Table on Assailants and Victims: Figures for murders come from *Uniform Crime Reports for 1990.* (Federal Bureau of Investigation, 1991). Those for rapes and robberies are derived from *Criminal Victimization in the United States: 1989* (Bureau of Justice Statistics, 1991). The tabulations refer to cases where the race of the assailant could be determined, and where the victims and the assailants were either black or white.
184 "median income . . .": *Money Incomes of Households, Families, and Persons in the United States: 1990* Series P-60, No. 174 (Bureau of the Census, 1991).
184 "unemployment rate . . .": *Employment and Earnings* (Bureau of Labor Statistics, 1991).
186 "has political intentions . . .": Eldridge Cleaver, *Soul on Ice* (McGraw-Hill, 1967).

187 " 'a social contract . . .' ": Bruce Wright, *Black Robes, White Justice* (Lyle Stuart, 1987).
189 "by law enforcement officers . . .": Professor James Fox of Northeastern University, quoted in *New York Times* (September 2, 1990).
191 "who had black victims . . .": *McCleskey* v. *Kemp,* 107 S. Ct. 1756 (1987).
192 "Goetz's exoneration was supported . . .": *Newsday* (June 28, 1987).
197 Table on prison inmates: *Race of Prisoners Admitted to State and Federal Institutions: 1926–1986* (Bureau of Justice Statistics, 1991).
198 " 'corporate crooks . . .' ": *Fortune* (April 25, 1988).
204 "Dinkins . . . 91 percent . . .": *New York Times* (November 9, 1989).
204 "Wilder . . . 95 percent . . .": *Focus* (Joint Center for Political Studies, November–December 1989).
204 "Jackson . . . 92 percent . . .": *New York Times* (June 13, 1988).
206 " 'what you did to us . . . Louis Farrakhan, quoted in *New York Times* (March 29, 1990).
210 " 'representatives of their choice . . .' ": For a full analysis of the Voting Rights Act see Abigail Thernstrom, *Whose Votes Count? Affirmative Action and Minority Voting Rights* (Harvard University Press, 1987).
216 Alexis de Tocqueville . . . *Democracy in America*, translated by Henry Reeve and edited by Phillips Bradley (Vintage Books, 1956).
225–226 Table on Racial and Hispanic Populations. Unpublished printout (Bureau of the Census, 1991).
227 Table on Population Composition. *Historical Statistics of the United States* (Bureau of the Census, 1975).
228 Table on States Racial Rankings. Unpublished printout (Bureau of the Census, 1991).
229 Table on Black Populations of Cities. Unpublished printout (Bureau of the Census, 1991).
230 Table on Births to Unmarried Women. *Natality: 1988* (National Center for Health Statistics, 1991).
230 Table on Women Who Had Abortions. *Induced Terminations of Pregnancy: 1988* (National Center for Health Statistics, 1991).
230 Table on Families Headed by Women. *Household and Family Characteristics: 1990* (Bureau of the Census, 1990).
230 Table on Marital Status of Women. *Marital Status and Living Arrangements: 1990* (Bureau of the Census, 1991).
231 Tables on Children Living with Mothers and Children Whose Mothers Have Never Been Married. *Marital Status and Living Arrangements: 1990* (Bureau of the Census, 1991).
231 Table on Families Headed by Women. *Household and Family Characteristics: 1990* (Bureau of the Census). Plus adjusted figures from *General Social and Economic Statistics: 1980* (Bureau of the Census, 1983).
231 Table on Community Size. *Social and Economic Characteristics for Illinois* (Bureau of the Census, 1983).
231 Tables on Racial Ratios of Death Causes, Life Expectancies, and Infant Mortality Rates. *Advance Report of Final Mortality Statistics: 1988* (National Center for Health Statistics, 1990).
232 Tables on Black Representation in Industries and Labor Unions *Employment and Earnings* (Bureau of Labor Statistics, 1991).
232 Table on Blacks in Armed Services. *Who Defends America?* (Joint Centers for Political Studies, 1989).
233 Tables on Occupations and Employment, Unemployment and Education, and Unemployment and Marital Status. *Employment and Earnings* (Bureau of Labor Statistics, 1991). Plus *General Social and Economic Characeristics: 1960* (Bureau of the Census, 1962).
233 Tables on Families in Poverty and Black Share of Family Income. *Money Income and Poverty Status in the United States: 1989* (Bureau of the Census, 1990).

234 Table on Blacks Attending White Schools. *Change and Desegregation in Large School Districts: 1986–1987* (National School Boards Association, 1988).

234 Table on Educational Attainment. *Statistical Abstract of the United States* (U.S. Government Printing Office, 1990).

234 Tables on Undergraduate Majors and Degrees Conferred. *Digest of Education Statistics: 1990* (National Center for Education Statistics, 1991).

235 Table on Public School Enrollments. *Survey of Public Education in Urban School Districts* (National School Boards Association, 1991).

235 Table on High School and College. *Digest of Education Statistics: 1990* (National Center for Education Statistics, 1991).

236 Table on Prison Populations. *Race of Prisoners Admitted to State and Federal Institutions* (Bureau of Justice Statistics, 1991). Plus *General Social and Economic Characteristics: 1980* (Bureau of the Census, 1983) and *Uniform Crime Reports* (Federal Bureau of Investigation, 1991).

236 Table on City Police Forces. *Police Departments in Large Cities: 1987* (National Center for Justice Statistics, 1989).

ACKNOWLEDGMENTS

Two Nations owes its initial inspiration to Edward T. Chase, my editor at Scribner's. It was he who suggested that a book like this needed to be written and I should take on that task. During the five years required for its completion, he offered every kind of encouragement an author wants and needs. I have benefited from the expert assistance of two other Scribner's editors, Bill Goldstein and Hamilton Cain, as well as copy editor Estelle Laurence and designer Erich Hobbing. Lorrie Millman provided additional—and timely—help in shaping the manuscript and organizing the Index.

Parts of this book first appeared, in somewhat different forms, as review-essays in *The New York Review of Books*. I am grateful to that publication for permission to reprint this material. And I owe particular thanks to Robert Silvers and Barbara Epstein for their steadfast attention and incisive suggestions.

Members of the reference staffs at the New York Public Library and the Queens College Library were invariably helpful in tracking down government documents. Margaret Padin-Bailo, Beverly Wright, and Marie Morales of the New York office of the Census Bureau went out of their way to provide me with updated figures.

My agent, Robin Straus, assisted at every stage, from the original outline to those penultimate months when this book finally began to take shape. Her enthusiasm and support are reflected on every page of *Two Nations*.

INDEX

ABOUT THE AUTHOR

Andrew Hacker currently teaches political science at Queens College in New York City. Prior to that he served as a professor of government at Cornell University. His writings include studies in political philosophy, statistical research, and a widely reviewed book entitled *The End of the American Era.*

He has written extensively for scholarly journals, as well as publications including *The New York Review of Books, Time, Newsweek, Harpers, Atlantic, The Wall Street Journal* and *Fortune.*

Mr. Hacker lives on the West Side of Manhattan with his wife, Lois. He has a married daughter, who resides in Boston.

DATE			